C000150002

Britain's Productivity Problem, 1948–1990

Britain's Productivity Problem, 1948–1990

Mark W. Bufton

© Mark W. Bufton 2004

All rights reserved. No reproduction, copy or transmission of this publication may be made without written permission.

No paragraph of this publication may be reproduced, copied or transmitted save with written permission or in accordance with the provisions of the Copyright, Designs and Patents Act 1988, or under the terms of any licence permitting limited copying issued by the Copyright Licensing Agency, 90 Tottenham Court Road, London W1T 4LP.

Any person who does any unauthorised act in relation to this publication may be liable to criminal prosecution and civil claims for damages.

The author has asserted his right to be identified as the author of this work in accordance with the Copyright, Designs and Patents Act 1988.

First published 2004 by
PALGRAVE MACMILLAN
Houndmills, Basingstoke, Hampshire RG21 6XS and
175 Fifth Avenue, New York, N. Y. 10010
Companies and representatives throughout the world

PALGRAVE MACMILLAN is the global academic imprint of the Palgrave Macmillan division of St. Martin's Press, LLC and of Palgrave Macmillan Ltd. Macmillan® is a registered trademark in the United States, United Kingdom and other countries. Palgrave is a registered trademark in the European Union and other countries.

ISBN 1–4039–1279–3

This book is printed on paper suitable for recycling and made from fully managed and sustained forest sources.

A catalogue record for this book is available from the British Library.

Library of Congress Cataloging-in-Publication Data
Bufton, Mark W., 1968–
    Britain's productivity problem, 1948–1990 / Mark W. Bufton.
       p.   cm.
    Includes bibliographical references and index.
    ISBN 1–4039–1279–3 (cloth)
    1. Labor productivity—Great Britain—History—20th century. I. Title.

    HC260.L3B84 2004
    331.11'8'094109045—dc22

                                                               2004045621

10   9   8   7   6   5   4   3   2   1
13 12 11 10 09 08 07 06 05 04

Printed and bound in Great Britain by
Antony Rowe Ltd, Chippenham and Eastbourne

Contents

List of Tables

List of Figures

Definitions of Acronyms

AACP	Anglo-American Council on Productivity
AEUJ	Amalgamated Engineering Union Journal
AEUMJ	Amalgamated Engineering Union Monthly Journal
AFAP	*Association Française pour l'Accroissement de la Productivité*
AFL	American Federation of Labour (merged with the CIO in 1955)
ASSET	Association of Supervisory Staffs, Executives, and Technicians
AWA	Amalgamated Weavers Association
BEC	British Employers Confederation
BPC	British Productivity Council
BRPC	British Railways Productivity Council
BSRV	Bargaining Strength Reward Vector
CBI	Confederation of British Industries
CD	Co-determination
CEIF	Council of European Industrial Federations
CFTC	*Confédération Française des Travailleurs Chrétiens*
CGT	*Confédération Génénrale du Travail* (General Confederation of Labour)
CIO	Congress of Industrial Organisations
CNP	*Comité national de la productivité*
CNPP	*Comitato nazionale per la Produttività* (National Productivity Committee)
CSEU	Confederation of Shipbuilding and Engineering Unions
DAG	*Deutscher Angestellten-Gewerkschaft* (German Salaried Employers' Union)
DGB	*Deutscher Gewerkschaftsbund* (German Council of Trade Unions, German equivalent of TUC)
DP	*Deutsche Produktivitätsrat* (German Productivity Council)
DSIR	Department of Scientific and Industrial Research
EAC	Engineering Advisory Council
ECA	Economic Co-operation Administration
EPA	European Productivity Agency
ERP	European Recovery Programme
FBI	Federation of British Industries

FO	*Force Ouvière* (French Labour Federation)
FOA	Foreign Operations Agency
GDP	Gross Domestic Product
ICI	Imperial Chemical Industries
IRC	Industrial Relations Commission
JC	Joint Consultation
JPC	Joint Production Committee
LPA	Local Productivity Association
LPC	Local Productivity Committee
LRD	Labour Research Department
OECD	Organisation for Economic Co-operation and Development
OEEC	Organisation for European Economic Co-operation
OBAP	*Office Belge Pour L'Accroisssement De La Productivité*
MINTECH	Ministry of Technology
MITI	Ministry of International Trade and Industry
MRC	Modern Records Centre
NABM	National Association of British Manufacturers
NBPI	National Board for Prices and Incomes
NCMT	Numerically Controlled Machine Tools
NEDC	National Economic Development Council
NIC	National Incomes Commission
NPC	National Productivity Centre
NPI	*Norsk Produktivitetsinstitutt* (Norwegian Productivity Institute)
NUBSO	National Union of Boot and Shoe Operatives
NUGMW	National Union of General and Municipal Workers
NUM	National Union of Mineworkers
PARC	Productivity and Applied Research Committee
PBR	Payment by Results
PCAC	Productivity and Conditional Aid Committee
PEP	Political and Economic Planning
PES	Production Efficiency Service
PRO	Public Records Office
PW	Pleming-Waddell Report
PULI	Percentage Utilisation of Labour Index
RKW	*Rationalisierungs-Kuratorium der Deutschen Wirtschaft* (Rationalisation Committee or Board of the German Economy: effectively the German productivity headquarters)
SNCF	*Sociéte Nationale des Chemins de Fer Francais*
SNS	*Studieförbundet Näringsliv och Samhälle*
TBBPC	Target Bulletin of the British Productivity Council
TGWU	Transport and General Workers Union

TUC   Trades Union Congress
TWI   Training Within Industry
UAW   United Auto Workers
UPMA   United Pattern Makers Association
UPW   Union of Post Office Workers
USDAW   Union of Shop, Distribution, and Allied Workers
USTAP   United States Technical Assistance and Productivity Programme
VDI   *Verein Deutscher Ingenieure* (German Engineering Association)

Acknowledgements

This book began life as a PhD thesis and I therefore have many people to thank going back some years. The University of Exeter and its Wellcome sponsored Centre for Medical History directed by Professor Mark Jackson, and the Economic and Social Research Council gave financial assistance without which the research and production of this book would not have been possible.

Three individuals who were themselves involved in the productivity drive gave valuable reminiscences. John Whitehorn, Eric A. Runacres, and Alexander King generously and courteously allowed me their time to prod and probe their memories of this era. Their conversations proved fascinating and enlightening and they have provided me with fond and lasting memories. Janet Briggs and Kellie Cox of Exeter University's IT department provided tutelage in graphics and word processing. Luciana O'Flaherty of Palgrave Macmillan was supportive, patient, and gave sound advice. Greatest thanks must go to four individuals, Professor Stephen R. M. Wilks, Reader Joseph L. Melling, Professor Christopher Wrigley, and Dr Alan E. Booth. Stephen Wilks provided help with securing the grant from the Economic and Social Research Council for the penultimate year of research. Joseph L. Melling proved invaluable at keeping me motivated and on track at crucial moments in the completion of this work. Alan E. Booth provided many excellent comments and criticisms during the thesis stage. Lastly I would like to thank an anonymous referee of Palgrave Macmillan for superb comments and criticisms of how the manuscript could be improved. All remaining errors are of course the author's.

I would like to thank the following publishers and authors for their permission to reproduce the following copyright material. The Social Market Foundation for permission to reproduce Table 8.1 'Levels of real GDP per head for selected years and countries in international dollars of 1990'; Blackwell Publishing Limited for Table 6.2 'Academic qualifications of company directors for selected years, 1931–71'; Mary O'Mahony and the National Institute of Economic and Social Research for permission to reproduce numbers in Table 2.1 'Labour productivity in the 1980s' and in Table 2.2 'Average annual hours worked per employee in UK manufacturing industry 1979–93'; Oxford University

Press for Table 2.3 'Organisation and productivity'; Elsevier for Table 4.1 'Size of cyclical fluctuations for selected countries, total GDP (1870–1979)'; Thomson Publishing Services on behalf of Routledge for permission to reproduce Table 5.1 'Incomes policies 1966–78'. Blackwell Publishing for permission to reproduce figure 1.1. The MIT Press for permission to reproduce Table 6.3. The OECD for permission to reproduce Tables 3.1 and 3.2. Every effort has been made to trace all copyright holders; but if any have been inadvertently overlooked, the publisher will be pleased to make necessary arrangements at the first opportunity.

Foreword

After the Second World War the United States via the Marshall Plan laid the foundations for a Western European-wide productivity drive. Explicit within this productivity drive was the objective of transforming battles over the distribution of gains from economic growth into apolitical technical questions of production. The productivity drive's specific aim was to promote productivity growth by transplanting best-practice American techniques of production into Western European countries. It sought to accomplish this through national productivity centres and a pan-Western European productivity agency. Soon afterwards the British government also embarked upon its own productivity initiatives to try to increase Britains growth rate. Fundamental to the success of the productivity drive was not only responsive participation by those groups central to economic activity, organised labour, capital, and the government, but also their willing co-operation in the institutional and organisational changes necessary to induce accelerated productivity growth.

Although the UK saw unprecedented rates of economic growth during the Long Boom (1950–73), by comparison with its industrial competitors these were poor. In the now myriad accounts of Britain's post-War relative economic decline three groups have been blamed, two of which have attracted particular criticism. British trade unions and workers, managers and entrepreneurs, and the state have all received heavy criticism especially for their role in retarding institutional and organisational change. An abundance of studies across a range of industries now document how and why British unions, managers, and government retarded or failed to implement reform.

It is through the work of the productivity agencies that the conduct of British workers, managers, and entrepreneurs is viewed during the Long Boom. This perspective on the behaviour of these groups reveals that the picture of the way in which these actors have been portrayed in various institutional accounts of Britain's relative economic decline is in need of greater subtlety and refinement. The picture so often portrayed of obstructive worker attitudes to change is found wanting, but such a judgement also applies in part to management. Moreover the real underlying theme is not so much one of deliberate obstruction but more one of institutional legacies that act to delimit the response of managers and workers to what appears self-beneficial change. As concerns post-War British governments here the view is reinforced that they either perceived the alteration of the significant institutional boundaries governing the workings of the UK economy as unfeasible, or were unwilling to attempt such change.

1
Introduction: Institutions and the Quest for Productivity

Introduction: Britain's economic performance

As the title of this book implies it is accepted that from the years of the Long Boom (1950–73) until recently the productivity performance of the British economy could have been better than it was. The most impressive and comprehensive quantitative account of Britain's productivity performance has come from Broadberry who has shown that manufacturing productivity was poor during 1950–79 (Broadberry 1997a: 393; 1998). Booth has challenged the idea often made that there was large underperformance in productivity growth in UK manufacturing during the post-War years (Booth 2003).[1] Whilst it is widely accepted that many of the industrialised nations would catch up and converge with the GDP per head of the UK, it is not at all clear why many of them should have overtaken the UK on such measures, as countries like France and Germany did after the Second World War. Indeed one of Britain's most prominent economic historians, Crafts, has said that there remains an 'unexplained' shortfall of about 1 per cent per annum in total factor productivity (TFP) growth during the years of the Long Boom (Crafts 2002: 67). Clearly, something needs to be explained.

This book searches for explanations within three British institutions, those of British trade unions, management, and government, and looks at how they responded to successive attempts to strike a national, long-lasting and durable national productivity bargain in order to raise the rate of productivity growth of the UK economy during the years 1948–90. The initial and terminal dates have been chosen because they enclose a period when many commentators, scholars, governments, and both sides of industry perceived that Britain was falling behind its competitors in economic growth. The year 1948 was when Stafford

Cripps made a speech urging greater efforts to increase productivity and the Anglo-American Council on Productivity was established. The year 1990 was when Prime Minister Margaret Thatcher fell from power and so ended her explicitly ideological project to break the post-war institutional consensus on economic matters and reverse Britain's relative economic decline. Whether her years in power achieved this is something we shall interrogate in the coming pages.

During the 42 years, numerous attempts and methods were tried to solve Britain's perceived relative economic decline and we will focus on some of them. First, there came the productivity agencies, the Anglo-American Council on Productivity 1948–52 (hereafter AACP), the British Productivity Council 1952–73 (hereafter BPC), and the European Productivity Agency 1953–61 (hereafter EPA). Then in the 1960s came the Donovan Commission, the National Board for Prices and Incomes (NBPI) and incomes and prices policies, and the National Economic Development Council (NEDC). We will focus on their efforts to raise the rate of growth of British productivity and to create an enduring national productivity bargain between, labour, capital, and the state.

We will also investigate three industries as productivity studies, which are rarely covered in productivity case studies: telecommunications, the post office, and transport. Industries such as vehicle manufacture, shipbuilding, engineering, steel production, and coal extraction have received much attention, but as Broadberry has pointed out in his magisterial *The Productivity Race* (Broadberry 1997a) and in subsequent research (1998) Britain's post-War productivity failure may lay in services as well as manufacturing.

Institutions, economic organisations, and economic performance

There are various definitions of an institution and various schools of institutional economic analysis. Rutherford defines an institution as, '. . . a regularity of behaviour or a rule that is generally accepted by members of a social group, that specifies behaviour in specific situations, and that is either self-policed or policed by external authority' (Rutherford 1996: 182). Compare this with the definition given by North, 'Institutions are the humanly devised constraints that structure political, economic and social interaction. They consist of both informal constraints (sanctions, taboos, customs, traditions, and codes of conduct), and formal rules (constitutions, laws, property rights)' (North 1991: 97; see also 1994: 360). Although the definitions are similar they emphasise different factors. Indeed there seems to be little precise agreement on what an institution is except for the fact that, 'The only idea common to all usages of the term "institution" is that of some sort of establishment of relative permanence of a distinctly social sort.'[2] While noting the social dimension, institutions will be defined, following North, as structures, which constrain and govern not only human social interaction but also economic and political interaction. North and Rutherford distinguish between institutional arrangements and institutional environments or the institutional matrix. Institutional arrangements can take particular organisational forms but the rules will apply only internally to the organisation. The institutional environment or matrix forms the incentive structure of society and can be considered as constituting the general social and legal rules. Although organisations can be seen as institutions, they can also be treated as separate and distinct, as North does. An organisation is defined as a group of individuals bound together by some common purpose to achieve certain objectives. Organisations include political bodies, economic bodies such as firms and trade unions, social bodies, and educational bodies.

There are two schools of institutional economic analysis, the Old and the New. The Old school embodies the work of such authors as Thorstein Veblen, John Commons, and Clarence Ayers. This school focuses amongst other things upon the ways in which institutional schemes, social conventions, and vested interests can resist technical change and innovation. The New school embodies the work of authors such as Mancur Olson, Oliver Williamson, and the institutional economic history of Douglass North. These writers have examined how transaction costs, the activities of distributive coalitions (through rent seeking), and strategic behaviour can affect long-term economic performance. Neither tradition represents a unified whole, nor are they mutually exclusive, but they are not wholly complementary. The conceptual and analytical framework deployed here will use the analysis of both schools, thus taking note of Rutherford's point that, '...any adequate treatment of institutions cannot ignore points made by each, and that neither approach has a monopoly over the good or the interesting' (Rutherford 1996: x).[3]

A number of works have now emerged which place the institutional perspective at the heart of accounts of economic performance. Crafts remarks, 'Institutions can have important effects on productivity outcomes and on investment' (Crafts 1992b: 22). Olson explored how institutions as distributive coalitions can through rent seeking hinder economic growth (Olson 1982). North who has written extensively about the role of institutions in economic history has asserted that institutions in societies, '... are the underlying determinant of the long-run performance of economies' (North 1981; 1990: 107; 1999).[4]

Institutions together with the standard constraints of economic activity determine transaction (exchange) and production costs.[5] Transaction costs are a critical component in the feasibility of engaging in economic activity. Furthermore North argues that it is the interaction between institutions and organisations that shapes the institutional evolution of an economy and that, 'Institutions provide the incentive structure of an economy; as that structure evolves, it shapes the direction of economic change towards growth, stagnation, or decline' (North 1991: 97; 1993). Therefore institutions and their interaction with organisations emerge as fundamental to a country's economic performance.

North's ideas have been questioned. Hampsher-Monk has challenged the assumptions underlying North's (1981) explanation of the shift from hunter-gatherer societies to agrarian society on two grounds. First, arguing that the assumption of rationality was not consistently deployed, but was instead utilised in an ad hoc manner to build the model. Secondly, that North took outcomes and then worked backwards to derive suppositional statements about such vectors as prices, which was part of North's model to explain (Hampsher-Monk 1992: 54–7). The most sustained, systematic, and devastating critique of North's work comes from Gustafsson. Gustafsson has argued that North's theoretical framework is difficult to render operational due to insufficient formalisation, and methodologically and more fundamentally that it is not falsifiable because no criteria are given as to how inefficient or efficient institutions have to be in order to explain variations in economic performance (Gustafsson 1998: 23).

Let us then turn to Eichengreen's work on institutions. Like North's, this falls within the field of the New Institutional Economics, and in one particular approach Eichengreen uses game theory to view institutional behaviour and its impact upon economic performance.[6] He based his model upon an established vein of literature on game theory, institutions, and economic growth. Dasgupta states that 'Game Theory is concerned with strategic behaviour on the part of decision units in a situation where the action of each affects all. It can thus be read as a sort of multi-person decision theory' (Dasgupta 1989: 619). For his analytical framework Eichengreen drew heavily from Lancaster's explicit model of economic growth as an adversarial differential game between capitalists and workers, where each has to make strategic decisions. Lancaster modelled capitalism as a simple and dynamic two-period finite time horizon game. At the end of the game neither party has any interest in what happens after. Workers control the rate of consumption in each period and capitalists control the rate of investment in each period. The most significant way in which workers can determine their rate of consumption, between defined boundaries, is through wage bargaining, their wages being a ratio of output to consumption. Capitalists determine their rate of consumption as a ratio of investment to the output that was not consumed by the workers. If the capitalists invest all output that was not consumed by the workers in the first period they will have greater output and consumption in the second. However this holds only if the workers keep an appropriate and agreed wages and consumption 'time-shape' made with the capitalists.[7] Likewise if the workers forego a large part of their current-period wages and consumption, then they will have greater consumption and wages in the next. Thus each is faced with a dilemma, and the outcome for both groups is dependent upon not only its own intertemporal decisions but also the intertemporal decisions of the other (Lancaster 1973).[8] How can workers and capitalists be assured that the other group will honour an agreement to forego a low first-period consumption rate for a higher second-period consumption rate? Applying Lancaster's perceptive model to national economies is difficult because of the difficulty for workers and capitalists in ensuring that the other party will keep to an agreed consumption and investment 'time-shape' which will enhance future growth.

Eichengreen used a very similar framework to explain the differential performance of the Western European economies after the Second World War. The theoretical core of Eichengreen's model along with the Calmfors Driffill model (which we shall discuss shortly) is deployed through much of the book and examines the way in which organised labour and employers responded to the efforts of the productivity drive to promote faster productivity growth. His model will therefore be set out in some detail. Eichengreen has put forward an explanatory framework which relies on an initial high-investment and low-consumption choice, encapsulated in implicit institutional arrangements which were crucial to the creation of the Long Boom in the Western European economies after the Second World War. For Eichengreen, the historically high rates of investment and the rapid increase in world trade after 1950 gave rise to the rapid growth of the Western European economies. The increase in world trade was the product of institutional agreements such as the General Agreement on Tariffs and Trade and the Bretton Woods system. High investment was the product of immediate wage moderation by labour and immediate dividend restraint by management. Organised labour and management agreed, in effect, to intertemporal substitution or deferred present consumption for increased future consumption. Labour-wage moderation existed in the European economies because institutional arrangements had been put in place, which afforded little opportunity for labour and management to renege on commitment to moderation.

These three institutional arrangements or mechanisms were bonding, co-ordinating, and monitoring (between 1945–59), which effectively nullified what we may view as a prisoner's dilemma. Monitoring mechanisms allowed workers to assess management investment decisions, thus ensuring that workers would know if wage restraint was not translating into investment. The Co-Determination Law of 1951 and the Works Councils in Germany, which allowed labour representatives on the executive boards of companies, are examples. Bonding mechanisms were such devices as government subsidies to firms, which would be forfeited if the firm reneged on its investment plans. Another example would be social security schemes in return for wage moderation by organised labour as in Belgium and Austria. Finally, co-ordinating mechanisms were institutions that centralised wage bargaining in the hands of employers' associations and, trade union associations, with or without government assistance. The importance of co-ordinating mechanisms is that they prevented competitive wage spirals between unions. This process was also helped by what Eichengreen refers to as bonding. Unions accepted wage centralisation because of the wage compression (the narrowing of wage differentials between unions) that bonding brought and employers were provided with inputs at subsidised below market prices. The resultant wage moderation could be 'sold' to economic agents as a contribution to full employment, again facilitating bonding. In Belgium the *Programmation Sociale* of the 1960s narrowed regional and intersectoral wage differentials between men and women. Holland and Sweden also witnessed wage compression.

As in Lancaster's framework the prisoner's dilemma is caused by the incentive of a smaller, but immediate consumption for which labour and management have to forego a larger future consumption. For neither side can be sure that the other will keep to its commitment, thus there is a time or dynamic inconsistency problem. The time inconsistency problem is the continuing commitment to wage moderation by labour on the one hand and the continuing commitment to dividend restraint by management on the other. Thus both labour and management gained from this co-operation (and in sum the gain to the community was higher), because labour got long-term wage growth and management got long-term dividend growth. These institutional mechanisms were strongest in Austria, the Scandinavian countries, and West Germany. The UK, Ireland, and France are examples of where they were weakest (Eichengreen 1994; 1996b).[9] The virtue of Eichengreen's analysis should now be clear. It proposes and indeed plausibly suggests three institutional mechanisms that will ensure that organisations of workers and capitalists keep a commitment to an agreed wages, consumption, and investment 'time-shape' which will enhance long-term economic growth.

Eichengreen's ingenious model of economic performance is not, however, without criticism. Booth, Melling, and Dartmann have questioned Eichengreen's interpretation of the initial post-War conditions in West Germany, Sweden, and the UK. They argue that out of these three countries, Britain had the most favourable environment for the building of a productivity coalition that would enhance long-term growth. They note that the post-war German trade union movement was not 'inevitably destined' towards consensual polices. Although the unions demanded co-determination (*Mitbestimmung*) the employers resisted and strikes ensued. Only after severe industrial relations conflict was compromise reached and co-determination implemented, but only in the iron, steel, and coal industries. With respect to Sweden, Booth *et al.* argue that the productivity coalition contained within it serious tensions. The Swedish labour congress were not favourably disposed towards centralisation of wage bargaining and the largest exporting companies within the Swedish employer federation opposed the ambitious control agenda of Swedish labour (Booth *et al.* 1997). Booth, Melling, and Dartmann are surely right to question Eichengreen's interpretation of the recent past, particularly the initial conditions. However we are primarily although not exclusively concerned with the analytical institutional framework he implements with which to view institutions. His categorisation of bonding, co-ordinating, and monitoring mechanisms will be particularly helpful.

The use of institutions as a solution concept in economic analysis of a game theoretical kind is also not without criticism. Mirowski amongst others has argued that such analysis assumes constancy of player or economic agent rationale, in other words there are no learning effects, which would presumably change agent rationale. However learning effects may break the constancy assumption. Mirowski has also argued that it assumes constancy of rules of interaction, and finally that it assumes stability of the objectives of agents and stability of the environment (Mirowski 1986; Rutherford 1996: 20–1). Here again however, the attractiveness of Eichengreen's framework should be visible. Eichengreen uses the constancy assumptions only in a very weak sense. Economic agents constantly need to be reassured that they are not being deceived, that the agreed wages, consumption, and investment 'time-shape' is being adhered to, hence the mechanism of monitoring. The constancy of economic agent rationale and rules of interaction will not be broken but reinforced; agents will soon learn if they are being deceived. The stability of the environment assumption is important, for changes in the environment do indeed bring to an end Eichengreen's analysis of the differential economic performance of the Western European economies. Yet, it is precisely the changing environment, which destroys the three institutional mechanisms of monitoring, bonding, and co-ordinating. Hence the conducive, 'time-shape' wages, consumption, and investment pact for fast long-run growth is smashed.

One of the ways in which the environment can change and thereby destroy the institutional mechanisms is through conflict over property rights, which determine particular wealth distributions (Rowlinson 1997: 37–8). Taking this point Knight has argued that institutional development is not best explained as a Pareto superior response to collective goals, such as North and others have argued, but that it is much more a function of the conflict over wealth and income distribution. Therefore institutional development is a contest among economic agents to establish rules that structure equilibrium outcomes most favourable to them. The determining factor in this contest is the relative abilities of economic agents or groups of agents to force others to act in ways contrary to their unconstrained preferences. From this struggle institutional development and change become an ongoing bargaining game among the members of a group or society.[10]

This contest over who gains the most substantive social outcome is one that we will explore fully in the following chapters. This approach ties in with those of the Old Institutional Economists such as Veblen. Veblen looked at how institutions can resist technical change by reference to their goals and aims, and the book will look at how economic actors attempt to structure institutions to achieve their aims (Veblen 1990). Lastly, institutions do not exist in a vacuum but in market environments (e.g. labour and product markets) and here we will place the analysis of how the institutions of capital and labour responded to the productivity drive within this context.

As we see in Eichengreen's model the presence of a co-ordinating mechanism helped ameliorate competitive wage spirals between unions, by co-ordinating and synchronising unions' wage bargaining. But wage bargaining and economic performance is also affected by the structure and number of unions in an economy as shown by the Calmfors and Driffill model where the quantity of unions and their structure has a large impact upon economic performance. Wage restraint is subject to the problem of collective action, for although collective wage restraint may be in the interest of all unions, such behaviour will not survive if the benefits of it are bestowed upon all unions indiscriminately. For instance, even though a union movement as a whole may have agreed to a policy of wage restraint it could be possible to obtain larger wage increases than the agreed norm without jeopardising the macroeconomic benefits of the agreed wage restraint, such as lower inflation. All unions would then face an incentive to maximise their own utility by demanding higher wages than the norm and could effectively 'free ride' on the wage restraint of others. If all unions followed this rationale then there would of course be no restraint at all. Theoretically, therefore, wage restraint, particularly voluntary as opposed to enforced or sanctioned restraint, would appear very difficult in environments of multi-unionism (Jones 1987: 142). More to the point, multi-unionism would lead directly to lower investment because if the firm undertook investment then it might face the prospect of the union appropriating the returns from that investment in the future in the form of higher-wage demands. Whereas if wage rates are determined centrally on an economy-wide level then the firm's decision to invest would not have to take account of this possibility. As Eichengreen says, '. . . competitive decentralised wage setting was ill suited to internalising the externalities for investment that spilled across sectors and over time. To the extent that such externalities prevailed, co-ordinated wage bargaining was required for efficiency. In the presence of externalities, competitive, decentralized markets did not suffice' (1996b: 44, 50).[11]

It needs to be pointed out that Eichengreen's corporatist framework with centralised and co-ordinated wage bargaining though similar to the Calmfors Driffill model is different from the hump-shaped relationship proposed by Calmfors and Driffill. Eichengreen is essentially proposing a highly skewed relationship where only (and that is the crucial difference) centralised and concertised (by both employers and employees organisations) wage bargaining will bring about wage moderation which is in line with productivity growth. Whereas Calmfors and Driffill argue that macroeconomic performance could be good under very decentralised and poorly co-ordinated or highly centralised and well co-ordinated wage bargaining as shown in Figure 1.1.

Those economies with either extensive decentralised wage setting or extensive centralised wage setting were better at containing aggregate

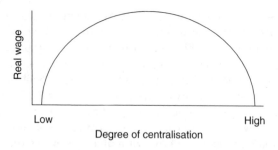

Figure 1.1   The hump-shaped hypothesis of Calmfors and Driffill
Source: Calmfors and Driffill (1988: 15).

real wage growth than those with intermediate centralisation of wage setting, at the industry and craft level, such as the UK (Calmfors and Driffill 1988).[12] However there may be a problem with this model. It is crucially dependent upon where countries fall in the ranking of centralisation and decentralisation and there is disagreement about rankings in such measures partly because of the small set of advanced industrial countries studied (Honkapohja 1988; Moene *et al.* 1993: 68–9). For example, it is suggested that countries like Switzerland and Japan, which have been categorised as highly decentralised may be better categorised as highly centralised because of the high levels of co-ordination between employers in the wage setting process. So if these two economic 'star performers' are taken out of the Calmfors and Driffill model the correlation between real wage setting and level of centralisation becomes much weaker. Nevertheless, as Crouch has documented, five other studies of centralisation rank the UK as relatively decentralised in its wage bargaining when compared to other Western European countries (Crouch 1993: 14). Moreover the Calmfors and Driffill model is, as Carlin and Soskice put it, a 'major intellectual advance', and what is important from our point of view is that it is still true that like the Eichengreen model it suggests that fully centralised and or highly co-ordinated bargaining is better than highly decentralised wage bargaining. This is because it produces lower equilibrium rates of unemployment due to fiscal externalities and union preferences (Carlin and Soskice 1990: 408–14).

The productivity drive

There is a significant amount of literature written on the post-War productivity drive, when narrowly defined, to include only the AACP,

BPC, and EPA. Carew wrote the first significant study of how organised British labour responded to transatlantic attempts at promoting productivity 'consciousness' among trade unions (1987; 1991). Tiratsoo and Tomlinson have written a volume which deals not only with the agencies of the productivity drive, primarily the AACP and the BPC, but also looks at how the Conservative governments of 1951–64 approached the problem of Britain's poor productivity growth rate. Their analysis and conclusion paint an underwhelming picture of the lacklustre and reluctant way in which the Conservative governments attempted to solve the perceived problem (1998a).[13] Tomlinson has written widely and extensively about the Attlee government's attempts in the post-War years to boost Britain's productivity and economic performance. Broadly he has argued that the Attlee government did all that it could within their own political ideology and the foreign constraints they found themselves operating under (Tomlinson 1995; 1997). It was however somewhat thwarted in its attempts by unenthusiastic and in some cases intransigent managers, employers, and their peak associations like the FBI and BEC (Tomlinson 1991a,b; 1992; 1993; 1994a,b,c; 1996b). Gourvish and Tiratsoo have produced an edited collection showing the variations between countries in their reception of American management practices and education (1998). Tiratsoo has written perhaps the first study of how the productivity drive in an institutional form faired in Japan (2000), while Clark has argued that the AACP was a failure because it had to work within the constraining influence of the prevailing institutional nexus between British industries (1999). One of the latest offerings is a comprehensive collection looking at the 'limits' of American influence in changing Western European and Japanese business practices and the adoption of American technology (Zeitlin and Herrigel 2000).

We shall also look at the broader canvas of the productivity drive including such initiatives as the Donovan commission, the National Board for Prices and Incomes (NBPI) (and incomes and prices policies and initiatives more generally), and the National Economic Development Council (NEDC) and analyse them through the perspectives of Calmfors and Driffill, and Eichengreen. The Donovan commission has received attention and analysis in various books and Middlemas has written one book on the NEDC (Middlemas 1983). We shall use these and other sources to provide material for our theoretical perspective. Fels and Mitchell both wrote accounts of the NBPI, Mitchell's was more a biography of the NBPI whereas Fels undertook analysis of its work and more particularly its reports but did not examine the broader context

(Fels 1972; Mitchell 1972). We will ask within a broader framework why in a country seemingly so in need of rising its productivity growth rate compared to its Western European rivals – a situation then perceived by many policy makers, business leaders, and trade unionists – the quest for increased productivity faired poorly. Tables 1.1 and 1.2 give a brief outline of the many productivity agencies and initiatives in operation during the 1950s and beyond.

Table 1.1   Productivity agencies in selected countries

Country	Productivity agency	Structures of decentralisation
Europe	European Productivity Agency (EPA) 1953–61	National Productivity Centres
Britian	Anglo-American Council on Productivity (AACP) 1948–52	De-briefing tours
	British Productivity Council (BPC) 1952–73	Local Productivity Associations In 1969, 148 LPAs in UK Local Productivity Committees
Germany	Deutsche Produktivitätsrat (DP)	130 local branches in Germany
	Rationalisierungs-Kuratorium der Deutschen Wirtschaft (RKW) – became German productivity headquarters in 1950	
France	Comité national de la productivité (CNP) Association Française pour L'Accroissement de la Productivité (AFAP); both founded in 1950	Eight regional productivity centres – Marseilles, Tunis, Strasbourg, Nancy, Toulouse, Montpellier, Bordeaux, Mulhouse
Italy	Comitato Nazionale per la Produttività (CNPP) – founded in 1951	Twelve provincial productivity centres, e.g. Bologna, Genoa, Sienna
Norway	Norsk Produktivitetsinstitutt (NPI) (founded 1953)	Local productivity branches, by 1963, 13 branches, especially in districts with small firms
Sweden	Studieförbundet Näringslivoch Samhälle (SNS)	Local Chapters in cities with small working parties
Belgium	Office Belge Pour l'Accroisssement De La Productivite (OBAP)	Several regional councils, e.g. Walloon, Flemish, with regional delegates and action committees

Denmark	National Association for the Progress of Danish Industry	Four productivity councils, e.g. industry, distribution, and building
Netherlands	National Productivity Centre	Vertical productivity centres for each industry, e.g. clothing, light, metal printing
Japan	Japan Productivity Centre 1955–62	Seminars and lecture series, five regional productivity centres, internal study visits

Sources: Derived from TUC, *Report of Annual Congress* 1969, p. 390. MRC.MSS.292/ 557.371/4, 'Community action in Western Europe: decentralisation of national productivity efforts on a regional and local basis', n.d. MRC.MSS.292/557.371/4, EPA, *European Productivity*, No. 29, June 1958, pp. 39–40. MRC.MSS.200/F/3/D3/7/13, 'Towards higher productivity in France: the French government's two productivity organs', n.d. p. 2. Amdam and Bjarnar (1998), Carew (1987), Gemelli (1995), Kuisel (1993), Link (1991), Tiratsoo (2000).

Table 1.2   British productivity initiatives 1948–90

Council on Prices, Productivity and Incomes (Cohen Council) 1957–60
Wage and price restraint

National Incomes Commission (NIC) 1962–65
Wage and price restraint

National Economic Development Council (1962–92)
Triparite co-operation between industry, unions, and
   government for faster growth
National Plan for growth

Donovan Commission 1965–68
Reduction in strikes and restrictive practices
Restructuring of trade unions and employers associations

National Board for Prices and Incomes 1965–70
Wage and price restraint
Productivity bargaining, and payment by results
Greater efficiency in work organisation

Thatcher's Reform Programme 1979–90
Trade union law reform
Profit sharing
Privatisation
Emphasis upon market solutions and freer markets

Institutions, the productivity drive, and technical change

In the Eichengreen model, which has at its heart the importance for fast growth of bargained organisational co-operation viewed from a game theoretical context, investment is a crucial factor. Although investment has been relatively lower in the UK than in other faster-growing continental economies this is not the only cause of Britain's relative economic decline. Crafts in his many explorations of Britain's relatively poor post-war economic performance has partly utilised the same framework as Eichengreen. Crafts sees productivity outcomes as the result of institutional bargaining between unions and managers over wages and work effort, and the framework within which this took place can be substantially altered by governments. Successive British post-War governments failed to reform the institutional structures of labour relations in which bargaining took place. They feared the electoral consequences. Thus governments focused upon short-run macroeconomic success so as to enhance their electoral chances, but this resulted in poor long-run growth. Post-War governments failed to attack the ability of trade unions to exercise restrictive practices and this restricted management's right to manage. Britain's poor performance has thus been the result of a low-level productivity bargaining equilibrium between firms and their workers (Crafts 1992b; 1995b). Crafts in his explanations, however, places stress not so much upon low investment as a result of this low-level productivity bargaining equilibrium, but instead poor returns on that investment, '...during 1958–72 the rate of growth of net output per unit of investment in Germany was 1.9 times the level in Britain while the German investment rate was 25 per cent higher' (Crafts 1992b: 26).[14]

The work of Eichengreen and Crafts lays emphasis upon two factors for fast growth. As we have seen Eichengreen stresses wage moderation by labour as a necessary precondition for high levels of investment by management. While Crafts acknowledges this, he also places importance upon the returns to that investment and a key determinant of this is labour's ability to impose restrictive working practices. Thus if workers can slow down the adoption of disembodied or embodied technical progress, then they could have profound consequences on the rate of a country's economic growth.[15] This relationship is succinctly summarised by Buchele and Christiansen, 'In the long run, the rate of growth of productivity depends on the rate of technical change and innovation. Workers can either cooperate with...technical change or they can resist it' (Buchele and Christiansen 1992: 79). René Richard who himself took part in the productivity drive wrote, 'It is not possible however to increase productivity without the support of labour...' (Richard 1953: 279).[16]

One of the central objectives of the AACP and other productivity initiatives was to encourage the acceptance of new, more efficient methods involving technical change; in other words to increase the returns to investment.[17] The productivity initiatives deployed various instruments to promote increased technical advancement in UK and Western European firms. These included advisory and promotional literature, consultancy work, and the holding of conferences and seminars, reform of collective bargaining, and income restraint.[18] Automation, mechanisation, and technical change were among the most important points emphasised by the productivity agencies. An analysis of the results of 58 AACP team reports was undertaken by the AACP. Forty-three team reports cited the extensive use of mechanical aids as the most important factor in achieving a high level of productivity in the USA. The fourth most important factor, which was mentioned in 26 of the team reports, was the extent of mechanisation.[19] The report of the Pressed Metal team of the AACP came to the conclusion that, 'The use of *Mechanical and Semi-Mechanical Handling Equipment* resulting in efficient utilization of labour could not be stressed too much. The Team emphasised that if the United Kingdom was to increase productivity, ... mechanical aids must be used as much as possible'.[20] The AACP's *Materials handling in industry* report also stressed that good materials handling was essential, '... One of the reasons why their [USA] standard of living is higher is because their materials handling is better' (AACP 1950b: 9).

The BPC in co-operation with the EPA and through the use of its LPAs and LPCs engaged in a massive propaganda exercise, attempting to promote acceptance of technical change and innovation amongst both workers and managers. The following examples should suffice. The Cardiff and District Productivity Committee organised a conference on automation and there were over 100 representatives of various organisations.[21] The Cardiff and District LPA ran jointly with the Welsh College of Advanced Technology a series of lectures given by experts, on automation, one of which was appropriately concerned with trade unions and automation.[22] The Watford LPC also had a half-day conference on automation, as did Barrow-in-Furness.[23] These examples are just a tiny fraction of the talks, tours, and conferences on mechanisation and automation that were organised under the remit of the BPC and attended by, in many cases, 'ordinary' shop-floor workers. Between September 1958 and April 1959 under the auspices of the BPC, 487 public meetings and conferences, 92 film shows, 161 work study functions, 180 circuit schemes, and 110 other miscellaneous activities were held. Many of these specifically focused on technical change.[24]

The Donovan Commission was also aware of the relatively low investment in the UK and that 'extreme union decenetralisation' combined with the reluctance to change was becoming more and more damaging to technical change and that technical advance was making traditional labour practices redundant, but did not lay primary blame upon the unions or workers (Cmnd 1968 3623). The attempts via income policies and the NBPI to restrain wage growth occurred because governments not only wanted to hold down inflation but also because they and firms did not want all productivity gains to be consumed by wage rises and thereby take away the incentives of firms to invest in new, more efficient technology.

Conclusion

The judgements made of the effectiveness of the productivity initiatives have been lukewarm. The productivity organisations, such as the AACP and or the BPC have gone down in history in a rather pessimistic light. Tomlinson said of the AACP that, 'In a simple sense we may say that the AACP failed because the weapon it used – basically the productivity teams and their reports – were hardly adequate to scale the problems of British industry' (Tomlinson 1991a: 89). Dartmann says the AACP failed completely because it was designed for the purpose of promoting a co-determination (similar to that created in Germany in the immediate years after the War) between British labour and capital (Dartmann 1996a: 4–5, 326, 335).

There is only one quantitative assessment of the contribution of the productivity agencies to British and indeed Western European productivity growth. Maddison estimates as a very crude proxy, that the efforts of the productivity agencies along with the dissemination of research and development activities contributed 10 per cent to labour productivity convergence after 1950 between the lead country, the USA, and the following Western European countries (Maddison 1991: 152–3). Broadberry and Crafts have attempted to estimate the contribution of the AACP reports to British labour productivity growth in manufacturing during the period 1954–63. They find the effects of the reports insignificant (Broadberry and Crafts 1996: 74–80). The Donovan Commission and the post-war incomes policies have also faired badly, many authors see the Donovan Commission as a failure along with the industrial relations acts that followed. So too have the incomes policies and the NBPI been seen in a pessimistic light.

Although the productivity drive and its initiatives do not appear to have been successful the recent ingenious theoretical advances of Calmfors and Driffill, and Eichengreen, allow us to look at these attempts to improve Britain's productivity growth rate with fresh eyes and ask from the vantages they offer what were the problems that held these schemes back; in contrast to previous authors who have examined these initiatives using traditional methods. As we outlined earlier there is general agreement that countries which established after 1945 successful co-operation and co-ordination between 'the social partners' appear to have had faster growth than those which did not and, secondly, a central concern of the productivity drive seems to have been to encourage mechanisation, automation, and faster technical change. The productivity initiatives therefore can provide a window on the two central elements in the growth process during capitalism's golden age: organised and effective collaboration between the state, employers, and workers and the problems of technical change.

In Chapter 2 British workers and the question mark that has hung over their unions and restrictive practices will be investigated via one of the most sustained and pervasive critiques of them by N. F. R. Crafts. In Chapter 3 we shall look at the ways in which employees and unions in comparison with their continental counterparts responded to programmes trying to improve British productivity. Chapter 4 will explore the ways in which British governments have intervened in the economy and are said to have caused poor performance. Post 1945, governments had little interaction with the productivity agencies of the AACP, BPC, and EPA, and what involvement they did have has been written about well by authors Tomlinson and Tiratsoo, and Carew; so in Chapter 5 we will instead look at the productivity enhancing measures of the Donovan Commission and incomes policies, which aimed to promote trade union discipline, lessen restrictive practices, and closely connect workers' pay with productivity. Chapter 6 surveys the functions and literature surrounding that other favourite of 'declinists' – poor British management; and in Chapter 7 we interrogate the way in which British managers and entrepreneurs along with their Western European counterparts received and responded to techniques to improve managerial ability and skills. In Chapter 8 conclusions will be offered.

2
British Workers and Britain's Relative Economic Decline

Introduction: the British worker question

There can be few organisations which have had so much opprobrium and blame loaded upon them for Britain's relative economic decline than the trade unions. As Nichols noted, set against the receding legacy of the Second World War, the post-War productivity drive, and the 'promise of productivity' (a reference to Graham Hutton's book *We Too Can Prosper*), the rise in competitiveness of other national economies served only to accentuate the perception of a poorly performing British economy, and give a yard stick by which British workers, were to be adversely judged (Nichols 1986: 20).[1]

Moreover the question of British workers and their relationship to production is highly controversial, as Terry has written, 'Few topics have aroused as much comment (and acrimony) as the issue of workers, unions, and job control. For some "restrictive practices", operated in industries such as engineering, by and through militant shopfloor union organisation are one, possibly the largest, key to Britain's economic decline' (Terry 1988: 17). Some authors have attributed Britain's relative economic decline almost wholly to the trade unions, such as and perhaps unsurprisingly, Hayek (1984).

Allen has noted that, 'All other industrial countries have suffered from labour troubles since the war [World War Two], but it is in Britain that they seem to have exerted the most damaging effect on production and so on living standards.' Both Allen and Phelps Brown believed that, '...our [the UK's] industrial relations remain the prisoners of their history'. Phelps Brown contended that British trade unions had resisted labour-saving changes and gave a high priority to job security because

18

of the legacy of hardship that they had gone through during the first industrial revolution (Allen 1979: 63–5; Phelps Brown 1977: 19).

Labour is seen as influencing productivity in two ways. One is the impact that trade unions can have in shaping behaviour and the other is the attitude of workers (Batstone 1986: 32). As Nichols has commented, many economists tend to explain lower British productivity by worker attitudes (Nichols 1986: 50). Given that the two are almost inseparable we will explore both in the coming pages starting with the writings of Crafts. Crafts has vigorously argued that British workers and their unions were a significant cause in Britain's relative economic decline. His arguments have consistently embodied and drawn on evidence from numerous authors who are also germane to our study. Given this, we shall discuss the assertions of Crafts in some detail and then examine the works he draws on.

Crafts and the British worker question

As we saw in the introduction, Crafts sees institutions as important to growth performance. We also saw that North defined institutions as the incentive structures in society. Crafts argues that institutional failings within Britain's industrial relations and the resultant poor incentive structures facing decision makers in business and government have been major causes to Britain's relative economic decline (Crafts 1996b: 85; 1999a: 28). We also noted in the introduction that Crafts views productivity outcomes as a product of bilateral bargaining between firms and their workers over wages and work effort (manning). Crafts asserts that the UK has suffered from a low-level productivity bargaining equilibrium between firms and their workers which was caused principally by two factors. First, there was the inherited craft or multi-union structure after the Second World War combined with monopolistic product markets, which successive post-War governments failed to reform because of the post-war settlement or 'social contract'. The post-war environment of low unemployment and an attitude of acquiescence towards trade unions by successive administrations coupled with multi-unionism, led to decentralised shop-floor bargaining. Much as the Donovan report asserted, as the post-war period progressed bargaining power shifted towards shop stewards and away from union leaders, although there were exceptions, such as the aggressive trade union leader Frank Cousins of the Transport and General Workers Union (hereafter TGWU). Multi-unionism is said to produce unions with narrow scope and low sophistication, they represent small numbers of workers, and are unable to effectively co-ordinate the interests of their members or to implement strategy. Unions of narrow scope are said to be more obstructive to productivity-enhancing changes than all-encompassing ones. Multiple unionism is particularly inimical to Eichengreen's idea of a co-operative and binding productivity equilibrium between labour and capital because individual unions have an incentive to 'free ride' on the wage restraint of others (Crafts 1988: xvi–i; 1991a: 88–9, 91, 94; 1991b: 273–5; 1992c: 32, 44–7, 52; 1993a: 1–2, 6, 8; 1994b: 45–7; 1995b: 246–7, 254–5; 1997: 44–6; 1999b: 60–1; 2002: 80–1).

There are a number of ways in which Crafts supports these assertions. First, he draws on a number of works such as those by Pratten, which alleged that behavioural causes such as strikes, overmanning, and other restrictive practices have in significant part been the cause of the relatively poor productivity of the British plant owned by international companies. Secondly, drawing on the work of Olson and to greater extent Batstone, it is asserted that small unions can lead to overmanning because each union does not have to withstand the costs that such a restrictive practice imposes upon the economy. Finally, in formal econometric models, Crafts and others have shown that multiple unionism will lower economic growth because of competitive wage demands by the unions, each union holds the firm to 'ransom'.[2] This industrial relations environment, says Crafts, should be contrasted with those present in Germany or Sweden. In those countries industrial unions of high scope and high sophistication with centralised bargaining, legally enforceable contracts, and an absence of multi-unionism and voluntarism facilitated a much greater degree of industrial co-operation between organised labour and capital. Lastly, the surge of productivity in the 1980s in which unemployment rose considerably and product market competition intensified is seen as confirming the relatively poor performance during the Long Boom and the contribution of the policy environment with its low unemployment and slack or uncompetitive product markets. Unemployment reduces workers' bargaining power, and increased product market competition reduces the rents available to firms and thus raises the costs of x-inefficiency (Crafts 1992a: 397–401; 1992b: 22–5; 1993a: 15; 1993b: 45–50; 1993c: 331, 344; 1994a: 41; 1995a: 444; 1996a: 175–7; 1996b: 85, 89, 91–3, 99, 102; 1997: 44–6; 1998b: 27–9; 2002: 79). However Crafts is not the only commentator to argue along these lines, others have too.

The 1980s productivity 'miracle'

The 1980s in Britain witnessed an acceleration of productivity growth so great that it has been labelled the 'Thatcher miracle', although this acceleration represents a rate of growth no faster than that which occurred in the UK in the 1950s and 1960s (Mayes 1996: 1). The average rate of productivity growth in the 1980s was 2 per cent per annum, which though not impressive in aggregate did contain rates of productivity growth for manufacturing which at 5.25 per cent were unprecedented over a long period (Guest 1990: 295). This is to a large extent where the claims for a Thatcherite productivity miracle rest. As Lansbury and Mayes note of this period, '... one fact which stands out is the striking improvement in labour productivity in manufacturing industry. Between 1980 and 1990 net output per head in 1985 prices increased by almost 60 per cent. This compares with 35 per cent and 17.5 per cent over each of the two previous decades...' (Lansbury and Mayes 1996: 20). But, as Cameron from his study of alleged productivity slowdown in the 1970s pointedly noted 'Any claim that the 1980s featured a UK manufacturing productivity miracle is dramatically weakened, however when one considers that the estimated trend rate of [TFP] growth in the 1980s is 2.75 per cent per year, compared with 3.04 per cent per year in the 1960s' (Cameron 2003: 136–7). Table 2.1 reports the dramatic rise in labour productivity during the 1980s as compared to the rest of the economy. Various theories have been advanced to explain this rapid growth rate in manufacturing-labour productivity and many focus on changes in the labour market and industrial relations.

Metcalf claims that there was a 'sea change' in the industrial relations environment in the 1980s, which transformed labour productivity growth in manufacturing. Metcalf, while acknowledging that unions can in

Table 2.1 Labour productivity in the 1980s (index numbers, 1993 = 100)

Year	Output per hour worked (whole economy)	Output per hour worked (manufacturing)	Year	Output per hour worked (whole economy)	Output per hour worked (manufacturing)
1979	71.4	53.6	1987	88.6	74.6
1980	70.6	52.1	1988	89.2	78.9
1981	73.5	54.5	1989	90.7	83.2
1982	76.9	58.1	1990	90.9	85.1
1983	80.1	62.5	1991	92.3	89.7
1984	81.3	65.7	1992	95.6	94.4
1985	83.0	68.1	1993	100	100
1986	86.0	71.0	1994	103.5	103.0

Source: O'Mahony (1999: 116–17).

principle be associated with rapid productivity growth in the firm, argues that in practice in Britain during the Long Boom, 'Union presence [was] generally associated with lower labour productivity in a workplace.' Metcalf cites three reasons as to why manufacturing productivity experienced a surge in the 1980s. First, employers in the early 1980s led an assault on union restrictive practices such as overmanning because they feared bankruptcy in the heightened competition in the product market. Secondly, employees were willing to co-operate because they feared redundancy due to the growing numbers of unemployed. Finally, increased product market competition made firms pay greater attention to labour costs (although this appears in effect to be the same as the first reason). Therefore productivity growth in the 1980s has been due to greater managerial control over the work process and more compliant unions (Metcalf 1989; 1990a: 286, 299; 1990b).

Oulton sees two institutions as retarding the UK's post-War productivity growth – the education system and industrial relations. Oulton argues that the UK industrial relations system had four distinctive features and although other countries may have possessed one or more, no other country possessed all four. These were, first, the high and rising union density before 1979; secondly, the dual system of negotiating both at national and company level with union staff, and at plant level with shop stewards; thirdly, a historical legacy of trade union organisation on craft lines which produced multi-unionism; and finally, British trade unions enjoyed a large number of legal immunities such as the right to secondary picketing which unions in other countries did not. However in the 1980s union power was reduced due to a fall in union density (the most telling measure of union strength), a decline in union recognition, and the imposition of legal constraints on the right to strike and picket. Although as Figure 2.1 shows, falling union density was common to all major industrial nations during the 1980s and Italy experienced a very similar fall to the UK. The growth of contracting out in the public sector also weakened union power by reducing union density; this along with other factors helped to raise productivity growth (Oulton 1995). Haskel too found that the increased product market competition of the 1980s contributed to the productivity surge. This, Haskel suggests, could have been due to the increased pressure on managers not to concede wage claims to unions because of pressure on their profits (Haskel 1991). This evidence would seem to support Crafts's contention that managers had less scope for allowing x-inefficiency in the 1980s. There are many issues here and we will explore some of them in this and the next chapters.

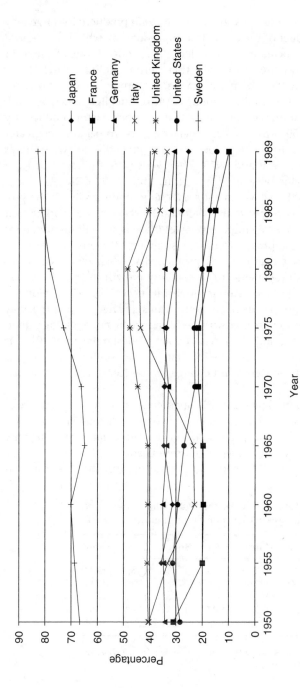

Figure 2.1 Percentage net union density at five-year intervals
Note: Data for the United Kingdom for 1989 is taken from 1988.
Source: Derived from Golden *et al.* (1999: 200).

However, it now looks possible that the 1980s productivity surge may have been a product of the estimation procedures by which the Central Statistical Office calculates value added. Value added is one of the most common measures used to obtain that output growth (Total Factor Productivity Growth) which cannot be accounted for by growth in factor inputs, that is, capital, labour, and to a negligible degree land. Quantitatively the impact of this is that, '...total factor productivity growth in the 1980s was less than a percentage point per annum greater than in the 1973 to 1979 period and was probably below the rates achieved between 1959 and 1973. The 1980s were therefore far from the Thatcher productivity miracle...' (Muellbauer 1996: 233–4).

A challenge to the view that the weakening of unions led to the productivity serge has come from Nolan and Marginson. They argue that studies such as those by Knight on strikes (a study we will discuss soon) and the 'Harvard' approach to unions show that there is no necessary relationship between unions and productivity. Nolan and Marginson stress that the improvement in productivity growth in the 1980s may simply be a function of labour intensification – labour is working harder. It might not be due to efficiency gains; further, as such this may be detrimental to long-run growth performance by encouraging under-investment in plant and equipment (Nolan and Marginson 1990). It is very difficult to measure labour effort but evidence on hours worked per employee suggests no significant change for the 1980s. Table 2.2 reports some findings.

The figures reported in Table 2.2 superficially at least give credence to the Nolan and Marginson argument about increased labour effort, for with little increase in hours worked it seems plausible that labour productivity growth could indeed be due to increased labour effort. One of the pieces of evidence used by some authors to support the assertion that

Table 2.2   Average annual hours worked per employee in UK manufacturing industry 1979–93

Year	Hours	Year	Hours	Year	Hours
1979	1756	1984	1751	1989	1743
1980	1726	1985	1746	1990	1714
1981	1728	1986	1738	1991	1661
1982	1721	1987	1763	1992	1667
1983	1741	1988	1759	1993	1671

Source: Reproduced with permission from O'Mahony (1999: 107).

productivity has increased because of increased worker effort is the Percentage Utilisation of Labour Index (hereafter PULI). Started in 1971 this index purports to measure human exertion per hour by factory operatives using standardised units of measurement, essentially work study techniques. The index in 1979 stood at 100.5 per cent and in 1988 was at 105 per cent, thus recording a rise in labour effort. Yet such measurements of worker effort are highly subjective, and so is the term itself. Guest strongly critiques the PULI asserting that it is not reliable because of the socially constructed nature of effort measurement and the essential inability to measure working times for identical work practices. First, because work practices vary over time, and are never constant, being subject to large or indeed tiny variations, thus introducing time variance into the PULI index. Secondly, effort is itself subject to peer group influence and personal perception, and so are those who measure it. Finally, those trained to measure working times frequently record large (greater than 10 per cent) variations amongst their measurement times (Guest 1990).

Institutional support for the Crafts argument

Two studies have been widely used by authors such as Crafts to provide theoretical sustenance to the claim that British productivity growth has suffered from a legacy of small sectional craft unions which have retarded innovation and constrained wage moderation. One is the work by Olson, in which it was argued that politically stable societies would over time accumulate a mosaic of rent seeking distributive coalitions. These coalitions can continue to exist only if they provide incentives for their members to remain. Thus they must extract more from the economic system than they put in (rent seeking).[3] However when such coalitions become very large (encompassing) their incentive for rent seeking declines until they will gain nothing from it. This is because they will become so big as to encompass most of those who would have to bear the costs of any such behaviour. The UK is seen by Olson and others as a country with a long lineage of political stability, thus ripe for the build-up of distributive coalitions, and one such form would be strong labour market interest groups, like small sectional craft trade unions. Olson sees Britain's competitors such as Germany or Japan as having most of their distributive coalitions destroyed by the ravages of the Second World War (Olson 1982).[4]

Secondly, the work of Batstone is cited as giving empirical support to Olson's notion of institutional sclerosis. Batstone draws on Olson's framework for his notions of organisational sophistication and scope.[5] Union or employer confederations with high sophistication co-ordinate members' interests and develop and implement strategies. Batstone argued that broad scope was usually a precondition for high sophistication. Institutional sclerosis simply referred to Olson's idea that over a stable period of time special interest groups were likely to develop and achieve considerable interest representation, such as trade unions. As we can see from Table 2.3 Batstone considers the UK to have a narrow scope and low-sophistication industrial relations environment, which was aligned with comparatively poor productivity growth (Batstone 1986).

Table 2.3   Organisation and productivity

	Power of employers associations	Productivity growth (GDP per man hour) 1950–73	Productivity growth (GDP per man hour) 1973–79
High sclerosis broad scope, high sophistication			
Netherlands	4	4.4	3.3
Norway	5	4.2	3.9
Sweden	5	4.2	1.9
Belgium	3	4.4	4.2
Mean	4.3	4.3	3.3
Narrow scope, low sophistication			
Canada	1	3.0	1.0
USA	1	2.6	1.4
United Kingdom	2	3.1	2.1
Australia	2	2.6	2.6
Mean	1.5	2.8	1.8
Low sclerosis broad scope, high sophistication			
Austria	4	5.9	3.8
Finland	4	5.2	1.7
West Germany	4	6.0	4.2
Mean	4	5.7	3.2
Broad scope, low sophistication			
Japan	2	8.0	3.9
France	2	5.1	3.5
Italy	2	5.8	3.5
Mean	2	6.3	3.3

Source: Batstone 'Labour and Productivity', Oxford Review of Economic Policy (1986), 2, pp. 32–43, by permission of Oxford University Press.

Although the table seems to show a strong relationship for the period 1950–73 it appears less strong there afterwards. Olson's theory also is not without criticism. Germany may have experienced institutional continuity not discontinuity after the Second World War. Olson's theory also seems unable to account for the worldwide productivity slowdown after 1973, amongst other problems (Paqué 1996; see also Booth *et al.* 1997; Maddison 1988; McCombie and Thirlwall 1994: 81–7). Moreover the Batstone framework reported in the table cannot and does not take account of other factors affecting productivity growth, such as catch-up and convergence, markets, or resource endowments.

A number of authors and case studies now seem to give empirical support to the Batstone and Olson arguments. Elbaum and Lazonick have argued that managers were unable to take control of such factors as manning levels and work loads because of the institutional rigidity imposed by craft union control of the shop floor (Elbaum and Lazonick 1986: 4, 8). Overbeek argues British unions and their workers have helped retard the implementation of an entire production system namely that of Fordism. Fordism was a new way of organising the labour process, on the shop floor and in society at large. In most European countries restructured capital along Fordist lines led at an early stage to the restructuring of the trade union movement as well. However this restructuring was retarded in Britain because British union structure retained a very specific character up to the late 1970s. Overbeek concludes that in Britain, 'Fordism ... did not develop fully in the post-war decades ... As a result the growth of productivity and the growth of real wages have all lagged behind developments in comparable economies.' Overbeek cites the reason for labour's retarding effect as its craft and decentralised origins (Overbeek 1990: 126, 140). Others explicitly state that Britain is an example where, 'A strong labour movement, defending precise skills, tasks and job rules, can block most of the productive potential associated with modern management methods. This can be called *flawed Fordism*' (Boyer 1995: 29).

Kilpatrick and Lawson argue that when mass production methods arose in the twentieth century it became difficult for management to implement them because of difficulties in overcoming craft workers' control of the shop floor. Furthermore, because no centralised collective bargaining system arose in the UK and hence bargaining between trade unions and employers stayed in its traditional craft union, decentralised mould, then this too constrained productivity growth. British trade unions have, it is said, through their degree of craft work place control been able to retard the introduction of new technology in the industries of shoe production, textile manufacture, and the motor industry (Kilpatrick and Lawson 1980). Lewchuk's examination of the twentieth-century British motor industry concluded that UK trade unions and workers have held back the introduction of Fordism. The British motor vehicle industry grew up out of bicycle manufacture with its skilled craft workers. Motor manufacturing hence also contained the same tradition and was organised on similar principles such as the gang system, piecework, and an absence of close managerial monitoring and supervision. Lewchuk argues that, '... in the late 1930s there were signs that production institutions had evolved and that labour had laid the basis for a post-war challenge to managerial authority'. Managers in the motor industry in the interwar period did not switch to Fordism because they believed that workers would not accept the fast work pace, abolition of piecework and payment by day rates, and close supervision that it necessitated. They felt essentially that workers would be un-co-operative and this would produce a poor effort–wage bargain. After the Second World War managers believed that they could introduce Fordism because automation allowed them to control the effort–wage bargain. However motor vehicle manufactures were wrong, and automation did not give them the control of the work process that was required to make the Fordist, machine intensive, mass production techniques profitable. Motor manufactures would have been better to keep to the British system, which although giving lower potential long-run market share would have given greater long-run profitability (Lewchuk 1986; 1987: 177).

Lazonick's work on why the British cotton industry was so slow to adopt the ring frame and the Northrop automatic loom in the late nineteenth and early twentieth century partly places the blame on the structure and organisation of industrial relations in the industry, and the power of the unions. The unions were powerful enough to determine piece rates unilaterally, and to also insist on the maintenance of wage lists, and the numbers of machines per worker, and this reduced the incentive of mill owners to introduce the new weaving technology (Lazonick 1986).

In the shipbuilding industry, trade unions have been seen as a cause in the decline of an industry in which Britain once held undisputed world pre-eminence. A large number of craft unions, had grown up with the growth of the shipbuilding industry, and their strength was such that they could resist the employer using semi-skilled workers in areas of craft work. Craft unions controlled the number of apprentices entering the trade, and they controlled manning levels. Such control hindered the adoption of mid-twentieth century work techniques, such as welding, burning, and prefabrication (Lorenz and Wilkinson 1986). Perhaps the most obvious and stark example of trade union resistance to change in the form of new technology occurred in the printing industry in the 1980s. The union of print workers, the National Graphical Association as it then was, bitterly contested the transfer of newspaper production from Fleet Street to Wapping, where a direct input system of production was to be used. Such a system was the first of its kind in the UK. It did not require typesetters thus dramatically reducing the demand for labour. The union lost the dispute and today Wapping continues to operate (McLoughlin and Clark 1994: 1–2).[6] Indeed Willman concludes that in the industry, 'Overall, therefore, the implementation of new technology in national newspapers has been substantially delayed by union resistance, in the form both of strike action and of the imposition of costs (severance payments and retirement)' (Willman 1986: 129). While in shipbuilding and printing, trade unions may have caused serious problems, but as Gospel has pointed out, it is difficult to assess how widespread and harmful such practices really were (Gospel 1988: 89).

It has been pointed out that one of the reasons why British labour has possibly been more restrictive than that in other countries is because such restrictions enhanced their bargaining power and was their only way to reap rewards from increases in productivity growth. Thus this is essentially a defensive attitude (Hyman and Elger 1981: 145). The distribution of gains is of course part of the Eichengreen framework, for bonding is one of the mechanisms that ensures material benefits to labour in return for co-operation in the form of wage moderation. Again this is an issue we will explore in the next chapter.

Empirical works used to support the Crafts thesis

As we saw, one of the works which has often been cited to justify claims that British workers retarded productivity growth is that of Pratten's. Pratten obtained detailed information from 100 international companies with plants in Germany, France, USA, and the UK. However he was only able to make quantitative comparisons for 71 plants in the UK with plants elsewhere. These plants then employed about 10 per cent of the workers in manufacturing industry. Pratten found that differences in behaviour such as strikes and other restrictive practices accounted for in some cases 40–50 per cent of the productivity differences between British plants and German or American plants of the same company. Pratten's information was almost exclusively obtained from management (Nichols 1986: 59). When he asked management for reasons as to the productivity differentials, as he did of those in the motor industry, the replies focused on trade unions as a cause of overmanning, and negotiating problems due to the organisational structure of UK unions. Some reductions in manning could be negotiated at local level while others would have to be raised at national level (Pratten 1976: 62).

Pratten in another study also noted that output per employee was about 50 per cent higher in France and Germany than in the UK and that in the US output per employee was about 100 per cent higher than in the UK. This was because, '...for comparisons of UK plants with German and French plants of international companies, it was clear that there were on balance, differences in efficiency – that the less efficient manpower and other practices applied more often at UK factories'. This report draws on evidence from 25 studies (some international comparisons) conducted in industries such as shipbuilding, chemicals, printing, motor vehicle, mechanical engineering, and textiles. These studies such as the Ryder and Central Policy Review Staff Reports on motor vehicles or the AACP team reports documented that inefficiency in the use of labour (crudely, overmanning) was a cause of poor productivity growth. Two causes of this inefficient use of labour were trade union restrictive practices such as strikes and trade union structure. The conclusion of this study reported that a valuable aid to increasing productivity was industrial co-operation (Pratten and Atkinson 1976: 574, 576). Prais studied productivity performance in ten industries in the UK, the USA, and West Germany in the 1960s and 70s and found that in UK, productivity growth in six of them was seriously hampered by firms having difficulty in negotiating manning levels with unions over new working practices when technical change was introduced. Prais also found that when plant size rose above 5000 employees nearly twice as many working days were lost due to strikes when compared to the USA and 20 times as many as in Germany and that strike frequency was almost directly proportional to plant size, a very remarkable fact thought Prais (1981: 61–2, 80).

Pratten, Pratten and Atkinson, Prais, and many other studies that have often been cited as evidence that British labour is restrictive and is a drag on productivity growth are not however without criticism. Indeed these studies and others, particularly the Ryder Report on the British Leyland Motor Corporation, have been subjected to strong methodological criticism. Nichols argues that these studies do not meet three elementary criteria needed to make comparative productivity assessments between plants in different countries. These 'ABC' requirements were that comparisons should specify whose productivity is being compared (and the quality and duration of their labour), that the physical means of production should also be specified, and finally that comparisons should report on working practices. None of the above reports met all of these criteria. Pratten and others disregarded the effects upon productivity of differing layouts of plant and the use of space and did not investigate how British managers compared with their continental counterparts in terms of ability in marketing, organisation, supervision, training, and quality control. No account was taken either of the fact that in some countries such as Germany a large pool of immigrant 'guest' workers was drawn on, mainly from countries such as Turkey, Spain, and Italy. These 'guest' workers were more compliant because they were not subject to the same legal rights as the indigenous workers. This was primarily because although such conditions and pay were relatively poor when compared to those of the indigenous workers they were better than those they would have obtained in their country of origin (Nichols 1986).

The issue of restrictive practices has often figured in debates on the effects of unions upon productivity growth. One of the most frequent claims made against British workers in this area, is that they have been comparatively very strike-prone. It is difficult to be precise about strike activity because of varying definitions of strikes between countries, non-reporting, differential strike rates amongst industries, and the uneven distribution of industries between countries (Crouch 1985: 115; Gilbert 1996: 130–3). However as Richardson says, '...the best available evidence suggests that by international standards the UK is affected only to an average extent by strike activity' (Richardson 1991: 432). Wrigley argues similarly, 'Contrary to notions of strikes being a (or even the) "British disease", the British pattern has been little different from that of other countries...' (Wrigley 1997: 23). Moreover Figure 2.2 should confirm that Britain did not suffer unduly from strikes in the period of the Long Boom. Indeed countries such as Italy and France fared about the same as the UK.

There is also another point that needs to be drawn here with respect to strikes. It is also not at all clear that strikes constitute a serious damage to productivity performance. Knight used a simple production function to test the effects of strikes on labour productivity. Using strike data for 1968 (a year of high strike activity) Knight sought to establish if strikes displaced an estimated production function, and whether that displacement was positive or negative.[7] Strikes may not be harmful to productivity for a number of reasons. For instance, they can act as a safety valve that reduces tension in the workplace thus enhancing managerial and labour co-operation once the strike is over. Of course strikes could also damage labour productivity by imposing upon the firm irrevocable output loses. Knight however concluded that there was no negative displacement effect on the production function, strikes did not lower labour productivity; thus generalising from the study, Knight thought it

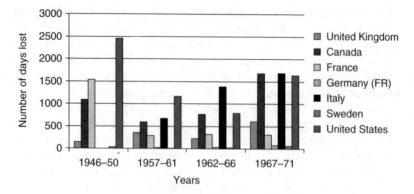

Figure 2.2   Working days lost through strikes in selected countries, 1946–71 (working days per thousand employees per annum)
Note: Selected industrial sectors; mining and quarrying, manufacturing, construction, transport, storage, and communication. Figures show five-year average, not weighted for employment. The series for France does not include 1968.
Source: Derived from Gilbert (1996: 132).

prudent to argue that for the 1960s the impact of strikes upon labour productivity was neutral (Knight 1989). Finally, Dintenfass and others have argued that some employers may have seen strikes as a way of equilibrating market conditions with firm conditions, in other words of bringing supply in line with demand, for example in the motor industry (Anthony 1986: 12–13; Dintenfass 1992: 31–3).

Thus as Phelps Brown has pointed out, 'The idea that British workers as a whole are prone to strike...is not borne out by the facts' (Phelps Brown 1977: 15). Richardson has also stressed this point, '...in spite of the very considerable political debate they have generated, strikes can hardly in aggregate have led directly to the damaging economic consequences frequently claimed' (Richardson 1991: 432). If strikes were a problem for the British economy during the Long Boom and after, then it can only be said with respect to very large manufacturing plants.

Before we proceed further however, we must attempt to define what exactly a restrictive practice is. For it is the degree of control which British labour has exercised over the shop floor, through restrictive practices, which to many writers has been the source of Britain's inability to take up Fordist mass-production methods or indeed any production innovation. This issue cannot of course be disconnected from union structure and indeed is intertwined with it. Trade union restrictive practices can take many forms and some of the more explicit ones that are designed to sustain or increase employment, have been referred to as feather-bedding. Examples are, restrictions on the amount of hours a union member works, limitations on the numbers of those allowed to enter an occupation, such as apprenticeship to a skilled trade, demarcation rules, and the refusal to allow technical change. Other restrictive practices would be the imposition of overmanning by insistence upon the employment of more workers to do a particular job than management might think necessary (Rees 1985: 298–302). The above is in no way a comprehensive definition, indeed it might well be impossible to give such a definition. Nichols points out that virtually all commentators would allow for some restrictions on working practices, either to comply with the law or in order to meet safety standards. But what is a justifiable safety standard and who is to determine it? (Nichols 1986: 274–5) Others would argue with respect to restrictive practices that, '...the whole area is highly contentious, making any "objective" criteria very hard to construct'. Tiratsoo and Tomlinson make this plea with reference to four private and three state investigations into the extent of restrictive practices in private manufacturing undertaken during the Long Boom. Citing the work of Zwieg, Carter and Williams, and three government surveys which asked businessmen if they suffered from the effects of restrictive practices, Tiratsoo and Tomlinson concluded that, 'The picture that emerges from this evidence is, therefore fairly clear. Restrictive practices do not seem to have been a problem for most British employers in the period 1945–60' (Tiratsoo and Tomlinson 1994: 77–8).

The British worker question and technical change

Previously we have looked at the issue of restrictive practices in general, but now we should turn to the issue of technical change, unions and restrictive practices, as this issue is one amongst a number central our study. Theoretically there are a number of ways in which unions could effect the introduction of technical innovation. First, by pursuing a high-wage policy they could deprive the firm of the necessary capital to modernise, and a number of studies have found that unions reduce profitability, thus this could be important. Secondly, by threatening strike action or other forms of restrictive practice at, and or after, the time the firm is about to embark upon modernisation, it could place prohibitive costs upon modernisation. Thirdly, unions could make high-wage demands once installation of an innovation has taken place, which could in effect capture the profits from modernisation. The firm anticipating this could be deterred from modernising. This is of course an aspect of the Eichengreen framework. In this framework a successful productivity coalition for long-term fast growth can only be built if firms and their workers make a binding pact *ex ante* whereby firms know that a sufficient stream of profits, which makes the innovation profitable, will not be captured over a specified time horizon. Alternatively it is possible that unions could accelerate technical change or innovation by pursuing high-wage claims, which encourage the firm to substitute labour-saving technology for relatively expensive union labour. The bargaining and grievances procedures or 'voice effects' of unions could also aid modernisation by reducing workers' fears and resistance to change and making them happier and more co-operative, further still there may be no single union effect. In other words whether unions retard or promote technical change and innovation could depend upon the type of change undertaken, the economic and political environment in which it is undertaken, and the type of union effected, either craft, firm, or industrial (Keefe 1991: 261–4; Machin and Wadhwani 1991: 324–5; Wadhwani 1990: 372; Willman 1986: 5–6). From this we may deduce, as Addison and Addison do, that, 'Obviously, whether unionism's impact on productivity is negative or positive is an empirical question' (Addison and Addison 1982: 146).[8]

Numerous highly quantitative studies have been conducted on whether unions have lowered the level of investment and innovation in British industry and consequently had a negative impact upon productivity. Denny and Nickell found in their study which included data from 72 industries gathered from a census of production survey and two Workplace Industrial Relations Surveys that firms which recognised unions suffered a gross 23 per cent lower investment rate than an equivalent firm which did not have a recognised union. However this figure is derived while holding wages and productivity constant. Given that unions influence wages, usually by pushing them up, then when they take this union wage and productivity effect into account they find that the net reduction in investment is only of the order of between 4 and 13 per cent (Denny and Nickell 1992).

Wadhwani's study concludes that unions appear to have neither a positive nor a negative effect upon investment, productivity growth, and employment. Wadhwani used data from the 1984 Workplace Industrial Relations Survey and company accounts data for the period 1972–86. With respect to productivity growth Wadhwani found that unionised firms experienced faster productivity growth between 1980–84 but did not experience slower productivity growth over the periods 1975–79 and 1985–86. In searching for explanations, Wadhwani believed that the faster productivity growth may have been because of the severe recession in the early 1980s which caused unionised firms to shed their restrictive practices, which they probably had in greater amount than non-unionised firms at the start of the 1980s (Wadhwani 1990). Therefore it is difficult to believe that the Thatcher anti-trade union legislation of the early 1980s was a cause of the faster productivity growth in this period, because if this was the case then why did not pro-union legislation in the 1970s reduce productivity growth.

Since the beginning of the industrial revolution, numerically controlled machine tools (hereafter NCMT) are amongst the most important types of production machinery and they are the most labour saving.[9] Hence here any identifiable union effects would be very important. There are few studies, which focus on this sector specifically, and those that do are studies of the US NCMT sector. However these studies have revealed interesting evidence. Taymaz found that US engineering unions had no effect upon the rate of diffusion of NCMTs in the period 1979–84 (Taymaz 1991: 305). In another study conducted in 1983 on 835 establishments, specifically related to seven types of advanced engineering technology in use in American manufacturing industry, Keefe found that unions had no apparent effect on the use of advanced technology. Hence while it was true that unionised firms were more likely to be found using advanced technology, this was because of their larger size and not union status (Keefe 1991).[10]

The research discussed so far does not draw explicit conclusions about how different types of unions may effect innovation in differing product and labour market contexts. The state of the product and labour markets needs to be taken into account. If firms face a highly competitive product market, then this may severely curtail a union's ability to appropriate rents. Competitive product markets will put greater pressure on management to resist union demands because it reduces the profit surplus which can be bargained over. From the labour market perspective, a tight labour market will increase unionised workers' ability to appropriate rents from innovation, because workers will not find it difficult to gain other employment if their demands are not met (Haskel 1991). These postulates of course formed parts of the foundations to the Crafts argument we discussed earlier. Theoretical studies on how differing unions might affect innovation in differing market contexts highlight factors that will figure in the following chapter. For instance Tauman and Weiss identify conditions under which unions may encourage the adoption of 'mild' technical improvement. Their analysis was of an oligopolistic market situation with non-unionised and unionised firms in competition. They found that if demand is high or demand elasticity of labour low, and assuming effective threats of entry then this would put pressure on unions to moderate their wage claims. This could of course promote innovation by allowing firms to keep profit levels high (Tauman and Weiss 1987). Dorwick and Spencer say that craft and industry unions are faced with a more inelastic labour demand, than enterprise-level unions. Thus if members of craft and industry level unions lose their jobs through technical redundancy, they will find it more difficult to acquire another. Whereas a peak-level union body representing a very large number of workers in an economy is more likely to favour change because of substantial utility gain to its members from a real income increase due to price reductions from the innovation (Dorwick and Spencer 1994).

Conclusion

In this chapter we have reviewed a number of authors who provide a representative sketch of the many ways in which it has been argued that British labour has retarded productivity growth. Indeed the literature in this area is massive and therefore we have only paid attention to the most relevant, salient, and influential. We have also looked at the theoretical literature on how unions can affect productivity and innovation and some of the case studies in this area. Yet it is difficult to see a clear answer emerging from this literature as to whether unions do or do not retard innovation, given the many other factors that play a part in how unions behave towards technical change. Moreover it is not difficult to find examples of workers and unions in other countries resisting changes in their production methods, and there are more examples than the graphic and famous one of the silk-weavers of Lyon throwing Jacquard into the Rhône for inventing his automatic loom.[11] American farm workers took strike action in the late nineteenth century in order to support their wage levels, which were being pushed down by the falling demand for farm labour due to the introduction of tractors and harvest-reaping machines. In some states farmers had their machines destroyed and others received threats that their machines would be destroyed. Such action did dissuade some farmers from adopting the new technology (Pursell 1995: 118–20). Staying with the United States but moving to the post-1945 period, a US labour union has been blamed for the technical stagnation of the steel industry because of its high wage demands (Tauman and Weiss 1987: 478).

Indeed one can find examples were British trade unions have not only fully co-operated with techniques for productivity enhancement but also initiated it. The Electrical, Electronic, Telecommunications and Plumbing Union fully co-operated with the modernisation of the electricity supply industry. The Post Office Engineering Union in the 1960s took the initiative in pursuing productivity bargaining with the Post Office. The leadership of the National Union of Mineworkers helped to promote the principle of pit incentive schemes as a method of boosting productivity in the mines (Taylor 1982: 143). Therefore it is more probable that whether a trade union retards or promotes technical innovation is as we saw a contingent empirical question. Some of the latest research states that with only small changes in the assumptions concerning the macroeconomic environment it is almost impossible to tell on an *a priori* basis how trade unions will affect microeonomic outcomes. The only conclusion that seems to hold in most circumstances is that trade unions will raise wages above the alternative 'wage' (Manning 1994). As we discussed union type and product and labour market contexts need to be brought into the analysis.

A number of scholars have now stressed that, 'Willing co-operation is the *sine qua non* of economic growth . . .' (Pelling 1996: 72). It is precisely the absence of such willing co-operation that British workers have been said to exhibit. They have had in other words an attitude of non-cooperation or simply indifference. One particular study by Yankelovich and others noted that UK workers had less loyalty towards their company than US unions, and that the trade unions and class divisions of the UK made it more difficult to build a consensus for working together to promote growth (Yankelovich *et al.* 1985b: 20). It should be remembered however that there are methodological problems with studies of this kind, such as differing questions in the countries studied and differential representation of occupational groups (Batstone 1986: 32–3). As we saw from the assertion of Nichols, social scientists see this as an important bearing on productivity outcomes. Given this, attitudes towards change will be heavily examined in the next chapter for there is little explicit work on this for the period and issues in question.

As two respected economists have concluded, 'There is now a plethora of case studies that support the widespread view that unions have been a major factor in Britain's slow rate of innovation over the last century.' However they further state that, 'The extent to which trade unions may be held accountable for the United Kingdom's slow rate of growth is still controversial' (McCombie and Thirlwall 1994: 92–3). We are left then with a situation where although it is often claimed that British unions have retarded innovation it is by no means proven. In the next chapter we will go on to explore unions and innovation in a comparative context, through the Eichengreen perspective.

3
British Workers and the Productivity Drive: A Comparative Perspective

Introduction: trade unions and the productivity drive

As the 1950s wore on, trade unions were coming under increasing criticism for Britain's relatively poor economic performance (Middlemas 1986: 318; Taylor 1993: 1; Wrigley 1996b: 1–2).[1] As Jones wrote, 'Throughout the period 1951–64 the trade union movement was frequently portrayed in the media as a force which had become too strong and irresponsible' (Jones 1987: 63). Trade unions as a cause of Britain's economic troubles have been a consistent thread through Conservative interpretations of British economic history from the 1950s onwards (Tomlinson 2001: 55–8). As we will see in Chapter 5 in the 1960s the setting-up of the Donovan Commission was a product of the growing perception that unions were slowing down Britain's growth rate. The productivity agencies and trade unionists were aware of the need to increase Britain's productivity growth rate and improve Britain's economic performance. Various issues of the BPC Bulletin, carried articles telling its readers the following, 'Germany's productivity is now rising fast. She has not passed us yet, but she promises to do so...'[2] One reader of Target, the BPC Bulletin, wrote to its editor saying '... our official advisers keep reminding us that the increase in Britain's productive rate is not as great as that of either Germany, Russia, America or France'.[3] In 1965 the newly appointed chairman of the BPC told his readers that, 'In fact, the need to raise productivity will always be with us, as with every country. The trouble has been that, in general, our chief competitors have been making, for various reasons, a better job of it than we have.'[4] Trade unionists and workers were subject to growing criticism as the post-war period wore on, they were also a heavily emphasised factor in the pursuit of productivity growth by the agencies. Carew has gone so far as to say that the AACP reports were directed more at labour than management (Carew 1991: 57). While Tiratsoo and Tomlinson have seen it as another instalment in blaming the British worker for Britain's poor productivity growth (Tiratsoo and Tomlinson 1993: 138–9). A number of authors have also commented on the prominence given to labour as the key factor in productivity, for instance Dartmann, 'It was clear that whenever productivity was used in the late 1940s and early 1950s, what was under consideration explicitly or implicitly was *labour* productivity' (Dartmann 1996a: 337).[5] We should though have some sympathy with the emphasis upon labour productivity for in the long run the wealth and income of everybody can rise only if labour productivity does (Oulton and O'Mahony 1994: 1).

When asked why the TUC contributed to the BPC, Edwin Fletcher, Secretary of the Production Department (set up in 1950) said that, '...we feel the Trade Union Movement here has as much to gain through industrial efficiency as the employers'.[6] Moreover, Vincent Tewson, General Secretary of the TUC from 1946–60, held the view early on in the productivity drive that the, '...T.U.C. was doing all it could to create the right atmosphere. In recent years there had been a revolution of the thought in these matters in the trade union movement'.[7] In notes prepared for Hugh Gaitskell who was to make an appearance with Harold Macmillan at a BPC rally on the 16 April 1959 to urge the cause for higher productivity, the TUC drew attention to the fact that, 'Trade unions have their part to play as well – [they] have an enormous job; while much more needs to be done, a lot more is being done than is some times realised.'[8]

In 1963 Patrick Fisher, who had superseded Robert Harle as the TUC's Production Secretary, told the Cannock and District Trade Council that in withdrawing from their National Productivity Year Local Committee they had contravened Congress policy. More significantly he argued that it would be far easier for trade unionists to achieve their fundamental and traditional role of advancing the interests of their members when national prosperity was increasing and not decreasing.[9] In 1964 the TUC's Organisation Department was to tell trade unionists that the TUC General Council was convinced that the BPC was serving a useful purpose; and that trade unionists should participate in LPA's for their own interests, not for the interests of government or employers.[10]

One particular example highlights the emphatic lengths the TUC went to in trying to engender co-operation from those in the lower echelons of the trade union movement. In 1963 Crawley Trades Council boycotted the BPCs National Productivity Year Local Committee. Its Vice-Chairman was on the managerial team of the second largest establishment in the Crawley area. This enterprise was in dispute with 350 workers who wanted work sharing. It was also, according to the trades council, attempting to reduce staff but maintain production levels, and it was attempting to reduce wages through the introduction of a bonus scheme. Such measures would of course boost productivity by increasing output per man and lowering unit labour costs. The TUC asked the Trades Council to change their minds saying that, '. . . improvement was not likely to be achieved by standing aloof from the National Productivity Year Committee'. This appears to have failed and a year later the TUC sent one of its productivity experts along to try to persuade them to take part in their LPC. The Trade Council however told Sullivan at a rancorous and angry meeting that the BPC was a 'waste of time' and that 'The policy of the T.U.C. [was] to increase productivity by all means', adding 'You expect to suck the workers' brains. For what? For redundancy?'[11] The above evidence would seem to give clear support to the assertion that throughout the period under study the TUC was publicly supportive of the productivity drive, even if for purely instrumental reasons.[12]

What is perhaps truly surprising is the degree of co-operation the TUC gave the productivity agencies such as the BPC, considering union feelings about some of the most prominent individuals within it. Graham Hutton, economic consultant to the BPC did not please the TUC who thought some of his writings stupid and demeaning to trade unions.[13] On one particular pamphlet issued by the BPC (Productivity and the £), the view of the TUC was that it showed Hutton's political leanings (right wing) and oversimplified economic relationships.[14]

The TUC directed some of their strongest criticism against the Pleming–Waddell report – 'The foundations of high productivity' (hereafter PW). 'The foundations of high productivity' was written by Norman Pleming, the Managing Director of Associated Industrial Consultants, London, and Harry Waddell, Editor of Factory Magazine, New York. This report was initiated by the AACP Council and the ECA. Its supposed aim was to analyse 15 AACP team reports and expose those underlying fundamental factors which were common to all the reports as the reasons for the higher level of productivity in the USA. The PW like many of the AACP reports contained very general statements like, 'Americans have a deep desire for a higher and higher standard of living – for more and more, newer and newer material things.'[15] Yet, unlike so many of the AACP reports it lacked technical rigour and detail. This was to annoy those in the TUC, who considered the PW to be therefore, '...little more than a survey of public opinion, and cannot be the "contribution of major consequence" suggested in the foreword'. In all, there were 73 criticisms of the 74-pages report, many were detailed and some were searing. Overall, the TUC felt the PW report erroneously simplified the issues.[16]

Trade union leaders not only urged support for the productivity drive, but also urged co-operation with management. Tyneside Productivity Committee put forward the view that if workers co-operated with good management then dramatic increases in productivity could be gained.[17] Subsequent commentators have had little doubt about the TUC's support for the productivity drive. Tomlinson wrote that, '...certainly at that "peak" level, union support for the government's productivity drive was strikingly enthusiastic' (Tomlinson 1991c: 96–9; 1992: 48). Carew believes that, 'Among the inner core of the TUC General Council, especially, support for the productivity initiatives was unqualified' (Carew 1987: 201).[18] Further support for this argument comes from Booth, who sees union leaders as willing to back any way to higher productivity between 1947 and 1950; and after 1950 union leaders may have tried to push the blame for the poor performance of British industry on to managers, but they still believed in the pursuit of productivity growth (Booth 1996: 52–3).

There is evidence that the TUC view was not shared by all trade unionists. One of the few cases about dissent from the TUC line on productivity within the trade union movement to attract attention is the case of the controversy which surrounded a speech made by Edward (Ted) Hill.[19] Ted Hill was General Secretary of the United Society of Boilermakers, Shipbuilders, and Structural Workers. In a speech Hill delivered at the opening conference of the BPC on 19 March 1953 he said he would not 'lift a finger to improve productivity', unless it improved workers' standard of living, a reasonable sentiment.[20] Hill acknowledged that, 'We expect the employer to want a decent profit, that is a natural sequence.'[21] The TUC however passed a motion deploring Hill for his remark about 'not lifting a finger', but he did however receive substantial support from some members of his own union, who disliked as they saw it, '...THE SHUT YOUR GOB mentality', and from many trade councils who wrote to the TUC in support of Hill. All in all the TUC received some 50 letters from trades councils supporting Hill and his controversial speech.[22]

The Bromley Trades Council was seething in its condemnation of the TUC's treatment of Hill, saying that they rejected, '...the servile and spineless attitude of the other trade union leaders present at the conference, and who were prepared to help the employers increase their profits without any guarantee of increased wages for employees'. They also wanted the General Council of the TUC to take into account as they put it, '...the activities of the parasites who throng the expensive hotels of London and flock to join the summer parade at "Royal Ascot" etc., and this at the expense of the blood, toil, tears and sweat of the productive worker'.[23] Those representing the employers took a very dim view of Hill's speech, but also highlighted its insignificance to the productivity drive. Sir Norman Kipping in his memoirs recounted about the conference that Hill's views had little long-run impact (Kipping 1972: 117). Even then, some trades councils such as Tonbridge, Croyden, and the Manchester and Salford took a dim view of the ERP and calls for employees to work harder and the idea that the USA offered a model of industrial relations.[24]

Even trade unionists like those above who took a strong dislike to the productivity campaign could however prove beneficial to its dissemination. In 1954 one manufacturer at an LPC conference declared with reference to the local Circuit Scheme that, 'We have strong and militant trade unionists. A militant trade unionist is the very type of man who will, if he is convinced, make a useful contribution to productivity. The man who has no interest in his trade union won't be of any help and won't be listened to by his colleagues.'[25] As should be evident from the above, although there was significant dissent from some trade unionists towards the productivity drive, the TUC consistently tried to persuade its members that they should be fully supportive. Indeed even when the BPC was to be closed down in 1973, Alfred Allen of the United Shop Distributive Allied Workers (hereafter USDAW) led a delegation to see Edward Heath to try to prevent this.[26]

Having taken account of the above we shall examine how organised labour responded to the productivity drive from within this spectrum of views, by looking at four key issues: unemployment, consultation and monitoring of the production process, wages and the distribution of productivity gains, and technical change and restrictive practices. We shall compare the attitudes of UK labour with those of the USA and Western Europe and we will view union behaviour as, '...the product of four broad influences that are constantly interacting upon one another: the desires of the members, the nature and abilities of the leadership, the capacities and opinions of subordinates, and the pressures of the environment' (Bok and Dunlop 1985: 218).

Particular attention will be paid to union attitudes to technical change within the productivity drive and it will be argued that trade union policy on this specific issue was dependent upon four aspects: the percentage of members affected, the economic condition of the industry concerned, the nature of the technical change, and the stage of development of the technical change (Willman 1986: 10). Therefore we have a variety of factors that need to be taken into account when analysing trade union responses to technical innovation. We shall investigate how peak associations, trade union leaders, and 'ordinary' trade unionists viewed the issues of automation and mechanisation within the context of the Long Boom, and the programmes of the productivity agencies to increase the use of these two methods of production. An important issue to trade unionists was that of employment and unemployment.

Trade unions and employment

In one of its first major policy statements on automation the TUC recognised that technical change was not a new phenomenon, and that, '…displacement of manpower by machines [was] as old as industry, and, in view of Britain's dependence on international trade, problems might be more acute if industrial change did not take place' (TUC n.d.a.: 8). Trade unionists were concerned that productivity gains through factors like automation would not hurt their members. In 1953 Tewson, said when addressing trade union officers, 'Experience [has] showed that industrial inefficiency had been a cause of unemployment…'[27] Edwin Fletcher of the TUC told the Institute of Production Engineers 1955 conference that, 'Trades unions have been prepared to co-operate, provided that their members have adequate protection from factors such as unemployment…'[28] In 1959 Victor Feather, Assistant Secretary of the TUC told a North Wales Productivity Committee at Chester that, 'Every worker has at least one concern at the back of his mind which is even more important than the size of the pay packet; that is, the regularity of his pay packets, the security of his employment. The question is, rightly, more a concern of his than it is the concern of anyone else.'[29] Employees were also aware that automation could cause significant unemployment, the National Union of Bank Employees stated, 'It is a fair and tenable conclusion that a serious redundancy problem would arise if there were to be a large scale switch from existing office machinery within a short span of time.'[30]

Unemployment may have been one of the reasons why workers were unwilling or reluctant to co-operate with the productivity drive. As Tewson recognised, people who had experience of the 1920s and 1930s had genuine fears about unemployment and may have seen greater efficiency as tending to increase rather than lessen the number of unemployed.[31] However, Tewson publicly at least wanted it to be known that he thought maximum efficiency in industry was indispensable to maintaining full employment, perhaps to calm labour fears.[32] The Mond-Turner Talks of 1927–33 had previously thrown up the issue that rationalisation and reorganisation could lead to displacement of workers in the short term and that in some way workers would have to be compensated (Gospel 1979: 186; McDonald and Gospel 1973: 816). Certainly some economists believe that one of the reasons why unemployment was so low in the 1950s and 1960s was precisely because workers having lived through the interwar depression had from then on acquired an acute aversion to mass unemployment, which might confirm Tewson's views (Newell and Symons 1990).[33] Indeed according to Middlemas, Tewson blamed the growing industrial unrest in the 1950s on the younger generation, which had never known mass unemployment (Middlemas 1986: 234). Those workers who had experienced the high unemployment of the interwar years would therefore be very wary of any measures, which threatened to bring back such conditions. As Peter Lange has written, workers' expectations come from two sources, 'One is institutions in the society, most importantly, the unions and government. Union officials are likely to be particularly prominent. The second major source would seem to be the recent experiences of workers themselves' (Lange 1984: 117).[34] Trade union leaders called for government intervention; Lewis Wright, General Secretary of the Amalgamated Weavers Association (hereafter AWA) was of the opinion that, '...the government have a responsibility in ensuring that their economic policies make for full employment and that fiscal and monetary policies make for full employment and that their fiscal and monetary policies will allow automation to develop smoothly'.[35]

However, as we saw from the Bok and Dunlop quote, trade union behaviour and policy is determined not only by what the leaders want, but also by the environment, that is to say market conditions. Thus, the General Secretary of the Topographical Association reported that, 'My council is fully aware that progress and development in automation will inevitably reduce very considerably the amount of labour required for jobs. So far, however we are happy to report that this Association has not experienced any redundancy resulting therefrom, notwithstanding the increased productivity of modern machinery.'[36] This can be seen as an assertion that the pace of automation was acceptable in prevailing market conditions. Fletcher agreed saying that British industry had easily absorbed automation because of post-war full employment.[37]

These views are confirmed by Batstone and Gourlay's study where they noted that the job affects of new technology have most to do with market forces (Batstone and Gourlay 1986: 181). The degree of competition in a market affects the bargaining power of those who operate in that market (Knight 1992: 15). From the statements above, trade union leaders obviously saw the prevailing tight labour market as a critical factor in ameliorating the possible harmful effects of technical change and as such advantageous to their members. Yet such conditions would also enhance their bargaining power with employers because employers would face a smaller effective labour pool from which to choose workers.

It was not until Wilson's Labour Government introduced the Redundancy Payments Act of 1965, an act intended to increase labour mobility in the face of technical change and reduce overmanning, that unionists and workers might have had less to fear from technical advance. Redundancy payments were of course not new to some UK workers; the 1920s and 1930s saw the beginnings of compensation for workers who were made redundant. Yet such payments were the exception and mainly confined to the largest firms such as Imperial Chemical Industries (hereafter ICI), Lever Brothers, Ranks, and Spillers. Gospel argues that these firms saw such payments as a way of getting worker and union co-operation over rationalisation and closure. However firms were uncertain as to the principle underlying these schemes, were they payments, for a recognition of lost job rights or a relief for hardship (Gospel 1992: 68–9). The 1965 Act introduced compensation for redundant workers who had worked more than 21 hours a week (Maguire 1996: 54; Taylor 1993: 115, 160). It has been claimed that this Act helped to overcome workers' deep-seated fears of redundancy, and was supported by management because they believed it would overcome resistance to the restructuring of British industry (Gospel and Palmer 1993: 249).

Dore on the other hand has claimed that this Act made redundancy more difficult for employers by strengthening workers' sense of job rights and making redundancy seem like an offence and, '...a proper object of resistance...', to the extent that employers have had to offer *ex gratia* payments above those statutorily necessary in order to soften union resistance to dismissals (Dore 1990: 94). Organised labour also had to accommodate the fact that British employers faced few restrictions over the hiring and firing of labour in contrast to their counterparts in other parts of Europe. The British state and the unions put few barriers in the way of management's control over redundancy. British shop stewards found it particularly difficult to stop redundancy (Salmon 1988: 210).

To compound this was the fact pointed out by Goodman that on the Continent dismissals were often regulated by joint works councils which had statutory or agreed rights in dealing with them, but joint production committees (hereafter JPC), the nearest equivalent the UK had to works councils, were slowly on the decline in post-war Britain (Tiratsoo and Tomlinson 1993: 107).[38] Streeck has argued with regard to Germany that co-determination (hereafter CD) effectively turned labour into a fixed factor of production and made it almost as difficult as fixed capital to dispose of. Large German firms also faced a policy of employment protection, which limited their ability to access external labour markets. This employment security and resulting identification of workers with firms made for comparatively easy acceptance of technical change and co-operative attitudes among workers (Streeck 1992: 32, 159). Looked at from an Eichengreen type perspective if workers have no institutional facilities like CD in which they can monitor management, and they have no other mechanisms by which to impact upon redundancy then why should they trust managers not to fire them in the second period of an institutional pact for fast growth, given the various incentives managers might have to do this, such as higher dividends and higher profits (Hargreaves Heap 1991: 40).

Historically British employers also had a history of externalising the labour market rather than develop their own internal structures (Gospel 1992: 11–12). One implication of this was that, 'They hired and fired as market conditions dictated . . .' (Gospel 1988: 110). No wonder then that British workers were fearful, and given that trade unions will rarely forgo the employment of even a few of their members, it is perhaps not surprising that trade unions made so much of this issue and looked for strong reassurances (Batstone and Gourlay 1986: 13). The fear of British unions that participation in agencies to promote productivity growth could lead to unemployment should be placed against that of the German unions, which shunned the RKW between 1950 and 1952 for fear of unemployment (Booth *et al.* 1997: 433).[39]

American unions took the same attitudes when it came to the employment effects of automation. A representative from the American Federation of Labour (hereafter AFL) said that there must be protection for those workers displaced by automation. Walter Reuther, Leader of the United Auto Workers Union (hereafter UAW) called for a shorter working week in the face of automation so as to ensure employment.[40] In 1955 the UAW joined the Congress of Industrial Organisations (hereafter CIO) and together they wanted any agreements with multi-plant corporations to have enshrined within them the condition that any workers displaced by automation had the right to inter-plant transfers.[41] The French unions also revealed their fear of unemployment from automation. In a survey of 750 workers it was found that, '. . . trade unionists are almost unanimous in their fear of unemployment, which is consequently still their principal objection'. One of the conclusions of the survey was that, 'Technical changes must improve [the] material conditions of work and must not lead to dismissals' (Richard 1953: 290, 292). Here it seems then that British unions were not acting unreasonably in their demands when set in a comparative context.

It may be insightful to end this particular issue on a remark made in 1951 by Senator William Benton before the Anglo-American Press Association. Before we do so however, it will be useful to reflect back on the remarks made by the likes of Barnett and others in Chapter 2 on how obstructive British unions were to technical change. Place these remarks and some of the assertions made about British trade unions against the following: 'Last week in England I was glad to re-affirm that the powerful resistance of the great unions to improvements in technology, due to fear of unemployment in the 1930s, is rapidly passing away.'[42] It is difficult to conceive of a political motive as to why Benton should have said this unless he believed there to be some truth in the observation.

Consultation, control, and monitoring of the production process

As we saw from the Eichengreen framework, if employees are to keep a pact for fast growth then they need to be frequently informed of managements' decisions and managerial knowledge and British union leaders were often pressing for workers to be given more information about the plans of companies that they worked for. Carron, President of the Amalgamated Engineering Union, and member of the TUC's General Council, speaking at a one-day conference in Cardiff on the problems of automation, told 120 industrialists and trade unionists that while they welcomed raising living standards and the eradication of laborious jobs they feared the consequences of rapid and uncontrolled change without consultation.[43] Thomas Williamson, General Secretary of the General and Municipal Workers Union, expressed a similar view, 'It is also of the utmost importance that the unions should actively seek consultation on all industrial changes. Here a change of emphasis is desirable: consultation should be at the point of executive decision on policy rather than at the point of implementation of policy.'[44]

It was not only at the apex of union structure that unionists were calling for consultation, so were shop stewards. At a one-day conference of shop stewards in the motor industry, held at Cowley, on automation, the call was made for, 'Full consultation between unions and management on the working conditions and rates of pay...'[45] Shop stewards in the engineering and allied trades also said, 'We are not opposed to the introduction of new technical advances but insist that full consultation should take place at shop-floor level prior to their introduction.'[46] However according to an EPA report, there was counterbalancing evidence that trade unionists, particularly the unskilled on the shop floor, may have been rather indifferent to the practice. The EPA report, based on a study of joint consultation in 157 firms in the UK, came to the conclusion that, 'In the shops it [joint consultation] was strong among workers' representatives, fair among shop stewards and weak among rank and file' (EPA n.d.: 31). The TUC itself was to hear that, 'One of the strongest factors to contend with in the encouragement of Works Councils was the apathy and opposition of union members.'[47] Goldthorpe and his colleagues in their study of 229 male manual workers between the ages of 21 and 46 working in Luton in the early 1960s in Vauxhall Motors Ltd, Skefko Ball Bearing Company Ltd, and Laporte Chemicals Ltd, came to a similar conclusion. They discovered that the majority of workers, excluding craftsmen, did not see the function of trade unionism as a way to greater worker participation in the affairs of the firm (Goldthorpe *et al.* 1968: 113).

The importance of joint consultation lies in Eichengreen's contention that the creation of monitoring mechanisms helped to bond capital and labour together in the successful post-war European economies. During 1951–52 the German *Bundestag* passed two Acts, the Works Constitution Act and the Co-determination Act, which forced all companies of the joint stock form and with more than 500 employees to allocate a third of the seats on their management and supervisory boards to worker representatives. This is commonly referred to as enterprise level co-determination (*Mitbestimmung auf Unternehmensebene*). It deals with the enterprise's general economic decisions. The Works Constitution Act of 1952 made legal workplace co-determination, (*Betriebliche Mitbestimmung*) which is exercised through works councils, and applies to all companies with more than five employees, it deals with matters relating to manpower and employment issues (Streeck 1992: 137–9). Co-determination allows workers to monitor firms' decisions and in the case of enterprise level co-determination workers can have a significant input into the company's decision-making processes. As Berghahn declared with respect to Germany, 'For some unionists ... *Mitbestimmung* represented primarily a means of gaining strategic control and participatory rights in the areas of economic policy making and planning at the level of the enterprise' (Berghahn 1986: 208).

In Holland the PBOs (*Publiek Rechtelijke Bedrijfsorganisatie*), brought representatives of government, workers, and firms together and in France labour–management plant committees (*comités d'enterprise*) were required by law after 1945 for those companies with more than 50 workers.[48] In Norway there were planning councils (*Bransjerad*) and production committees (*Produktionsutvalg*) (Eichengreen 1996b: 47–8). In America, according to Harle, there was relatively little joint consultation and everything 'hung around the contract', which went into immense detail covering such things as fringe benefits and pensions.[49] Southwell in his study noted some very significant differences between joint consultation in the UK and the rest of Western Europe. He pointed out that in both most information went to the workers via management and consultative bodies such as works councils and joint production committees whose terms of reference were limited by agreement. He also asserted that on the Continent there was much less contact between management and the unions inside factories, there were no shop stewards and that which required union attention was dealt with by management and full time union officers from outside the factory. However Southwell recognised that there were some full-time union officials inside European factories and they came into negotiations with management much earlier and more frequently than was the case in the UK. He also observed that the law intervened much more widely in the field of industrial relations in Western Europe than it did in Britain.[50]

In the late 1940s the TUC had been dissatisfied with the progress that had been made towards the formation of joint production committees and while they accepted that lack of progress was partly the fault of the workers themselves, most blame was placed upon the employers and managers, particularly junior or shop managers. The TUC were also irritated by the fact that some managers insisted on having non-unionists on those committees.[51] However the TUC may have worked to emasculate joint production committees fearing lest they should be 'captured' by communist elements within the workforce (Hinton 1994: 76–85, 121, 200–5). Certainly those at the peak of the trade union movement did want to exercise some sway over management, for the question was raised at one peak level meeting, 'Are there any avenues worth exploring to allow trade unions to exert greater influence on management and employer opinion, through, for instance, the British Productivity Council and its local productivity committees?...'[52] The issue of influence over LPAs was to prove controversial as the productivity drive matured. The Watford Trades Council in 1969 decided to disaffiliate from the South West Hertfordshire Productivity Association and it cited as one of the main reasons the lack of, '...any real progress towards the ideal set out by the [BPC] of equal representation from workers and management at the seminars organised by...[the LPA]'. It also claimed that no amount of seminars would achieve greater productivity unless a more democratic atmosphere prevailed within industry.[53] The view of the Watford Trades Council gains resonance when compared with the opinions of a 1962 TUC circular, which expressed concern that LPAs were regarding themselves solely as management organisations. The Shirebrook Trades Council said that they were beneficial so long as management did, '...not try to hoodwink the Trade Union side'.[54] It was also believed that the absence of joint consultative machinery in engineering and ship-building at the industry level was a serious shortcoming.[55] According to one influential trade unionist, the real fear for his members was not automation itself but who controlled it.[56]

Some union leaders were well aware of the lack of discussion and information that flowed between management and labour and its consequent negative effects. A. W. Allen General Secretary of USDAW said that the speed with which new techniques of production were introduced into the UK was too slow because management and labour distrusted each other. He went on, 'We fail to exploit our assets simply because as people, we do not work well enough together.' Allen also highlighted the significance of the past in the inherited antiquated division in industry between management and labour.[57] George Woodcock, who replaced Vincent Tewson as General Secretary of the TUC in 1960, gave an interesting example of how production may have suffered from lack of consultation when he criticised managements for resenting unions which expressed interests wider than wages and conditions: 'I am told that one of the difficulties of increasing our exports is failure to meet delivery dates. Why does not management discuss this with workpeople?'[58] The issue of consultation is important because CD gives workers large incentives to be both innovative and co-operative in the production process, because they can be assured that management will not appropriate workers' innovations and claim them as their own. Thus the worker who was the originator of the innovation gains the credit and possible reward for it (Smith 1990). Therefore the British industrial heritage seems to have been unhelpful in this respect.

However in few sectors foreign observers were to remark on how well British consultation worked. An International Report on technical change in the postal and telephone services revealed that unions and management in Britain had a well-tested machinery for finding agreement on the solution to problems arising from new technology and automation in the Whitley Council system, under which productivity committees had been established. Employee representatives were consulted on all phases of mechanisation, from the planning to the actual installation and operation of the machinery. No machine was placed into operation unless it had the approval of the union. Two joint committees had been founded composed of union and management representatives to oversee the process. The study group also reported that every effort was being made by the management to, '... relate the pace of the mechanisation programme to the absorption in other work of people – particularly highly skilled – who are rendered surplus by the changes in methods'.[59]

Similar positions existed in some other Western European countries but with crucial differences. In Belgium, Bell sorting machines had been installed to mechanise postal services. As in Britain there were committees, which dealt with productivity matters. Established in 1954, a primary committee had members from trade unions, the Minister of Finance, a representative from the Ministry of Communications, and representatives from postal management; this committee was assisted by other sub-committees. No mechanised programme could be placed into effect until these committees had been consulted. Unlike in the UK, Belgian unions appear to have had no veto over installation.

According to the team, in Germany, '... there existed among large groups of employees a certain amount of suspicion and prejudice against all efforts to promote rationalization and increased productivity'.[60] As in Belgium and the UK there were productivity committees, although they were exclusively the unions' preserve. One of the functions of these committees was to ensure that telephone operators made redundant by the change from manual to automatic exchanges were provided with new jobs. However a key difference was that the planning of the installation of automatic devices was undertaken prior to consultation with the unions. It was therefore apparently very difficult for the unions to bring about changes or modifications. This evidence supports Dartmann's point that in Germany co-determination and the wider productivity drive removed the control of both work and technology from the bargaining arena, in sharp contrast to the situation in the UK (Dartmann 1996a: 77).

In France there were no committees whatsoever on productivity, and according to the study group, labour–management negotiations were conducted in what appeared to be an atmosphere of suspicion. However *Postes Téléphone* authorities told the group that consideration was given to the welfare of workers before work processes were mechanised. French trade unions were initially against the motorisation of letter carriers and they took the view that efficiency and productivity were secondary to human values of freedom and dignity.[61] More generally, European trade unions desired to be consulted about the introduction of automation, a position, which seemed sensible to employer representatives.[62] In the UK the TUC in its response to the Donovan Report said that, '...the notion of a binding legal contract becomes more and more unacceptable as the process of technological change accelerates'. It continued, '...the onus must be on managers to ensure that new productive process are not introduced before the agreement has been re-examined in the new context' (TUC 1968: 17–18). In other words not only did the TUC not like the idea of bargained agreements between workers and employers, but it sought re-negotiation and thereby consultation before technical advances in production could be implemented.

What is interesting about the above examples from the same industry, is that the UK seems to have been unique in one respect, that British unions could effectively block, albeit temporarily the introduction of new technology. This evidence would seem to give support to the contention of Williams, Williams, and Thomas that the problem with UK manufacturing firms has been poor management control over the labour process; unlike Germany or Sweden where unions do not claim the right to negotiate staffing levels for new technology (Williams *et al.* 1983: 29, 34–5).

While British unions may have wanted to negotiate manning levels there is evidence that British unions had no desire to retard the introduction of new machinery (Lorenz and Wilkinson 1986; McLoughlin and Clark 1994: 1–2). The American study group that reported to the EPA said of British trade unions that in the main they were not hostile to technical change. The study group's conclusion on the UK was that, 'The unions of Great Britain have generally welcomed technological development subject to full consultation with the Administration about its effects and the maintenance of strict standards of safety. They believe that technical change opens the way to better pay and conditions for their members.'[63] Significantly it went on, '...the policy of the unions encompasses; co-operative planning with management on mechanization programs and the human problems involved; participation by unions and management in placing mechanization programs into effect; and an assurance that the worker receive a fair share of the economic benefits made possible by increased productivity'.[64]

We have now surveyed a range of elements concerning this aspect of production and a number of salient points have emerged. First, UK unions were aware of the potential improvement to productive efficiency that consultation could potentially bring; reconsider the remarks of Allen on labour and management discussion and failure to meet delivery dates. However most impetus for joint consultation came from trade union representatives rather than workers who had indifferent attitudes towards joint consultation. Secondly, virtually all other Western European countries had mechanisms for joint CD and their unions in this sense were able in some degree to monitor management behaviour. In the UK, JPCs were on the decline in the 1950s and only in industries with the Whitley councils did unions have an established machinery for consultation. Finally, Williams *et al.* have asserted that UK unions negotiate with management over manning levels.

Yet as we saw from the findings of the EPA study, UK unions were not hostile to technical change, but did want consultation in advance of it. However, a potential ability to impede technical change through, say, negotiating manning levels (consultation) in no way implies that unions will retard change. Indeed the comments of Allen imply quite the opposite. That is, British unions saw consultation as a way to enhance efficiency and from the remarks of various trade union leaders, that we saw in the introduction such as those of Fletcher the Production Secretary, it is manifest that union leaders emphatically wanted to see greater efficiency. Here then lay a substantial impediment to creating a viable politics of productivity at the shop-floor level. Given that UK unions did not have CD there is little incentive for workers to be innovative. The absence of CD means that workers may not receive any gains from their suggestions to enhance efficiency.[65] It is precisely this aspect, worker and union gains from increased efficiency and productivity that we will now explore, and to probe how and to what extent trade unions saw themselves as material beneficiaries of the productivity drive.

Trade unions, wages, and the distribution of productivity gains

The TUC thought that it was of vital importance that the existing industrial relations machinery should have the ability to deal with the problems of automation (TUC n.d.a.: 12). One factor that was of concern to the TUC was the impact upon wages and working conditions right across industry. The TUC thought unions would seek to spread the advantages from automation to all areas of industry but the problem for unions would be how to fit the piece-meal introduction of automation into existing wage structures which did not necessarily reflect automation's 'ability to pay'.[66] As far as the TUC were concerned, 'if...workpeople think, rightly or wrongly, that they personally are going to be worse off as a result of automation it would be idle to expect their willing acceptance or co-operation' (TUC n.d.a.: 13). The TUC believed that workers had the right to share the results of higher productivity in order to increase their purchasing power and standards of living (TUC n.d.a.: 15).

The disposition and attitude of French trade unions was very similar to that of the British. The CGT-FO issued a document – 'The Foundations of an Economic and Social Programme' – in 1950, which stated that it was essential for the working class to associate itself with productivity problems. Without the co-operation of the workers problems could not be solved. But the profits derived from higher productivity must be shared in order to provide an incentive to the workers to co-operate (Richard 1953: 281–2). Levard, the Deputy General Secretary of the *Confédération Française des Travailleurs Chrétiens* (hereafter CFTC) was of the opinion in 1952 that French workers were ready to help in the productivity drive so long as they were allowed to share the benefits. He wrote that, '...a generally acceptable productivity programme must be conceived as part of a far wider policy than that of taking technical action and no more; that has been done already and, from the social standpoint, has yielded negative results...' (Richard 1953: 291). It is worth noting that CGT-FO passed a motion in 1952, which called for their representatives to withdraw from the trade union centre for the study of productivity and the other agencies for increased productivity, such as the AFAP, unless they gained guarantees concerning the awarding of productivity bonuses that had to be covered by special works agreements. None of the major British trade unions ever took such an equivalent action.

In the case of Germany, Dartmann informs us that the *Deutscher Gewerkschaftsbund* (hereafter DGB) in initial discussions on the brief of the RKW succeeded in getting an RKW sub-committee to agree that the distribution of the 'fruits' of faster productivity growth had to be fixed through bargaining between those involved before the particular productivity enhancing measures could begin. Although this never came about, the German union peak associations tried another tactic (Dartmann 1996a: 345). The *Deutscher Angestellten-Gewerkschaft* (hereafter DAG) wanted future ownership rights in the employers' capital if their members could not get immediate wage increases. Referring to the increase in the capital of German industry between 1950 and 1956 from reinvestment of 60 billion Deutsche, Marks Cynog-Jones suggested that the restraint of trade unions in asking for lower pay increases than they were justified in asking for, and consumers paying higher prices, had made this possible. Cynog-Jones said that if workers had received higher pay increases and if consumers had paid less for products, the money available for reinvestment would have been much less. Workers and consumers had increased the wealth of owners of capital. Cynog-Jones therefore asked whether there was not a case for letting workers and consumers share in the ownership of the capital increases they create.

The DAG were calling for an Act of *Bundestag* which would recognise the right of trade unions to negotiate with employers about the ownership of new capital created every year. The DGB argued that since 1948 German industry had been largely self-financing about 80 per cent of its investment. The DGB asserted that this was made possible by the, '. . . surplus created by the labour of the workers and by consumers paying too much for the product'. The DGB did not however want a guaranteed increase in future wages but a guarantee of future shares, issued on a yearly basis, in the new capital created by the investment. They argued that the combined shares of the workers should amount to a 50 per cent ownership of all new capital created that year.[67]

Looked at from Eichengreen's dynamic two-period perspective, German peak associations sought therefore to ensure that they would gain from immediate wage restraint with future long-term wage growth, as in the case of the demands of the DGB. With respect to the attitude of the DAG we see that if this cannot be obtained, then German labour wanted guarantees that they would gain through the acquisition of capital in the second period, when fast growth begins to materialise. The remarks of Cynog-Jones however suggest that first-period labour wage moderation was achieved in Germany not so much because of agreement between the social partners, but more possibly because of the balance of power in the labour market which favoured capital, as German unions do not appear to be enthusiastic about initial wage restraint (Kramer 1990: 209–12). The Eichengreen model and the balance of power between labour, capital, and the state is an issue we will return to in the 'Conclusion'.

American unions also expected higher wages as a result of productivity increases. Goodman, a member of the British Electrical Development Association, an industrial specialist, and a contemporary expert on automation wrote, 'American trade union leaders...have welcomed automation but have coupled their interest with demands for higher and guaranteed annual wages and a shorter working week, together with full consultation before changes are made. They have demanded, too, severance pay for redundant workers and retraining schemes.'[68] The CIO did not oppose automation, but was, '...strongly determined that the workers in industry shall share the benefits in the form of higher wages and shorter working hours...' The CIO president with reference to new machines at a Ford plant in Cleveland, stated that 'The machines are good as long as we get the benefits of the machines by higher living standards and shorter work hours.'[69] In a resolution adopted by their 1955 congress, the UAW-CIO wanted a guaranteed annual wage, the upward revision of rates for automated jobs and the '...union [was] demanding that individual classifications and wage rates reflect specific productivity changes'.[70]

An EPA mission to study directly US trade union attitudes towards automation included Robert Harle who superseded Fletcher at the TUC's Production Department. Harle noted that: 'The only philosophy they [American trade unions] are interested in, they say, is that employers can always pay higher wages. The unions believe wage pressure increases productivity and efficiency...'[71] He based his analysis on the conferences he had attended, speeches he had heard, the union officers he had met, and the literature the AFL-CIO had produced for its members. Harle described how in America, union–company employment contracts were very detailed covering factors like fringe benefits and severance pay. The challenge to unions and management was to design structures and agreements which permitted the control of the working situation and were resilient enough to accommodate the impact of technology and other forms of innovation. However, the guaranteed annual wage is intended to maintain employment stability at the expense, if necessary, of technical development.[72]

Some of those in the lower levels of the British trade union movement did feel annoyed that they were often exhorted to co-operate and work harder for the productivity initiatives, yet received little in return. In 1953 Tonbridge Trades Council was aggrieved at a BPC booklet which seemed, '...another call to work harder...', yet as far as they were concerned production and productivity had increased continuously since the end of the War but real wages had fallen. The trades council felt if real wages increased as a result of increased production the workers would have more interest in increasing productivity.[73] While the assertion of a 6 per cent drop in consumption is surely wrong, the quotation reflects a central issue for organised labour, namely that they desired what they saw as adequate returns from increasing productivity. In 1956 Lewis Wright also put the case that while the need for increased productivity and production may be constantly reiterated by those at the peak of the trade unions, this increased productivity may not be, '...fairly shared among the people of a country and in particular that workpeople may not receive their rightful share'.[74] Earlier in 1951 Lincoln Evans, General Secretary of the Iron and Steel Trades Confederation, had told his readers that until there was acceptance of the idea that gains from labour-saving devices or new techniques should be shared there could not be the confidence needed to encourage the maximum use of new methods.[75] In response to a particular piece of BPC literature the Southport Trades Council and Labour Party passed a resolution calling for the BPC to look at the issues more from the workers' perspective and that workers should receive their fair share of the 'fruits' of their labour towards increased productivity.[76]

The Morecambe and Heysham Trades Council wrote, 'This Council deplores the unqualified support now being given by the T.U.C. to the National Productivity Committee. We urge that any future support should have as its basis the principle that higher productivity in industry should be matched by an equivalent increase in the standard of living of the people.'[77] The Trade Union Advisory Committee to the EPA, a committee made up of trade unionists from most of the participating EPA countries, took a similar position. Not only did it insist on consultation but unless, '...workers directly benefit from the increased productivity and unless there is effective consultation with the trade unionists at all levels, European, national, industrial, factory and workshops, their co-operation in the [productivity] campaign is impossible'.[78] In mid-1950 Watford LPC sent a memorandum to the BPC saying that it was unreasonable to ask trade unionists to participate in the productivity drive without assurances about a fair and equitable sharing of the gains from productivity increases.[79] In formulating its reply the BPC was to reveal one of the dilemmas, which struck at the very heart of the productivity drive. 'It is implicit in the "Objective" of the Council...that the results of higher productivity shall and indeed must benefit all sections of the community...It is necessary, to make quite clear that the Council is not, however, an appropriate body to concern itself with the details of this policy apart from endorsing the general principle.' The reason for this was that if the council did concern itself with wage bargaining then it would be duplicating and impinging upon the methods of negotiation and collective bargaining already in operation.[80]

In 1958 according to an answer given by the BPC to an EPA Question-naire on Britain's national productivity centre, the BPC stated that it was, '. . . in no way concerned with stating views about the distribution of "the benefits of productivity", wages or conditions of work. These are matters which are left entirely to the collective bargaining system'.[81] Some years earlier the TUC had concurred with this view. In a letter to the Monmouthshire Federation of Trades and Labour Councils, Edwin Fletcher had written that, '. . . rewards to labour in terms of wages and salaries in distributing and service trades as with all trades including manufacturing are the domestic affair of the union concerned'.[82] The TUC was also somewhat concerned when it became aware that the Hull Productivity Committee felt that wages and working conditions were at the root of productivity, according to a report in the *Manchester Guardian*. Edwin Fletcher cautioned the Committee against getting involved in such matters as this was not an area in which the TUC, like the BPC, had any remit.[83] If wages and working conditions are detached from and not allowed to become part of productivity discussion then it prevents increases in wages or improvements in working conditions being used as an incentive to motivate workers into working harder or more effi-ciently for greater output. It also reduces the incentives workers have for putting forward suggestions to improve efficiency (Tiratsoo and Tomlinson 1993: 107).

From our evidence for the peak level of British trade unions it appears we may conclude as Willman does, '. . . TUC policy, far from being one of opposition to change has consistently been concerned to encourage innovation, however this commitment has not been unqualified but has rested on the development of collective bargaining strategies for adjust-ment . . .' (Willman 1986: 21). Whilst Noble has pertinently pointed out, union officials tend to be in favour of technical change, so long as this change gives a 'bigger slice of the pie' to the workers, while not threatening their jobs (Noble 1978: 317).

Finally, an interesting point of comparison should be made here. In the UK there was a relative lack of wage and working practice contracts as existed in America and began to appear in France, for example at the Renault works in 1955 which guaranteed wage growth and other benefits in return for work reorganisation.[84] The Renault agreement became the basis for a number of work contracts in the metal, coal, and food indus-tries in France.[85] However a small number of examples can be found for the UK in which workers were assured of a share in productivity increases resulting in co-operation for enhanced production. In 1959, 321 workers at the Nailsworth Board Mills received their share of £12,000, which had accumulated over the previous year as part of the 'Share of Production Plan' which the firm operated, each worker received a one-off payment, which averaged about £30 net in their wages. A representative of the National Union of General and Municipal Workers who had been with the company, Chamberlains, for 25 years said that it was one of the best things that had ever happened to the company, because it gave everybody an incentive to 'do' their job and the union liked it because it lessened their work. The representative believed it had increased wages by a shilling an hour for the entire year. Leslie Chamberlain said that, '...the chief advantage is...that it has brought everybody together – management and work – people – to work as a team'. Under the plan workers earned a monthly bonus if they produced 5 per cent more than they had the previous month without an accompanying increase in labour costs, in 1957 and 1958 substantial total wage increases were gained. Other companies in the area considered or adopted the plan.[86] In Leicester, Shield Engineering a small firm employing only 20 people also adopted an incentive bonus scheme after production innovation, and was held up by the BPC as a success story to be modelled by other small firms.[87] These companies are not unusual. At a gas by-product manufacturing plant in Huddersfield 300 workers boosted productivity by 25 per cent and this was partly attributed to the introduction of an incentive bonus scheme.[88]

Before we leave this issue we must however take note of a development which occurred in the 1960s – productivity bargaining. Productivity bargaining developed as a response to the perceived problems of poor industrial relations as a source of the slow productivity growth of the UK economy. Productivity bargaining involved explicitly linking specific changes in working practices, such as greater interchangeability amongst workers, reductions in overtime, and reductions in manning levels with wage increases. The most widely noted example of these, are the productivity deals that occurred at Esso's Fawley refinery in the 1960s. The management concerned about the refineries' relatively low productivity attempted to negotiate with the trade unions for a reduction in a number of practices, such as demarcation and working times. From these negotiations emerged the Blue and Oranges books: two weighty documents that went into much detail about the restructuring of work and the resultant pay structure which was to emerge. These documents Flanders refers to as productivity package deals, which embodied a high wage, low overtime, and flexible working approach (Flanders 1964).

According to Gospel, by 1969 there were 3000 productivity deals in the UK covering 6 million workers, which amounted to a quarter of the workforce. It is has been argued that these deals did not achieve the desired goals for management, with some arguing that bargaining merely increased workers' control of the shop floor (new restrictive practices were created in place of the old) and gave no increases in productivity. Yet as Gospel argues such conclusions could be ill founded for management felt the reforms were worth having (Gospel 1992: 121). This in itself could have given management a new source of confidence. The earlier examples from the 1950s are designed to show that workers were prepared to bargain over productivity and that management believed positive results ensued.

EPA studies of workers and technical change

In May 1955 the EPA organised a seminar designed to help trade unions study automation and its economic and social repercussions.[89] It was hoped to aid trade unions in adopting courses of action, '...most appropriate when exercising their full prerogatives'.[90] The seminar provides us with rich and detailed comparative information on Western European trade unions and their attitudes and behaviour towards automation. It also offers us a valuable yardstick by which to assess how British trade unions approached automation and it gives us something by which to assess the claims about the retarding impact of British trade unions on innovation.

The report contains three case studies, two on France (concerning Renault and the *Sociéte Nationale des Chemins de Fer Francais*, hereafter SNCF), and one on the UK concerning automation in the glass industry. The Renault motor vehicle manufacturing group was nationalised in 1945 by the French government, and consisted of 11 works employing about 50,000 people, of which, about 36,000 worked in a single plant at *Billancourt*. According to Serge Colomb, a trade unionist and adviser to the EPA on automation, Renault and the Billancourt works were sensitive social and economic barometers, and they were also a stronghold of labour and had a tradition of labour problems.

The *Billancourt* works underwent considerable automation in the late 1940s and 1950s, with the regrouping of machining processes, the use of flow production, turn tables, automatic lathes, and multiple spot welders. Most importantly of all there was large-scale installation of transfer machines, considered by many to be one of the defining transitions on the road to automation. The installation of the transfer machines was in three steps, the experimental phase, then their wider application, and then their full implementation – automation. In one shop, the introduction of automation resulted in the increase of numbers of maintenance staff by 100 per cent, machine-setting staff decreased by 20 per cent, production and handling staff went down by 83 per cent, and electrical staff increased by 100 per cent.[91] These developments affected the workers in a number of ways. First it was reported that transfer machines had made work more arduous. Workers were compelled to follow the prescribed tempo of the machines, but safety was improved. Workers became more isolated from contact with each other in the plant (work became more dehumanised), also automation did not reduce the hours worked. Workers were placed on a wage classification system whereby wages were calculated as follows:

(Basic rate × average performance) + fixed component

Workers did earn more under the new system and there was little technical unemployment. Unfortunately Colomb did not relate the specific trade union reaction to these developments, but considered the reaction of the CGT-FO to automation in general. They wanted a guaranteed wage, shorter working hours, earlier retirement, planning of industry, reform of technical education, an improvement in the social relations between management and labour – instead of the atmosphere of conflict – and facilities to be given to trade unionists to undertake their research and studies.

The Renault agreement between management and labour that came into effect in 1955 ensured labour a number of benefits. These were three-weeks paid holiday for everyone, full pay for general (bank) holidays, the possibility of a pension scheme, sick pay, compensation for accidents at work, codification of wage payments, and a four per cent increase in all wages from 1955, with a guarantee of further increases of at least four per cent in 1956 and 1957. What is more the trade unions had been 'fighting' for ordinary workers to enjoy the same advantages as the technicians had received, although unfortunately Colomb does not say what these were.[92]

Mechanisation had first been introduced into the SNCF in its administrative departments some 30 years earlier, in the form of punched card, simple calculating, and accounting machines. By 1945 the south Western office equipment pool of the SNCF became the last to be automated with the introduction of punched card machines. Pierre Liénart, a member of the trade union CFTC studied the introduction. This episode consisted not only of the introduction of punched card machines but also accounting machines, computers, collators, and reproducers. The result was a reduction in the office staff pool of 125, or 25 per cent. The effect on employment does not seem to have been significant, for the permanent staff had a guarantee of employment, and the reduction was brought about through natural wastage. The changeover also increased the pace of work, and it appears that there was no reduction in working hours. Liénart thought that the introduction of the new machinery and the consequent reorganisation of the office had raised substantial personal problems for the staff in areas such as redeployment and housing. There was some resistance by older staff to adapt themselves to the new techniques. The wage systems seem to have been somewhat complex, with workers receiving a rate, which corresponded to their grade, an efficiency bonus, and other incremental bonuses depending upon seniority and efficiency. There were also bonuses and penalties depending upon the quality of the work.

The trade unions did not oppose automation although they were concerned especially about possible unemployment. Like the Renault workers, they wanted shorter hours of work, in this case a 40-hour week. They also wanted a revision of training – to give greater prospective for promotion, a reclassification of jobs, and a reform of the payments system amongst other things. Liénart concluded by saying that trade unions wanted full information on SNCF projects and that technical progress should be linked to 'social advancement'. Under these conditions railway personnel would co-operate with the development of automation in the railway industry.[93]

McLaughlin a representative of the National Union of General and Municipal Workers (hereafter NUGMW) reported on automation in three Pilkington plants in the British glass industry, claiming that this represented a very good example of the problems that came with automation.[94] Automation consisted of the introduction of an elevator that took the raw materials after delivery to hoppers and then to a conveyor belt. They were then taken to the mixer, mixed, placed into a storage batch, and then held until a furnace was available to process them. All this was monitored from a control room by signal lights. Previously this work had been undertaken by workers with spades, and was extremely physically arduous, thus highly suitable for automation.[95] From the beginning the union was kept informed and agreed to the company's actions on advertising for staff for the new plant. Certainly the new methods required less labour and the displaced workers were absorbed into other parts of the plant. Regrettably McLaughlin gives us no information on what happened to hours of work. However, before the plant came into being the NUGMW signed an agreement with Pilkington

Brothers on the procedures to be followed in dealing with all cases of labour transfers, job dismissal, the duties of shop stewards, and many other matters.[96] This information tends to support the assertions we have already made concerning the unemployment, consultation, wages, and distribution issues and illustrates that British unions like their foreign counterparts wanted binding agreements to ensure protection from adversity for their members.

Previously, mention has been made of the 1952–53 OEEC EPA study of steel workers' response to technical change in Belgium, France, Italy, Holland, and the UK. The study compared a single large steel plant in each country, except for Belgium, that had undergone a fairly intensive period of embodied and disembodied technical change involving in most cases the reorganisation of whole departments and the displacement of hundreds of workers. Tables 3.1 and 3.2 illustrate what was studied and the workers' responses.

As we can see the study reported higher percentages of workers unfavourably disposed to technical change in Germany and the Netherlands than in the UK. Again under the 'Favourable' heading the UK was by no means the best performer, but not the worst. The report however found the UK unusual in two ways. First, in the UK workers for the new plant were selected on the basis of seniority by management in consultation with the unions, not by some form of aptitude tests as undertaken in other countries except Belgium. Secondly and as mentioned earlier the

Table 3.1 Types of modernisation studied

Belgium	Comparative study of changes in three firms:
	1 Modernisation of a tin plate mill (extensive mechanisation)
	2 Modernisation of maintenance workshop
	3 Erection of a continuous rolling plant (extensive transfers of personnel)
France	Rolling mill for the manufacture of steel plate
Germany	Seven technical innovations ranging from the introduction of a new machine into an existing department to the introduction of a completely new mill
Italy	Replacement of heating furnaces by others of an improved type
Netherlands	Replacement of an old mill by modern continuous wide strip mill
United Kingdom	Reorganisation of an old smelting shop

Source: Adapted from EPA (1959: 12). Copyright OECD, Steel Workers and Technical Progress, 1959. Reproduced by permission of the OECD.

Table 3.2 Attitudes of workers to particular technical changes (figures are percentages)

	Favourable	Unfavourable	Other replies
Belgium	79	4	17
France	90	7	3
Germany	71	15	14
United Kingdom	67	10	23
Italy	87	6	7
Netherlands	57	26	17

Source: Adapted from EPA (1959: 39). Copyright OECD, Steel Workers and Technical Progress, 1959. Reproduced by permission of the OECD.

workers disliked continuous shift working. Therefore here it is apparent that British workers cannot be seen as excessively obstructive to technical change compared to their continental counterparts as many other sources seem to assert as was noted in Chapter 2; although the disinclination to shift working can certainly be seen as a hindrance, if not obstructive, to productivity.

Trade unions, restrictive practices, and evidence from the productivity agencies

We saw earlier how British trade union structure was asserted as one of the causes for the UK's poor productivity growth. Bean and Crafts in particular have argued that multiple unionism should be more conducive to restrictive practices than encompassing industrial unionism (Bean and Crafts 1996). In the previous chapter we also gave definitions of restrictive practices that included restrictions on the deployment of labour and strikes. Remember that in the discussion in Chapter 2 we looked at the impact of strikes upon labour productivity in British manufacturing and we saw that although it has often been claimed that strikes have hurt the UK economy the theoretical and empirical evidences cast doubt upon this. So does evidence from the productivity drive. Although members of the AACP's British section asserted that good relations between management and labour were evident in American industry, US businessmen were to estimate that in 1949, 7.76 hours were lost per worker in the USA through disputes as compared to 0.75 hours for the UK. The result was a 20 per cent loss in productivity in the USA (Carew 1987: 144–5). Moreover, Graham Hutton one of the chief disseminators of the merits of the productivity drive noted in his publication of 1953, *We too can Prosper*, '. . . industrial relations as a whole since 1945 have been better in Britain than in America, where days lost through strikes and stop-pages due to "labour troubles" have been much greater (in proportion) than in Britain' (Hutton 1953: 41).

One particular strike which occurred in the 1950s has often been seen as symbolic of the obstructive way organised labour responded to technical change, the 1956 strike at Standard's Banner lane works. Standard Motors had decided to invest heavily in transfer machines at the tractor works at Banner lane. It was envisaged that 2500 would be made redundant, the installation however happened to coincide with a recession in the motor industry. About 2000–3000 workers were laid off which constituted about 40 per cent of the work force. During the course of the strike a prominent TGWU official was sacked and the redundancies included a large percentage of the shop stewards. The redundancies were not based on seniority or personal circumstances. According to Salmon, management at Standards saw the strike as one over automation, but the Standard stewards were not against automation in itself. The stewards however had a policy of no redundancy, something management would not accept. The Standard stewards also firmly believed the benefits of technical change had to be shared amongst employers, shareholders, and workers. It could also have been the case that Standard's management were worried that the introduction of such capital-intensive production methods would give greater power to the shop-floor workers. Standard had large work gangs and thought that they were inflexible in the face of technical change and wanted to introduce smaller gangs so as to lower their bargaining power and relate work effort more closely to reward. Indeed Lewchuk has gone so far as to say, 'Effort norms were at the heart of managerial concerns.'[97] Thus the hard-line approach of Alan Dick the Standard Chairman, in laying off so many men in one go. Whatever we may make of this episode, it is clear that the issue of distribution of benefits from technical progress was important and this example re-affirms the argument that technical change can have major effects upon workers. Technical change can only proceed smoothly if management approaches the organisational and institutional changes with sensitivity (Donnelly and Thoms 1989: 107–8; Salmon 1988: 201; Thoms and Donnelly 1985: 169; Tolliday 1986: 213).[98] This conclusion is reinforced by the opinion of Austin Albu who was at one time works manager of an engineering company, and was Deputy Director of the British Institute of Management and a member of parliament. Albu thought that if management did not discuss with employees production changes then workers would resist changes and this had led to the Standard strike (Albu 1956: 258).

There is evidence that some British workers did resist attempts at the promotion of efficiency, namely work study. The BPC enthusiastically embraced what was known as work study, setting up its own work study department in 1954. From 1956 to 1960 the BPC's Work Study Unit gave 222 one-day conferences and 133 five-day appreciation courses, which were carried out on the premises of local firms. Members of the BPC's Work Study Unit, such as Speakman and Jones, gave many lectures on work study around the country at colleges and meetings of shop stewards and managements.[99] Work study is composed of two elements – method study which examines methods in use and then tries to produce greater efficiency, and work measurement which calculates the times for the various methods, thus enabling the most time efficient method to be chosen. Lewis Wright member of the BPC, phrased it as, '...finding the easiest and most efficient way to do a job'. According to Wright what worried trade unionists about work study was that in the past it had resulted in jobs temporarily being lost.[100] In 1951 the TUC recommended that 'Unions should seek to co-operate in the application of "scientific management" which, even if not an exact science, can make a valuable contribution to increasing productivity in industry', of which work study was an integral part.[101] The TUC were however worried that work study could turn into indoctrination (Carew 1987: 187).[102]

Work study was applied to traffic operation in British Railways and although in many parts of the country staff did accept these studies, in some they did not. In passenger stations at Thorpe (Norwich), Stirling, and Oxford, work study was either not introduced or stopped due to the requests of staff. At the goods terminal of Kilmarnock, at the freight yard of Wyre Dock, at carriage cleaning in Cambridge, Birmingham, and west London, and at motive-power servicing in the Reading, Southall and Didcot areas, staff again declined to accept work study, or in one case, Wyre Dock, it was withdrawn on the advice of the National Union of Railwaymen.[103] Thus while work study may have had official if reserved support from the TUC there was disparity between peak and shop-floor level. This was noted by Jones of the BPC's Work Study Unit who wrote with regard to the application of work study in industry that whilst those at the top of trade unions may approve of work study it did not mean that those at shop-floor level would accept its implementation.[104]

British Railways also appeared to have some staff that were not keen on the introduction of new machinery, according to the British Railways Productivity Council (hereafter BRPC). The BRPC was founded in 1955 because of the strong competition that British Railways perceived to exist from other forms of transport. The BRPC's objective was to consider ways that would make the railways run with the highest possible efficiency.[105] The BRPC reported that due to difficulties over manning agreements some new machines introduced into railway workshops had been laying idle for months. The BRPC thought that such disputes generated a lot of bad publicity and promoted a picture in the public mind that such restrictive practices were common in British Rail.[106] Trade unions after consultation gave their co-operation for the introduction of mechanical handling on British Railways, such as at Southampton (where a new transit shed had been installed), Hull, Hartlepool, and Middlesborough. Overall however, the BRPC came to the conclusion that restrictive practices 'as usually understood' were not a severe impediment to productivity improvement on the railways.[107]

According to the 1956 BPC *Review of Productivity in Freight Handling*, it was possible to find organisations where equipment for the mechanical handling of materials could not be introduced partly as a result of the refusal of operatives to consider the redeployment of labour. However the review stated that such reactions were not as common as the reports on industrial action would suggest. One area that loomed large in the public mind concerning organised labour's attempts to block productivity-enhancing measures was of course in the dockyards. The BPC *Review of Productivity in Freight Handling* looked at the dockyards and gave some prominence to the opinions of Lord Waverly, who in the 1950s was chairman of the Port of London Authority. Waverly thought that the often cited criticisms of dock workers as idle, undisciplined, and constantly on a 'go slow' untrue. The report found that, '. . . in isolated cases there has been opposition to working with mechanical equipment'. Dock labour has of course at times faced accusations of restrictive practices and they have been a contentious matter in the dockyards, but there were many other far more important factors impinging upon the dockyards' productivity.[108] Other ports such as Rotterdam and Hamburg had the advantage of being completely rebuilt after the War with the latest facilities. The report also noted that there was an unwillingness by labour to depart from the one-shift system, sometimes coupled with a limit on the amount of overtime worked. It also reported that many men insisted on waiting at the conclusion of a job until the call for the next job came, before they would report for another job. Manning ratios were another area were dockyard workers were reluctant to change. The introduction of handling equipment brought about a reduction in the numbers of men required in a gang, and some were reluctant to accept this, though the reluctance was not universal. The report concluded that: 'So long as the memories of pre-war days and of the attitude of mind towards casual employment endure the likelihood of close co-operation between employers and dock workers is almost bound to be an ideal rather than a practical goal.'[109]

The legacy of casual employment in the docks could well have affected labour's attitude towards industrial co-operation. For although the Dock Labour Scheme was introduced in 1947 which established a guaranteed minimum wage for registered dock workers, casualisation did not come to an end until 1967. Dock workers now had to attend the docks every morning and afternoon and accept whatever work they were offered. With this measure dockyard workers experienced a tightening in disciplinary codes, but labour market structures, work organisation, and industrial relations retained their pre-1930 character (Mankelow and Wilkinson 1998: 233, 235).[110] Set within these market and industrial structure conditions it is not hard to see why workers may have had difficulties in adjusting to more capital intensive production conditions.

There is an aspect of this that needs elaboration. 'Continuous' shift working can affect the effort–reward bargain of working because of the need to maximise the utilisation of capital equipment. If wages and work effort are equilibrated within an enterprise, any technical change that shifts the wages–work effort bargain may increase work effort and lower the bargaining power of organised labour (Willman 1986: 102–3). Here is a possible reason as to why British workers may not have liked this new form of shift working, because it had the possibility to change the effort–reward bargain in favour of the employers (Batstone and Gourlay 1986: 231).[111] However if 'continuous' shift working both raised the intensity of work and increased rewards to labour then workers may react favourably to this although it could seriously affect their social life.

Another possible reason as to why workers may have disliked 'continuous' shift working is because it may have put an end to the excessive reliance on policy overtime working in British industry. This could have reduced workers' earnings but left them working at the same amount of effort as before, thus in effect shifting the effort–reward relationship in favour of the employers. Of course a lot hangs on what we mean by effort and how we attempt to measure it. 'Effort' is a highly ambiguous term and should not be conflated with throughput or work intensity.[112] In our case 'continuous' shift working could have increased throughput but not work intensity or worker effort whilst lowering earnings, from the ending of institutionalised overtime (Caves 1980: 145–6; Matthews 1986: 914). Here we may be seeing organisational inertia in the face of institutional change that workers do not like because of its distributive effects. 'Continuous' shift working can be seen therefore as an institutional development that has the possibility to alter distributive outcomes. As we saw in Chapter 1, actors will seek to establish institutional equilibrium, which put them at greatest distributive advantage. It is then perhaps no wonder that organised labour would be less than enthusiastic about this new institution given its ability to alter distributive outcomes in favour of the employers.

Conclusion

As we saw in the introduction to this chapter, Fletcher told his European counterparts that the TUC sought to take part in the productivity drive because they believed that it was in the best interest of their members. This view was to prevail throughout the period 1948–73. In 1964 Patrick Fisher wrote to Oxford and District Trades Council and reaffirmed an instrumental attitude towards the productivity drive: by arguing that determined battles had to be fought in order that trade unions gained higher living standards from increased productivity but acknowledge that success would be greater in industries that were highly efficient.[113]

The importance of the phrase 'fight determined battles' should not be lost, for the productivity drive and its agencies were meant to forestall precisely this, indeed turn back to the concerns expressed by Watford LPC about having to fight for a share of the benefits from productivity growth. Consequently after 16 years of its operation, trade unionists were still of the frame of mind that they could only gain what they saw as their rightful rewards from increased industrial efficiency if they fought for it. It is clear from the issues of unemployment to wages that British trade unions were demanding and asking for no more than their Western European counterparts. Indeed Western European and North American unions saw the productivity drive in the same instrumental fashion as the UK unions.

Consider now the proposition we outlined in Chapter 1 concerning institutional change: that institutional change is not simply a function of moving from one Pareto outcome to another, but it is also a product of distributive outcomes. If trade unionists saw co-operation with the productivity drive as altering their present or future share of national product, possibly to less advantageous ones, then it is hardly surprising that co-operation would not be forthcoming. We have frequently examined unions' suspicions of productivity increases without any mechanism for ensuring that workers will benefit or be consulted about the pace and scale of technical change. British trade unions may not have been alone in this position. Carew has pointed out that American productivity specialists knew that European trade unions were disposed (more so than management) to accept the logic of the productivity programme, but they did not have the organisational strength to guarantee themselves benefits from the gains of increased efficiency. Organised labour was reluctant to disturb the existing equilibrium by moving in a new direction (Carew 1987: 166–7).

The above analysis graphically illustrates the problems faced by a productivity drive operating within the context of an unreformed industrial relations structure (Tiratsoo and Tomlinson 1993: 109).[114] In this respect trade union leaders and the TUC were faced with a fundamental problem. Given the voluntary nature of British industrial relations, union leaders could not force their members into co-operating with any measures to increase productivity (Clegg 1970: 343–9; Gospel and Palmer 1993: 158–9, 260; Maguire 1996: 59–60). Moreover, even today collectively bargained agreements are still not legally binding as they are in many other countries (Gospel and Palmer 1993: 260). In other countries the productivity drive was pursued within a context of reform albeit in some cases limited. Moreover the historical legacy of UK industrial relations was particularly unsuited for the productivity drive because of its decentralised and voluntarist traditions. As Tom Williamson said, 'It might be borne in mind that our institutions operate within a democracy, and that trade unions are voluntary organisations. The membership can be neither coerced nor driven, and it is no easy task to persuade millions of trade unionists.'[115] The TUC also wished to see the existing machinery of voluntary negotiation and collective bargaining preserved (Panitch 1976: 16–17, 25, 90–1, 169, 276; Tiratsoo and Tomlinson 1993: 97). All the TUC General Council could do was insist that unions, '...pay regard to the realities of the economic situation in framing their policy...'[116] Eichengreen's three institutional mechanisms to promote productivity growth were either absent (co-ordination of wage bargaining) or only weakly present (the bonding and monitoring mechanisms associated with CD). Organised labour had no new mechanisms to ensure returns from co-operation, and therefore had to rely upon its pre-established pattern of decentralised voluntary collective bargaining. The unions may have fought hard to retain the voluntary system but they also found themselves in a political position that led them to reiterate the need for co-operation.

As we saw from many of the statements of the TUC and notable trade union leaders, they went to extensive efforts to co-operate with the productivity drive, so too did many of those at the grass-roots level.

There were a significant and vocal number who did not. The TUC and assorted trade union leaders played their part to the full in the productivity drive and its attendant promotional bodies. Nevertheless, to preach the necessity of productivity was difficult, as Carron, President of the AEU noted: 'He [Carron] thought that the influence which the council [the BPC] had had on trade union leaders in leading them to preach productivity something which was not always easy for them had been very valuable. The attitude of mind which the Council's activities had created in many areas had had a considerable effect.'[117]

Thus, the productivity agencies were in the end forced to work by exhortation, it was not what was originally intended.[118] Trade unionists at all levels were active in this respect, from the leaders noted above to ordinary union members of productivity teams.[119] Here North's conception of ideology, as an instrument in institutional change should not be overlooked. For trade union leaders in this respect certainly tried to manoeuvre their position within the institutional workings they accepted and fought to keep. Academics such as Booth, Carew, and Tomlinson have all noted how enthusiastic the TUC was for the various productivity initiatives and the productivity drive in general (Booth 1996: 52–3; Carew 1987: 201; Tiratsoon and Tomlinson 1993: 142, 164; Tomlinson 1991c: 96–9; Tomlinson 1992: 48). The ability of union leaders to elicit co-operation from their members is contingent upon their degree of unity and discipline (Knight 1992: 202). The success of the productivity drive has been seen to be contingent on the degree of unity and discipline that it could engender from trade unionists, and as we have witnessed in some cases this was precious little. Hence it is possible to see a cleavage emerging below the TUC as the productivity drive matured with many unionists taking part and others not. Moreover as E. P. Thompson wrote, 'No ideology is wholly absorbed by its adherents: it breaks down in practice in a thousand ways under the criticism of impulse and experience...' (Thompson 1981: 431). In the case of Italy for example the productivity drive, '...broke down against reality rather than against opposing ideologies' (D'Attorre 1985: 37). Certainly it looks as if the ideology of productivity broke down in many cases on the shop floor (Taylor 1993: 62) because workers may have appreciated that co-operation with the productivity drive could radically alter the existing distributive equilibrium in favour of the employers. This would explain Cannon's 1955 remark that many militant shop stewards and trade union officials were recommending acceptance of productivity-promoting schemes which would in the long run lead to increasing exploitation of their members (Cannon 1955: 91).

Although Fletcher of the TUC's Production Department may have thought that the EPA had brought about a '...marked change of attitude to productivity of workers' representatives...', it seems unlikely that this could be translated into productivity outcomes because of the aforementioned reasons.[120] Indeed consider the words of the Deputy Director of the EPA from 1956 to 1961, Alexander King, when he reflected on the productivity drive, '...the average working man had to see there was something in it for him. Not just something vague by him sacrificing in order to make the country richer. From which he might or might not profit...'[121] We should not see those trade unionists that were less than enthusiastic about the productivity drive as obstructive, as in other countries trade unionists sought distributive gain just as vigorously. Here, however, they may have been at less of a disadvantage than UK unions because of mechanisms which would ensure distributive advantage both in the short and long term; both France (consider the examples of Renault and SNCF) and American unions with their various wage and productivity contracts, could ensure agreed rewards at the micro level. Indeed recall the examples in the UK of Shield Engineering and Chamberlains where distributive gain was ensured. Here co-operation did materialise and productivity was enhanced. However British unions in comparative perspective were right to stress their desire for rewards, for in Italy the workers gained very little from the productivity drive (Romero 1992; 1997). In the north east of Italy at the Vicenza Productivity Centre, which was the 'capital' of the Italian productivity drive, firms like Olivetti took up some of the institutional mechanisms of the productivity drive such as suggestions boxes. In the case of Olivetti, a suggestion from a worker which saved the firm 40,000 lire per year gave the employee, '...the derisory lump sum payment of 10,000 lire' in return. Another suggestion, which saved the firm two million lire, was rewarded with the sum of less than 20,000 lire. In general, D'Attorre has called the politics of productivity in Italy nothing but 'superexploitation' (1985: 24, 37). While for France, Kolko and Kolko have argued that although productivity rose substantially in 1952, most of these efficiency gains went into profits (Kolko and Kolko 1972: 636–7).

We must, however, with respect to the case examples presented above hold in mind that they do not meet the demanding methodological caveat (the 'ABC' requirement) presented in Chapter 2 by Nichols. Yet as we saw none of the studies that reputedly show British workers as the main factor accounting for poor firm-productivity performance do either. In this respect our case examples are methodologically no poorer than those mentioned previously. Our evidence is at most equal to some of these studies because of its highly comparative nature and not just with respect to one comparison but a number. In this way we have shown via qualitative evidence and a number of case studies that the linkage between British unions and the UK's relatively poor post-War productivity performance (the quantitative outcome) is not so nearly as clear as other scholars have attempted to show. However there are other sides to this equation and we shall now move on to equally important ones – the state and management.

Hence a final and appropriate caveat is in order here before we turn to the next chapter. We took note in Chapter 2 of how many studies have claimed that British workers were obstructive to change and that this evidence was almost solely drawn from managerial sources. But it is not difficult to find British managers who expressed quite the reverse. Sir Graham Cunningham of Triplex Safety Glass and an FBI member stated in 1957 that:

> PRODUCTIVITY is as high in our factories as it has ever been and when people complain that the British workman is not capable of work I say that it is management that is largely to blame when it comes to work in an organised factory. I will back the British workman against any in the world, properly managed.[122]

4

Britain's Relative Economic Decline and the British State

Introduction: government and markets

Amongst the litany of explanations for Britain's relative economic decline, the British government and state have often been seen as partly the cause of the problem. Some authors have asserted that large state expenditure retarded private sector performance, while others have argued macroeconomic mismanagement slowed growth. For example, Middleton whilst not blaming successive British governments for Britain's relative economic decline has alleged that various administrations between 1945 and 1979 exacerbated relative economic decline by policy errors (Middleton 1996: 466–7).

There are numerous viewpoints on the nature of the state, and these perspectives to a certain degree predetermine how the state is seen to affect economic outcomes. For instance the state may be seen as simply a parasitic institution, the property of officials, which plays little role in economic production, and is thus merely a tool for the aggrandisement of bureaucrats. It could also be seen as an instrument of class rule for use by a particular class in a society, although whether any class could use it with equal ease is another matter. Alternatively the state can be seen as a factor of cohesion, reconciling or moderating class conflict through repression and or concession. Here distributive struggles may lie at the heart of analysis, with the state intervening in the economy to alter income distribution between groups. In Chapter 3 we saw how organised labour wished in some instances for the state to intervene in the economy and ameliorate or alter market distributive outcomes, which were thought would be harmful to workers, as in the case of redundancy. Lastly we could treat the state as simply a set of institutions and make no assumptions about its class character (Jessop 1977).

Some explanations for Britain's relative economic decline have focused on the nature of the state and the way it has intervened in the economy as a cause of poor performance. Gamble, for example, points out that some explanations have accused the governing elite in Britain of having an anti-industrial ethos, which accorded low status to industry and engineering. Another state perspective criticises the British government and state for failing to shed its world role with its heavy defence expenditure and instead take up the challenges of the markets of the European Union (Gamble 1981: 20).

Governments can intervene in economies by a number of methods, and here Middleton provides a useful taxonomy. First, intervention in a market economy may take the form of regulation. Governments may legislate to determine the conditions under which production and consumption can take place. Secondly, governments may engage in production themselves by owning the means of production and determining what is to be produced. Thirdly, there is financial intervention whereby the state may, through taxes and subsidies on both incomes and prices, alter resource allocation. In order to achieve any or all of these three types of intervention government and state can use a number of instruments at their disposal. Monetary policy operating through such mechanisms as interest rates is often used by governments to control the quantity of money in circulation, the exchange rate, or hire purchase terms. Monetary policy can therefore be used to regulate market activities. The 'inverse' of monetary policy is of course fiscal policy, and this operates chiefly through taxation and public expenditure programmes. This therefore can, like monetary policy, be used to manipulate both the supply and demand for factors of production and the supply and demand for a whole array of goods. Finally we may note the use of physical controls, such as legislation to control wages and prices, quantity restrictions on output or imports, and direct intervention in a firm's production activities and the distribution of goods. As part of this category we may include policies of exhortation, which rely upon the power of persuasion not legislation. This type of policy was widely used during the productivity drive (for example, Middleton 1996: 126–8). Our main area of concern in examining the state vis-à-vis the productivity initiatives is industrial policy, trade union reform, and incomes policies. However before we turn to these we need to investigate those aspects of policy on which governments focused heavily, that is, macroeconomic management and its alleged ineffectiveness. For industrial and business activity is often more affected by the general economic decisions governments take than by the decisions that form part of specific policies such as industrial policy (Corden 1980).

Government macroeconomic stabilisation policy

One of the first explanations given for Britain's poor growth performance was that government intervention in the economy, primarily by fiscal and monetary policy, had been destabilising. For example Dow in the mid-1960s stated, 'As far as internal conditions are concerned then, budgetary and monetary policy failed to be stabilising, and must on the contrary be regarded as having been positively destabilising' (Dow 1970: 384). Criticisms of this stop-go policy have come from others as well. The Musgraves argued that, 'To be sure, the stop actions . . . by British standards at least, were undesirably large', which they attributed to balance of payments problems (Musgrave and Musgrave 1968: 43). Other economists have also implicitly criticised macroeconomic policy for producing stop-go cycles in the British economy (Prest 1968).

One possible cause of 'stop-go' may have been the political business cycle. The ability of governments to generate political business cycles is a function of the extent to which they can manipulate state revenue and expenditure, and if necessary create highly unbalanced budgets. One of the most direct and malleable mechanisms by which it is asserted they can do this is by the use of Keynesian macroeconomic demand management techniques (Buchanan *et al.* 1978). Duncan MacRae argued in the 1970s that the business cycle was more of a policy cycle. Taking his evidence from the timing of elections and economic cycles in post-War America, Duncan MacRae argued that in democratic societies governments are assumed to want to stay in power and therefore pursue vote-loss minimising behaviour. In order to achieve this they seek to minimise unemployment and inflation but in pursuit of this they face a dynamic trade-off. In the manipulation of this trade-off governments generate a policy cycle, which may be stable or unstable (Duncan MacRae 1977). It is also argued that democratic societies can generate instability not only through incumbent politicians seeking re-election but, by vote-seeking politicians engaging in competitive outbidding at the time of election. This creates excessive expectations amongst the electorate and places pressure upon the elected political parties to implement policies via a Keynesian template, which are then damaging to the economy (Brittan 1988).

The policy-generated business cycle argument in its crude form has however not fared well, when applied to Britain. Hatton and Chrystal while not denying that prior to several post-War elections in 1955, 1959, 1964, and 1972–73 real per capita incomes did experience unusually rapid growth, agree that it is difficult to find any systematic evidence of fiscal expansions immediately before elections and hence conclude, '...electoral motives...have had little effect on the pattern of business cycles'. It is also unclear as to whether such expansions have the desired effect anyway (1991: 86–7). Recent research has however breathed new life into this intuitively plausible argument. Schultz has argued that previous research failed to find a significant relationship between election timing and business cycle peaks because the relationship between the two was incorrectly specified. Previous models operated with the crude principle that just before an election one would expect to see governments attempting to engineer an economic boom.

Schultz has convincingly teased out the relationship between business cycles and elections, highlighting that one must take account of the standing of governments in opinion polls prior to their entering an election campaign. If governments have high standings in opinion polls there will be little to be gained from engineering a peak in the economic cycle. Moreover there is a trade-off; to engineer a boom prior to an election when governments already have a significant poll lead would be to risk a highly marginal and possible unnecessary vote winning exercise, against possible long-term damage to macroeconomic performance. This deterioration in macroeconomic performance after an election had been fought and won would be to damage the re-elected long-term prospects of any government by undermining any future claims to economic competence. Ergo, given that there are long-term costs to manipulation, '...the degree to which a government will manipulate the economy prior to an election will vary inversely with its political security going into the election'. Using this hypothesis Schultz applied a regression test to government transfer payments in the UK between 1961 and 1992. Transfer payments were chosen because elected politicians have some direct control over their level. Moreover transfer payments have an instantaneous effect of raising real disposable incomes for recipients. Given that real disposable income is highly correlated with a government's popularity and its electoral success, Schultz found that UK governments tended to increase transfer payments by substantial amounts when they are trailing badly in the opinion polls. Indeed Schultz found that at 1985 values a government trailing by nine percentage points in the opinion polls prior to an election would be expected to increase transfer payments by £368 million (Schultz 1995: 87).[1] Whether such contingent manipulation of the British economy and business cycles in general, have been harmful is of course another matter.

One of the most damaging types of cycle is alleged to have been 'stop-go'. 'Stop-go' cycles were said to be detrimental to the UK economy in that in the upturn of the cycle producers could not increase their output due to short-run capacity constrains. However Wilson showed that many other countries experienced far greater degrees of fluctuations than the UK in this respect. For instance, Japan experienced exceedingly high instability but growth was much more rapid than the UK. Sweden experienced very minor fluctuations, but did not experience the rate of growth of the fast-growing countries, say Germany or France. Wilson concludes, 'By historical standards the post-war period has been remarkable for both stability and growth' (Wilson 1966: 28, 30–1).

Wilson's evidence was further supported by Whiting who asserted that stop-go was unlikely to have lowered the level of investment and firm efficiency. Here the argument runs that if the fluctuations are of a regular pattern, then businesses will get used to them and thus predict them. This implies that in the upturn of the cycle enterprises will be able to produce all that is required because they will have planned in advance for such output levels. Moreover as we saw in Chapter 1 it is not at all certain that lower investment *per se* has been the cause or a consequence of the UK's relatively poor growth rate. Whiting has further asserted that in some sectors of the economy there was massive capacity underutilisation. For in some industries such as electrical engineering, iron, steel, and motor vehicles, components machinery was productively used for only 50 per cent of the time, thus expansion of output under these conditions would not be difficult. Whiting measured cyclical volatility of net output in the manufacturing sector between 1955 and 1973 of seven countries, the USA, Sweden, Germany, France, Italy, Japan, and the UK, and it was the British economy, which showed the least variation from trend. Whiting thus proposed, '...cyclical fluctuations in the UK business cycle are extremely unlikely to represent an important causal factor of the UK growth performance' (Whiting 1976: 38). Identical conclusions were found in a National Economic Development Survey (NEDC 1976: 3, 37).

Wilson and Whiting have been criticised for their methodology by Boltho who suggested that their studies were measurements of variability and did not allow for differing degrees of capacity utilisation. However Boltho showed using no less than four different measures of variability and three different measures of cyclical fluctuations, that the decades of the 1950s, 60s, and 70s were much more stable than the periods, 1870–1913 and 1922–37. Boltho attributed the increased stability to a number of factors – a fall in the importance of agricultural production in the economies of the countries studied, automatic stabilisers, demand management (although as Boltho points out this is contentious), and knowledge by the private sector that governments would intervene in the economy. Indeed the countries which came out most stable are those in which governments did pursue policy activism, e.g. France, Norway, Sweden, Britain, and the USA, while those countries which came out less stable are those which did not actively seek stabilisation, that is, Switzerland, Spain, and Germany (Boltho 1989: 1724).[2] Table 4.1 reports Boltho's results; the data seems to present strong evidence that the UK in no way suffered exceptionally from large amplitude cycles either comparatively or historically.

Overall then the hypothesis that government intervention in the UK economy through policy activism to achieve stabilisation was inherently detrimental strains credibility. In that the alleged transmission mechanism of Keynesian demand management by which the cycles were caused has been shown at the most to be only weakly present and in that the cycles themselves were in no way unusual compared to those of the UK's economic competitors.

However, intervention by the British government in the UK economy has been said to be unusual in that it did not focus on the supply side of the economy. Aldcroft has pointed out that between 1950 and 1975 there were 47 changes in consumer credit regulations. This led to fluctuating demand in the car and consumer goods industries, but as he realises it is difficult to create consistent, long-term supply side policies. As to whether the government had a '...pathological obsession with demand management policies', as he provocatively phrases it, is a lot more difficult to judge (Aldcroft 1982: 43, 52). Aldcroft's focus on the car industry is well taken, for other authors have argued that government mismanagement of broad macroeconomic intervention has damaged the industry. Wilks has noted for example how in 1960 the reimposition of hire-purchase restrictions on cars by the then Chancellor of the Exchequer, Heathcoat Amory coincided with a slump in the US car market and a cyclical downturn in the UK consumer duarbles market, which was particularly bad for the UK car industry. Less specifically Wilks asserts that macroeconomic instability, particularly during the 1960s, has had a negative impact upon investment in the car industry (Wilks 1984: 78–9, 86). Here at least the negative impact of government intervention upon the economy looks more justified.

British Governments have intervened in the UK economy in more direct ways than through fiscal measures alone, most notably and directly through the nationalisation of certain industries, and some have argued that this has damaged economic performance. In using the nationalised industries as instruments of macroeconomic policy they have made long-term investments in these industries difficult and ministers have

Table 4.1 Size of cyclical fluctuations for selected countries, total GDP (1870–1979)

Country	Standard deviation of annual percentage changes in GDP			Coefficient of variation of annual percentage changes in GDP			Mean absolute percentage deviation of GDP from its log-linear trend			Mean percentage shortfall of GDP from potential, proxies by 'trend' through peaks		
	1870–1913	1922–37	1950–79	1870–1913	1922–37	1950–79	1870–1913	1922–37	1950–79	1870–1913	1922–37	1950–79
France	4.53	5.49	1.57	2.78	2.71	0.33	2.94	4.98	2.49	5.04	4.59	1.21
Germany	2.18	8.97	3.11	0.75	2.48	0.59	3.37	7.96	6.57	3.69	8.66	1.53
Italy	3.38	4.11	2.36	2.22	1.73	0.49	5.82	3.07	3.91	3.21	3.10	1.75
UK	2.35	3.35	1.94	1.25	1.30	0.81	2.02	3.16	2.12	2.51	2.95	1.75
USA	4.40	8.09	2.59	1.03	2.92	0.74	2.93	8.91	2.44	4.89	9.16	3.12
Canada	7.84	7.88	2.63	1.91	3.06	0.57	6.79	9.61	2.63	6.34	10.13	3.06
Japan	5.99	4.29	3.84	1.99	1.36	0.45	3.04	2.95	7.17	4.75	2.94	3.31

Source: Reprinted from *European Economic Review*, 33, A. Boltho, 'Did policy activism work?', pp. 1709–26, copyright (1989) with permission from Elsevier.

demoralised managers by cutting across their managerial authority (Dunkerley and Hare 1991; Middleton 1996: 613). This was particularly so in the 1970s when, according to Hannah, politicians in search of instruments by which to control the new economic phenomenon of 'stagflation' intervened repeatedly in the management of the nationalised industries to try and abate the poor economic performance. Be this as it may Hannah asserts there is, '... no *prima facie* case to see the degree of commitment to state enterprise (as opposed to the quality of state enterprise and its alternatives) as a major determinant of the poor economic performance of industrialised democracies like Britain'. The crucial point is how they are managed and here no definitive judgement can be made because some nationalised industries performed well while others performed poorly (Hannah 1994: 170).

The growth of public sector expenditure

The growth of the public sector and the rise in state expenditure have been held responsible for the UK's relatively poor growth by a number of writers and two notable economists, Bacon and Eltis. Their theory is that the growth of the non-market sector has crowded out and placed a huge burden on the market or wealth-creating sector of the economy (Bacon and Eltis 1978). The expansion of the non-market sector occurred most rapidly between 1961 and 1975. The non-market sector is defined as those goods and services, which are not sold and the market sector is defined as those goods and services, which are.[3] The non-market sector consists of broadly non-industrial output and the market sector consists of private industrial and service output. Bacon and Eltis's theory accounts for relative economic decline by arguing that Britain has excessively deindustrialised due to the growth of the non-market sector. Bacon and Eltis say that the increase in corporate and personal taxation and interest rates that has occurred to finance the non-market sector has squeezed industrial investment and led to slow growth. They argued that the scale of the detrimental effects on economic performance could have been lessened if workers had accepted that the increase in public sector employment represented an increase in state welfare provision and therefore moderated their wage claims accordingly. Moreover Bacon and Eltis assert that firms could not compensate for increased wage pressure by raising their output prices because of government prices and incomes policies and foreign competition in product markets. This fits in with Eichengreen's model where in other Western European countries increased welfare provision was tied to wage moderation and this allowed for increased firm investment which led to faster growth.

However Bacon and Eltis's theory was based upon an analysis of the 1960s and 1970s, and as such it draws its evidence from this period, but the empirical evidence of the 1980s should make us seriously question the validity of their theory. Although there was a company profits squeeze in the mid-1970s, company profit levels improved substantially in the 1980s and regained their former level of the 1960s. Nevertheless the size of the non-market sector has remained the same despite Thatcher's attempts to reduce it. It seems that non-market sector consumption has come at the expense of market consumption and not market investment. Companies keep their profit levels up by altering the real wage or the level of employment or both. Any trade union pressure to maintain or increase the real wage due to an increasing tax burden to finance the non-market sector will probably result in higher levels of unemployment and an increased non-accelerating inflation rate of unemployment, not falling firm profits (Crafts 1991b: 270–1; Crafts 1993b: 26–7).[4] It will be helpful briefly to review comparative data presented in Figure 4.1 concerning this issue. Only for the years 1950–59 does UK government expenditure exceed that of its major competitor nations while for the years 1960–87 the UK does not appear exceptional. Bacon and Eltis have tried in their own words to 'salvage' their theory but the rescue operation remains unconvincing.[5]

Although it is hard to defend the argument that the level of government expenditure has been a significant burden to the British economy there

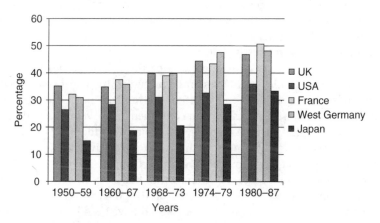

Figure 4.1 Government outlays as a share of GDP, 1950–87
Source: Derived from Crafts and Woodward (1991: 10).

are theories, which place emphasis upon its unusual composition as the problem. Barnett took aim at the amount of government expenditure post-War governments made on the National Health Service, housing, and social security in general. Barnett implied that the British level of spending was far higher than that of its industrial European competitors and that this money should have been spent on technical education and industrial modernisation as occurred in Germany (Barnett 1986: 240–3, 296–7). Barnett's argument has however been devastatingly criticised and now looks implausible. Barnett cited no data relating to levels of social expenditure in European countries which is readily available, for if he had it would have shown, as Harris has, that as early as 1950 Britain had a lower level of social security expenditure as a proportion of GDP than West Germany. By 1952 it was lower than France and Denmark and by 1957 it was lower than Italy, Sweden, and the Netherlands. Even if one only considers spending on the National Health Service, one of Barnett's most often cited totems of the burden of state expenditure on the national economy; the evidence does not lend support to his argument. In aggregate although during the 1950s and 1960s Britain spent more through central government on health care than other Western European countries, in total the per capita expenditure, both through local and central government, was higher for most other Western European countries. Although Barnett does not make the argument himself, the only way in which his thesis could have explanatory power concerns the unusual way in which the UK raised and spent its funds on public health. Britain was unusual in that most of the cost of welfare expenditure was financed out of general taxation and spent through means-tested public assistance, not through contributory social insurance as on the Continent. However, whether this peculiarity was detrimental to the economy is unclear (Harris 1990).

However, a pointer to the effect of a particular form of taxation has now emerged. Cooley and Ohanian have studied the effect of the high rates of ex post capital income taxation put in place in the 1941 budget to finance the British war effort and continued until 1980. The high rate of ex post capital income taxation particularly during 1941–59 when the rate was 36.7 per cent was put in place on the advice of Keynes and resulted in low rates of physical investment compared to the USA. They use counter factual modelling to show that had a tax smoothing policy been put in place to finance the War, as was the policy with previous wars, then the rates of physical investment would have been higher. In other words, the legacy of Keynes is responsible for Britain's slow growth up to 1980 (Cooley and Ohanian 1997). The argument is well made but lacks comparison with other Western European economies' growth and capital income taxation levels and it can only explain part of the problem because returns to investment were poor as well.

The scale of British defence expenditure has been frequently cited as a source of Britain's relative economic decline.[6] If one looks at the level of British military expenditure as a proportion of GDP (measured at purchases values) then one finds that the UK has a level second only to the USA. More especially, all the other advanced industrial countries have a level, which is below that of both the USA and the UK, only France comes close to having the same kind of expenditure level. Figure 4.2 shows levels of military expenditure across an array of OECD countries and it is clear that the UK does have a relatively high burden.

Although historically Britain had a legacy of relatively large defence expenditure with the outbreak of the Korean War, Britain embarked upon a massive rearmament programme, which it has been argued severely slowed economic growth. This, it is claimed set British defence spending on a higher plane for the next three decades. Members of the 1945–51 Labour governments had pretensions of maintaining Britain as a great power in the world. Ernest Bevin for instance believed that Britain should continue to play a great power role. Even Churchill stated that

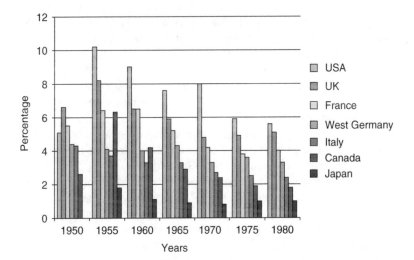

Figure 4.2 Military expenditure as a percentage of GDP at purchases values, 1950–80, for selected OECD countries
Notes: The NATO definition of military expenditure is used.
Source: Derived from Chalmers (1992: 113).

Labour's plans for defence spending were way beyond the British economy's capacity to bear (Chalmers 1985: 34–5, 54). Other British governments were not unaware of the burden such high spending had on the economy. Harold Macmillan for example, said that, 'For every rifle that our comrades in Europe carried we were carrying two. If we were to follow the European example, we would save £700 million a year. If only half of these resources were shifted into exports the picture of UK foreign balances would be transformed' (Chalmers 1992: 37).

Manser has identified one mechanism by which UK defence expenditure could have been harmful to growth. Manser believes that the economic policies of successive governments have constrained the growth rate of the British economy by deflating the economy every time a balance of payments crisis loomed. The balance of payments crises were caused by overseas expenditures, particularly on military related items, which consistently pushed the balance of payments on current account into deficit, when without these governmental expenditures the balance of payments on current account always had a commercial surplus. Hence the British economy has via the foreign policy of various administrations been kept under a permanent state of suppression and not allowed to grow at its 'natural' rate (Manser 1971).[7]

Blank has argued similarly, Britain after the War tried to maintain an international political and military position which was too extensive for its economic capacity to support. The domestic economy was sacrificed for foreign policy goals. The defence of Sterling via deflationary packages and the enormous rearmament programme in 1951, dealt heavy blows to the economy. Government policy especially in the 1950s and 1960s attacked the major sources of growth in the domestic economy. Blank lays the burden of responsibility for this on Britain's rulers, hence his remark that, 'Britain's economic problems have risen . . . from the impact of the attitudes, commitments, and politics of Britain's top political leaders.' All this has led to the fundamental problem for the economy of a lack of investment (Blank 1977: 714–17).

It is often argued that defence expenditure particularly on research has 'spin-offs' and helps the export sector if a country can export a significant proportion of its arms production, these arguments are open to serious question. The level of divergence between custom-built, low-volume, and highly sophisticated military products and the high-volume non-specialised products required for the civilian market, makes the scope for 'spin-off' from the military to the civilian sector very small, 'Moreover, the commercial spin-off from defence research has proved to be nothing like as great as the gains made from comparable expenditures on industrial research' (Alford 1988: 47). There is however the counter argument that defence spending helps Britain's balance of payments, in that money spent on military R&D products can thereby help make arms exports more competitive. Yet, British arms have been uncompetitive, especially against American competition, and countries which spent much less on their defence industries had an equivalent level of arms exports. Italy in 1979–83 had an equal share of the world's arms markets, yet spent 40 per cent less on its defence industry. For the same period, France spent a near equivalent level to Britain on defence but had a share of the world's arms markets two and a half times more than that of Britain (Chalmers 1985: 113, 120–3).

Smith provides the strongest evidence that military expenditure is inversely correlated with investment, and thereby slows growth. He studied 14 large OECD countries and found that the opportunity cost of military expenditure was foregone investment, this result was robust whether pooled, panel, time series, or cross section data was used.[8] He found for the years 1954–73 an almost total inverse correlation of −1. In Smith's model, military expenditure causes a reduction in government expenditure on public goods such as health and education and via an aggregate private-sector savings effect this lowers investment. Given that private consumption is composed of both private and public goods and that the two are close substitutes, and assuming that consumers have a target real income level, then any fall in public consumption causes an increase in private consumption financed by a fall in private-sector savings (Smith 1980).

It is of course argued that the example of France highlights the case that defence expenditure is not *per se* damaging to an economy. Indeed the figure above does convey the impression that France had second only to the UK and the USA a high level of defence expenditure. This proposes that it might not be defence expenditure in itself which is detrimental to an economy but instead that, '...we need to know more about the contrasting ways in which post-war British and post-war French governments tried to retain great-power status, and in what way their attempts impacted on their respective economies' (Marquand 1990: 318). Thus levels of defence expenditure have possibly no inherent drawbacks, indeed they may have been advantageous for a regime of Keynesian demand managers, in that it allowed them to stabilise the demand in the economy (Kidron 1970: Ch. 3). However defence expenditure was heavily concentrated overseas and here lay the problem. This resulted in a periodically weak external account on the balance of payments and placed governments in situations where they had to chose between internal economic growth and external equilibrium in the balance of payments. This underconsumption thesis of defence expenditure in which defence expenditure mitigates the business cycle can be considered as a form of disguised industrial policy. It is against the economic and political backcloth that we have detailed above of alleged poor macroeconomic management and excessive defence and welfare expenditure that the productivity drive occurred and it has therefore been examined accordingly. We shall now examine industrial policy (Middleton 1996: 616).

The British state problem and industrial policy

Before we begin our discussion it is perhaps necessary to precisely define what we mean by industrial policy and outline why it is important. We shall take industrial policy to be the guiding framework by which government uses, '. . . its authority and resources to . . . address the needs of specific sectors and industries (and if necessary, those of individual companies) with the aim of raising the productivity of factor inputs' (Coates 1996: 23).[9] Within this definition there falls what we may call direct and indirect industrial policy. Direct industrial policy is concerned with enhancing the performance of particular industries, sectors, or firms. Indirect industrial policy is concerned with the effects upon sectors of industry, which follow from more general economic and social policies.

Industrial policy is important because it bears directly upon the productivity and competitiveness of all sectors of an economy, particularly the tradable sector, which in the global market is important to the performance of the whole economy. The importance of the performance of tradables is highlighted by the fact that only 20 per cent of service output can be exported and for every 1 per cent decline in the UK's exports of manufactures, its exports of services have to increase by 2.5 per cent to compensate for this loss. To add to this a significant proportion of the service sector (e.g. financial services) is dependent upon the output of the manufacturing sector (Lee 1996: 33).[10] Many economists stress the importance of manufacturing, 'Historically, manufacturing in all countries has tended to experience faster rates of productivity growth. Market economies which have maintained relatively large shares of output in manufacturing have tended to have above average growth rates' (Muellbauer 1996: 220).

Industrial policy is set within the wider state framework or what many call state tradition and it is crucial to explore the nature of British state tradition for many authors have argued that it was the failure of a developmental state to emerge in the UK, in the twentieth century, which has been the most significant reason in its relative economic decline. The general idea behind the developmental state is that markets may fail to provide optimum economic outcomes, in other words there may be what economists call market failure.[11] In order to improve economic performance governments can embark upon an array of initiatives. In France for example there were national plans which had the aim of providing a consistent economic scenario by which firms could plan their investment decisions, although it is controversial as to whether this influenced France's growth rate. The Eichengreen perspective on economic growth should not be lost sight of here; as we saw in his model, long-term investment strategies are essential to economic growth. This strategy of planning for growth is based on the hypothesis that if firms have optimistic expectations about future economic growth they will invest and this then generates growth. This begets what one may call a virtuous economic circle through the operation of self-fulfilling expectations. One of the most often cited examples of a successful developmental state in operation is that of Japan. Japan, through the operation of amongst other things, its famed Ministry of International Trade and Industry (hereafter MITI), instituted a battery of economic policies to improve its economic performance. There were tax incentives, the government's unconsolidated (investment) budget, anti-trust policy, forums for exchanging views and reviewing policies, and an extensive reliance upon public corporations, to name but a few (Sawyer 1992: 262–4).

There are three recognised and distinct state traditions, they are the liberal or market-led; negotiated – consensual or corporatist; and the developmental, statist, or entrepreneurial (Coates 1996: 27; Katzenstein 1985: 20; Marquand 1988: Ch. 4). These state traditions, although ideal types help to clarify and focus a particular set of industry–state relations. There are now a number of works which assert that UK industrial policy has for at least a hundred years been subordinate to government polices which have attempted to placate the interests of what has come to be called the City–Treasury–Bank of England, financial nexus. Amongst these the Treasury has received enduring blame (Middleton 1996: 38). Newton and Porter, for example, have argued that over the last one hundred years every attempt to form a 'producers' alliance' between organised capital, organised labour, and the government, with the aim of increasing industrial productivity has failed because of the demands of the financial nexus. The supremacy of the demands of the financial sector over the needs of industry are exemplified by such government actions as the return to the Gold Standard in 1925, with the pound valued at $4.86 to the ounce and the unsuccessful attempts to maintain the pound's value in 1949 and again in 1967. Newton and Porter argued these actions were highly detrimental to industrial interests, and induced by the primacy of the financial nexus in the government's macroeconomic policy making. This core policy-making nexus with its three demands of the pursuit of free trade, the maintenance of the highest possible external value for sterling, and the balancing of the budget has, they argued, contributed significantly to Britain's relatively poor economic performance (Newton and Porter 1988).[12]

Marquand has remarked that, 'British economic agents have repeatedly failed to adapt to the waves of technical and institutional innovation sweeping through the world economy...' The reason for this is the failure of the UK to change its adjustment strategy. The problem for the UK economy was that every time a group of individuals or alliance of groups formed to promote adjustment via a state-led strategy it was nullified by an overriding financial orthodoxy. Thus Marquand cites the same examples as Newton and Porter. The Mosley Memorandum and Lloyd George's programme for public works were both neutered by the Treasury and Snowden the Labour Chancellor during 1929–31. In 1966 we have the example of Wilson's administration abandoning the National Plan for economic growth (Marquand 1988: 144).

The primacy of the financial nexus in government policy has been traced back deep into the roots of British history. Anderson has written, 'The fundamental origin of the decline of British capitalism lay in its initial priority...British industrialisation arrived without deliberate design, and triumphed without comparable competitors' (Anderson 1987: 71–2). According to Anderson, British capitalism could never fully develop due to the hegemonic supremacy of the English aristocracy and the City. The English Civil War and the Glorious Revolution placed the English aristocracy and the City in a commanding position thereafter. Even when industrialisation was in full swing and Britain was the 'Workshop of the World' profits from the City in 1880 were, 50 per cent of the total value of manufactured exports (Anderson 1987: 34).[13] Furthermore the City was over successive centuries colonised by aristocrats and when agrarian wealth lost its power, City money became the hegemonic form of capital. The Treasury was, '...after the City, the second great albatross round the neck of English economic growth', and '...determined to minimise government at home...' The '...Foreign Office of vice-regal horizons abroad...', could not help the British economy either (Anderson 1964: 51; 1987: 57).[14]

The most persuasive, detailed, and closely argued form of this argument has come from Cain and Hopkins. At the end of the First World War

British industry was too fragmented and bitterly competitive to counter the supremacy of the City in its coherence and simplicity. In the interwar period Lancashire took second place to London in the defence of Sterling, 'By 1921 the gentlemanly capitalists were in charge again, and their implicit internationalist assumptions once more guided British economic policy.' But the return to the Gold Standard in 1925 required an immense effort, which harmed manufacturing exporters and encouraged imports and accelerated Britain's relative economic decline. There was such close intimacy between the City and the Treasury that the City could in the interwar period veto 'unsuitable' candidates for the post of Chancellor. The 'gentlemanly capitalists' who ran British economic policy were arrogant in assuming that they knew what was best for British industry. Furthermore industrial capital had little influence upon the distribution of power or the formation of economic policy. British 'gentlemanly' values were pervasive and restoring London's position as the main international money market was their chief concern, resulting in high priority to the balanced budget, free trade, and the Gold Standard. The City was moreover better organised to provide capital to foreign countries than to British industry. The City represented the nation and industry was seen as provincial and self-interested. After the Second World War financial orthodoxy sought to rebuild the empire as an integral part of regaining Britain's position as a major financial centre which was vital to the economy. In the post-War world the ties, which joined Whitehall to the City were much closer than those, which joined Whitehall with Manchester. And by the 1970s there ran an intricate web of interlocking directorships which formed the chief decision-making body in the private economy which also had close ties with the elites of the civil service, and the wider, 'gentlemanly establishment' (Cain and Hopkins 1993: 4, 19–20, 30, 47–8, 53–4, 57, 61, 68–9, 70, 76–7, 92–3, 104–5, 198, 210–1, 234, 261, 268, 290).

To summarise the arguments deployed above, it is clear that the 'problem' of the British state towards industry has not taken the form of a direct and negative link but more one of an indirect link, in that industry was in some sense, 'neglected'. The state was too sensitive towards the interests of the City and finance, and therefore a low-level priority was given to the needs of industry. David Coates nicely crystallised much of the above when he wrote, 'Twentieth-century UK manufacturing went into decline under state policies which (as late as the 1950s) were still preoccupied with the defence of empire and sterling, and under a gap between industry and finance inherited from its nineteenth-century economic and social geography' (Coates 1996: 4–5).

Despite the wide-ranging arguments from various authors deployed above there is in no way an accepted consensus on the supremacy of the financial nexus as a retarding break on Britain's economic performance. Daunton has challenged many of the propositions upon which these arguments rest and claimed that there was no single and united coherent interest with a high degree of historical linearity, which we can refer to as the City–Bank–Treasury nexus. Moreover the landed aristocracy did not maintain closure against outside interests, there was no substantial division between 'gentlemanly capitalism' and 'industrial capitalism', individuals could and did move freely between the two spheres (Daunton 1989).

Alford has also challenged the idea of the financial supremacy of the City or 'gentlemanly' capitalists. Like Daunton, 'gentlemanly capitalism' is not seen as a coherent entity, and Alford asserts that from 1880 the family networks that are supposed to have been the pillar of 'gentlemanly capitalism' were breaking down. Merchant banking was not a closed preserve but relatively open and thus this sector did not constitute a ruling elite. Moreover, Alford claims that there were powerful industrial and provincial alliances which were not 'puppets' of 'gentlemanly capitalists', the state therefore had to take account of a number of competing interests, all equally powerful, and no particular social group reigned supreme in policy making (Alford 1996: 102–5).

While Daunton and Alford have attacked the idea that the City component of the financial nexus was partly responsible for relative decline, Thain has criticised another component, the Treasury. Thain has argued that the Treasury was itself a prisoner of the ruling consensus on economic policy, and did not contain a single, unified economic view. There resided within it many competing views. The Treasury was and is subject to the political control of ministers and in the end the prime minister; it does not dominate them. Although the Treasury should accept some of the blame for poor performance, ultimately decline has been in operation longer than the era of the managed economy; and anyway, the Treasury is only part of the decision-making machinery, it also has to continually struggle for dominance with other departments (Thain 1984). Capie and Collins have undermined another pillar of the financial nexus argument by persuasively showing that British banks did provide adequate long-term liquidity to industry but the problem, if anything, was that industry did not ask for the credit, moreover British banks have suffered no financial crises since the 1870s unlike countries such as the USA or those in Western Europe. British banks gave the best benefit of all to British industry financial stability (Capie and Collins 1992).

In the foregoing discussion we have considered the positions of a number of authors on the British state tradition and most would seem to conclude that Britain has failed to witness the emergence of a developmental state, and the corollary has been poor British economic performance for most of the twentieth century – particularly after 1945. Yet there are those who would contest the idea that the UK never had a developmental state or anything similar. Edgerton, after reviewing Britain's performance during the Second World War, its heavy investment in military, industrial, and civilian research and development, takes issue with those writers who have argued that the British state has been anti-technocratic, anti-industrial, and pre-occupied with a concern for issues of general social welfare. Edgerton asserts, '...in the twentieth century the British state has been a militant, industrial and technological state...' (Edgerton 1992: 111). Edgerton argues that a British national technical-industrial strategy is evident in the policy of the Ministry of Aviation in the 1960s which was a '...vast organisation, responsible for aeronautical and electronic R&D, procurement of aircraft and much electronics for the armed services, civil airports and air traffic control'. The Ministry also had seven major research and development establishments, such as the National Gas Turbine Establishment and the Royal Radar establishment (Edgerton 1991b: 103–7). Edgerton offers other examples, like the Ministry of Technology (hereafter MINTECH) which from 1964–70 developed from small beginnings, into the, '...most comprehensive production ministry Britain ha[d] ever had'. Tony Benn is even said to have referred to MINTECH as the first techno-economic ministry in the world. With respect to the Wilson administration of 1964–70 Edgerton writes, 'The whole model of decline believed in by many 1980s analysts – that Britain did not have a "developmental state" – implies that the real MINTECH (as opposed to an insincere initiative of 1964) could not have existed. And yet it did exist.' Edgerton has also drawn attention to fact that the UK has had a very high level of research and development expenditure saying, 'In 1960 Great Britain was without doubt, the scientific and technical powerhouse of Western Europe: research and development (R&D) spending whether industrially funded or government funded, was significantly higher than in any capitalist country other than the USA...' (Edgerton 1996: 65–7, 77, 53).[15]

Middlemas however portrays the formation of a different state tradition, which arose after 1945 that was neither liberal as asserted by Marquand and Anderson nor developmental, technocratic, and modernising as claimed by Edgerton. In this scenario both labour and management had learned incalculable lessons from wartime co-operation. The Labour government of 1945–50 believed that fundamental quarrels between both sides of industry and the state could be contained. Attlee and Cripps thus both envisaged co-operation between government, industry, commerce, and labour. Moreover the re-establishment of such bodies as the NJAC was meant to perpetuate the harmonious industrial relations, which had apparently dominated during the War, without giving either side influence over government policy. Middlemas emphasises that the post-War settlement between organised labour, organised business, and government produced an essentially consensual state, where the primary interests in Britain extended their natural competition into the centre of government. Middlemas says that this co-operation was essential if governments were to achieve economic growth and political stability. Middlemas too notes however that this model failed to provide sustained and comparatively good economic performance. Thus by the end of the 1950s it was beginning to crumble because of inflation and poor growth. This led to conflict between the tripartite partners over who was responsible (Middlemas 1986: 23, 67, 75, 119, 242, 349).

There can be not doubt however that government is responsible for setting the regulatory framework when it comes to competition policy and regulating monopolies, cartels, and restrictive practices. During the interwar period the UK government had actively encouraged cartelisation and trade association agreements as a way of encouraging efficiency through rationalisation. Moreover the general economic climate of that period was one of tariffs and international trading agreements, again this tended to promote cartels. Indeed Crafts and Broadberry have pointed out that during the depression, there developed widespread collusion among firms behind tariff barriers and that this collusion was promoted by government policies in the name of rationalisation. But while these policies may have had some success in alleviating the effects of the Depression in the short run, harm was done in the long run because it left an unfavourable legacy of entrenched restrictive practices and low productivity in the post-War world (Broadberry and Crafts 1990a: 5; 1990b: 603; 1990c: 398).

However after the War both Labour and Conservative governments slowly attempted to rid the British economy of such restrictive trading agreements with such measures as the Monopoly and Restrictive Practices Act 1948 and the Restrictive Trade Practices Act 1956. The implementation of these Acts was not particularly rigorous. The 1948 Act's principal measure was to establish the Monopolies and Restrictive Practices Commission. Mercer aligns the establishment of the Commission with the productivity drive arguing that the Commission was part of an education 'package' in the field of monopoly which had an aim therefore akin to that of the AACP's in the field of productivity. Mercer notes however that the Commission worked very slowly and by 1951 had only produced two reports on dental goods and cast-iron rainwater manufactures (Mercer 1992: 55; 1995: 122). Tomlinson has referred to the 1948 Act as a 'mouse' although he does believe that the 1956 Act did help to promote competition and technical change (Tomlinson 1994b: 182). In Germany on the other hand competition policy was much tougher (Tiratsoo and Tomlinson 1993: 132).

Broadberry and Crafts have attempted to assess the extent of competition and innovation in the 1950s by using the register of collusive price agreements set up by the 1956 Restrictive Practices Act. They found that although innovation was not stifled by collusion and high industrial concentration it did hinder the transformation of those technical innovations into productivity enhancement. In terms of governmental policy there was too much focus on the Schumpeterian idea that industrial concentration promotes technical progress and far too little account taken of the managerial failures which can lay uncorrected because of uncompetitive markets. This policy failure continued into the 1970s with emphasis upon subsidies to large companies and widespread state intervention. Only in the 1980s were these policy errors addressed and corrected with emphasis upon promoting competition (Broadberry and Crafts 2001). As Crafts has made quite plain, 'From the 1950s through the 1970s, Britain failed to exploit opportunities for rapid catch-up economic growth as fully as its European neighbours. The British government must bear a substantial part of the blame for this, in the form of misplaced interventionism and ill-conceived supply side policies' (Crafts 1998a: 204; 1999b: 56; 2002: 83).

Conclusion

This chapter has ranged across many aspects of the way in which it is asserted that successive British governments have restrained British economic growth. It should be evident that there is no settled agreement on if and how British governments have indeed retarded growth. The British economy did not experience unusually large post-War business cycles, nor was UK state expenditure unusually high in the post-War period, and though defence expenditure was set at a comparatively high level, the French managed to combine high levels of defence expenditure with fast growth. As for the nature of the state itself there is no fixed agreement on its type or how this impacted on performance.

The British state has been characterised as liberal, developmental, and consensual, but no agreed characterisation emerges. We do see however that lack of tough and effective competition policy is seen to have been a problem particularly in the early years. Whilst one particular form of taxation – capital income taxation – may have reduced the incentive to invest in physical capital, the return to investment is more the problem. Given this, in the next chapter we shall look at an aspect of government behaviour and governmental initiatives explicitly designed to improve productivity performance, that of incomes polices and the Donovan Commission.

These initiatives had to occur of course within as we have seen a British state frequently liberal in its outlook. This orientation was as we noted reflected in its desire to achieve external military and financial goals. Against this background, it looks difficult for Eichengreen type initiatives or reforms, designed to shift the organisational level at which UK labour bargaining occurs away from the middle of the Calmfors and Driffill 'hump', to be successful. However it would still be possible to conceive of a productivity drive within a liberal state tradition framework, but governments' involvement and aim of promoting income restraint and reform of bargaining institutions would be more difficult. Its functions could revolve around the moulding of producer groups towards acceptance and or acquiescence to new patterns of behaviour by persuasion, encouragement, exhortation, and finally law. As we have noted in the introduction, exhortation was a component of Middleton's taxonomy on government intervention in the economy. Given Britain's comparatively poor economic conditions and the failure of macroeconomic measures to accelerate the rates of growth and output and productivity, exhortation was the most likely tactic that essentially liberal British governments could deploy to improve industrial performance in the private, non-military sector of the economy. An exhortatory approach implies no direct intervention into the activities of private industry, but a widespread perception of economic, and especially industrial failure, can be expected to have pushed the policy-making apparatus to strain at the limits of accepted political economy. It is in this context that the state's involvement in the productivity drive via incomes polices and the Donovan Commission will be assessed.

5
The Government and the Productivity Drive

Introduction: government and the promotion of productivity after 1945

During the Second World War, the Board of Trade officials had developed a clear and pessimistic analysis of Britain's industrial backwardness and the prospects for the UK's competitiveness once the War was over. Barnett notes that during the War the Board of Trade conducted surveys into the prospects for British exports in peacetime, which revealed that chemicals, cotton, car exports, shipping, coal, and aircraft (amongst others) could all face stiff competition. In 1943 a Board of Trade memorandum said, '...our first consideration must be to raise the efficiency of industry as a whole, and particularly to stimulate the export industries'. One year later a Board of Trade report stated, 'One of our dangers, perhaps the main danger, is that this country will fail to see clearly and early enough the grave difficulties that lie ahead of British industry after the transition from war to peace' (Barnett 1986: 56–7, 252).

As the memory of the Second World War faded into the background British governments participated in and established various organs to try and raise the productivity growth rate of the British economy. There were the productivity agencies, the AACP, BPC, and EPA. There was also the Donovan Commission on industrial relations, and at least three attempts to try and control wage and price inflation, via the establishment of various institutions, that is, the Cohen Council, the National Incomes Commission, and the National Board for Prices and Incomes (NBPI), and National Economic Development Council and Office.

Such was the perceived importance of increasing Britain's productivity that in 1959 there was a joint declaration by none other than the

Prime Minister, Macmillan, and the Leader of the Opposition, Gaitskell. Both appeared on the same platform at a national rally of Local Productivity Committee officers in April 1959, in order to emphasise the bi-partisan approach to the problem of productivity.[1] Although it should be said that civil servants thought some ministers, '[paid] lip-service to the cause of increasing productivity...'[2]

As the post-War period progressed many commentators, observers and the public began to think there were major problems with the British economy. There was as far as the economy was concerned a 'What's wrong with Britain' panic in the early 1960s (Tomlinson 2002: 196). One of the problems most seen in need of rectification was the behaviour of trade unions and their propensity to strike, and their predilection for restrictive practices (Coopey and Woodward 1996: 20; Wrigley 1996a: 282). Influential commentators such as Eric Wigham who sat on the Donovan Commission and was labour correspondent for *The Times* in 1961, published a wide-ranging critique of British trade unions. In the critique, he drew attention not only to the restrictive practices of unions but also to the desire of some of their members for unofficial strikes led by truculent shop stewards (Wigham 1961). In the same year, the journalist and writer Michael Shanks published the first edition of his influential *The Stagnant Society*. Here too the unions were criticised for outdated behaviour and a drift of power from the centre to the shop floor (Shanks 1961, rev. ed. 1972). In 1962, the wide-ranging writer Arthur Koestler published his emotively titled *Suicide of a Nation*, which took the national fascination and obsession with decline and failure to new heights (Koestler 1963). In 1967, journalists and television-show makers Jones and Barnes who had promoted the idea of Britain's decline through their programmes published *Britain on Borrowed Time* a collection of essays in which the working practices of unions and management were criticised (Jones and Barnes 1967). The persistence of notions of pathological failure of the British economy resurfaced in 1978 when a collection of short essays by the likes of academics and politicians (including Stafford Beer and Sir Keith Joseph) entitled *What's Wrong with Britain* was published (Hutber and Home 1978). This again coincided with a high relative incidence of strike activity and 1979 was when working days lost through strikes reached an all-time post-Second World War high. Indeed Barbara Castle who in a cabinet reshuffle in April 1968 had been appointed to the newly created Department of Employment and Productivity said in her diaries that one of the reasons why the Donovan Commission had been established was because the Labour government were worried by the impact on public opinion of the increasing incidence of unofficial strikes (Castle 1984: 459).[3] This is the subject, which we shall now discuss.

The Donovan Commission

In 1965, the Labour government established the Royal Commission on Trade Unions and Employers' Associations 1965–68 (often referred to as the Donovan Commission after the Commission's chairman – Lord Donovan) to investigate the growing discord in British industrial relations and as its name implied, also to look into employers associations.[4] It set about its work by sending a survey consisting of 330 questions to all trade unions and employers associations. The Commission also published an invitation in the press for any member of the public to submit evidence to the Commission if they wished. Written evidence to the Commission was sent by 430 organisations, groups and persons and it took oral evidence for over 58 days. On behalf of the Commission, the government's Social Survey Department undertook interviews with 1400 shop stewards, 200 full-time trade union officers, 500 trade unionists, 400 non-trade unionists, 600 foremen, 300 works managers and 120 personnel officers. Research for the Commission was undertaken by the industrial relations academic W. E. J. McCarthy, one of the Oxford Group of academic–industrial relations specialists at the time.[5]

Obviously, the above facts testify to what a massive research undertaking the Donovan Commission represented. The Commission's most singularly important finding and the conclusion for which it is most, if only, remembered is that Britain had at that time two systems of industrial relations (Nevin 1983: 50; Pelling 1992: 254; Smith 1980a: 119), to quote the report, 'The one is the formal system embodied in the official institutions. The other is the informal system created by the actual behaviour of trade unions and employers' associations, of managers, shop stewards and workers.' The problem was that these two systems were at odds with each other.[6]

According to the Commission the British system of industrial relations was unique because it was based on voluntary agreed rules which could not be enforced in law, this was an 'outstanding' characteristic which distinguished it from many other systems. There were no legally binding contracts but as the Commission noted there was nothing to stop employers and workers from making legally binding contracts. However, it felt that this would be a radical departure from the long tradition of industrial relations in Britain and could not be supported. Commission member Shonfield however dissented from this view and thought that collective bargaining should be brought within the law so that unions and employers made legally binding collectively bargained contracts. If this occurred British management could more confidently undertake cost-reducing innovations or output-enhancing innovations without fear that trade unions would renege on dependable commitments to new working methods.[7] According to Eichengreen this is exactly the kind of commitment mechanism that promoted investment by management in other Western European countries and gave them fast growth.

The practices of the informal system was exerting more influence on the conduct of industrial relations than the formal system and the British system of industrial relations was ill fitted to improvements in the use of labour. Overmanning was caused by work groups using their power to hold or push up manning levels to protect jobs and the formal system offered no means by which to negotiate the relaxation of these and other restrictive practices. Another very important and damaging consequence of the formal–informal divide was the strikes and industrial action consequent of the British system of industrial relations working under full pressure. The pressure of full employment was not only encouraging factory-level bargaining but also leading to extreme decentralisation with power shifting to self-governing work groups which was breeding inefficiency, indecision, anarchy and reluctance to change. This was particularly damaging to the rate of technical change. However restrictive practices (such as that of the craftsmen's mate) which often led to serious under-employment were not, the commission thought, the fault of the trade unions and workers, workers just wanted to protect their jobs, and resistance was deep-rooted. Restrictive labour practices were the result of technical change and changing circumstances.[8]

The strike problem was predominantly that of increasing unofficial strikes (that is, strikes not officially sanctioned by trade unions), the quantity of which was much bigger than official strikes. Between 1964 and 1966, there were 2171 unofficial strikes and 74 official strikes in British industry. These unofficial strikes had nothing to do with industry-wide agreements and were the consequence of methods of collective bargaining and especially methods of workshop bargaining and an absence of speedy, clear, and effective dispute-solving procedures, in essence inadequate conduct of industrial relations at company and plant level. Here the CBI in its evidence to the Commission drew comparison with and advocated an approach along the lines of Sweden where the Swedish Collective Agreements Act made it the duty of trade unions to endeavour to prevent their members from committing unlawful offensive actions. The Commission rejected such a proposal because it would not lead to a rapid diminution of unofficial strikes, because work groups took action without regard to the procedures of collective bargaining. This was caused by the structure of the British system and the economic conditions under which it had operated since the Second World War. Obviously, the Commission wanted to see the number of both types of strike reduced and thought the way to achieve this was through reform of the collective bargaining system. This was fundamental to the improved use of manpower in British industry. For the Commission, collective bargaining was the best method of conducting industrial relations. But, industry-wide agreements argued the Commission should be replaced by company level agreements. The Commission stated that bargaining within the factory was all but de facto anyway.[9]

The Commission looked at the structure of British trade unionism and concluded that it was extremely complex. Commission member and industrial relations expert Hugh Clegg said just after the end of the Donovan Commission that British trade union structure was 'complex beyond belief', diverse and higgledy-piggledy (Clegg 1971: 79–80). The complexity arose from the extent and nature of multi-unionism. Two types of multi-unionism were in operation in British workplaces. One was where each occupational group had its particular union, such as technicians, clerks, operatives, the other type of multi-unionism was where unions competed for the same occupational group of workers. According to the Commission, four-fifths of British trade unionists worked in multi-union establishments. The bargaining taking place in these workplaces was fragmented and outside the control of employers associations and trade unions, leaving a façade of industry-wide bargaining. This resulted in piecemeal and competitive sectional wage adjustments. Industry wage structure was often the cause of strikes because employees' actual earnings were not determined by negotiations at industry level but at plant level. Levels of overtime were high in British industry to make up for low basic pay as industry-wide agreements were always set at the minimum level.[10]

The Commission therefore considered what advantages might accrue to the UK if industrial unionism was adopted. Here it drew comparison with Germany, but rejected advocacy of industrial unionism on many grounds, including these – that workers might want to unite on an occupational not industrial basis and that industrial unionism ties unions to particular industries, which if they decline take the union with them. However there was need for trade unions to merge to reduce multi-unionism. For example, in coal mining, the docks, shipbuilding, and vehicle manufacture there was strong fragmented bargaining with anarchic wage structures. The Commission thought the TUC should promote amalgamations between unions and noted that since 1964, 53 Trade Unions alone had merged.[11]

Integral to the functioning of British trade unions in the work place was the shop steward and the Commission examined their role, which since the War was increasingly seen as one of militant reaction against managerial prerogative. In the UK in the 1960s, there were roughly 17,500 shop stewards, compared to 3000 full-time trade union officials. Shop stewards dealt with issues of pay and working conditions. The Commission concluded however that shop stewards were not an inflammatory influence on shop-floor conflicts between management and workers, but more a restraining influence on those workers who were confrontational and strike prone. Managers and shop stewards got on well with each other. The vast majority of managers surveyed felt shop stewards efficient at their job and helpful, and likewise most shop stewards felt management reasonable to deal with. However, the Commission thought unions did not have sufficient influence on the workplace situation. It wanted to see more full-time union officers and thereby a lower ratio of union officers to trade union members as was the case in countries such as Germany, the USA, France, and Italy. The TUC had a wider compass over its affiliates than the CBI had, but TUC authority was more limited than that of the TUC's equivalent peak-level organisations in West Germany or the Scandinavian countries.[12]

With respect to employers associations the Commission thought they should merge (in 1965 according to the Commission there were 1268 employers associations) and thus there was a strong case for amalgamating smaller employers associations. It also thought that the recently formed CBI should widen its scope and exercise influence on companies in matters of collective bargaining and incomes policy. The Commission thought industry-wide bargaining required association among employers and drew attention to Sweden where employers negotiated a framework agreement with the central trade union organisation. Employers associations should also register with a newly created Industrial Relations Commission. Four out of five officials of employers associations said that they had enough influence over their members.

As regards management the report said management were accepting low standards of performance and that there was a great deal of confusion between the functions of shareholders and the board of management. The TUC in their submission to the commission wanted workers to be involved in management in three ways. First, they wanted a work people's representative to sit on the body, which regularly met at plant level and took decisions on the running of the plant. They also wanted trade union representatives at higher levels of management, that is, at regional or functional level. They also wanted to see trade union representatives sitting on boards of directors.[13]

The Commission found that managers preferred informal rather than formal agreements for four reasons. First, in times of dispute or production change formal agreements would constrict managements' ability to alter bargains made on the shop floor. Secondly, future shop stewards may abuse formal bargains made previously with former shop stewards. Thirdly, once the process of formalisation began where would it end, in essence would all agreements become formalised? Fourthly, board level management might not be prepared to formally admit concessions made to the workers, as it might look like incursions had been made into their managerial prerogative and managerial structure.[14]

In order to solve these problems the Commission made substantial recommendations. It advocated the passing of an Industrial Relations Act, which would oblige companies of 5000 employees or above to register collectively bargained agreements with the Industrial Relations Committee (IRC). The purpose of this was to emphasise that the responsibility for the conduct of industrial relations and the framework of collectively bargained agreements lay with the company's directors. The Act was to also make provision for the establishment of an Industrial Relations Commission (hereafter IRC) with full-time staff, which would at the direction of the Department of Employment and Productivity investigate and report on problems with the registration of collective agreements. Trade unions were also to register with the IRC and to be given corporate status although the benefits of this were administrative and there was no penalty for non-registration.[15]

One of the important developments of the time and one which was seen as offering a way out of the perceived lag of Britain's productivity growth rate compared to other advanced nations was productivity bargaining and productivity agreements. The report made favourable comments about such agreements like Esso's Fawley refinery agreement where productivity was said to have risen by 50 per cent in two years; or British Oxygen Corporation's productivity agreement. However, it was noted as with the case of the BOC agreement just how much work union officials had to put in to 'sell' such agreements to workers. The Commission's report put forward the idea of the factory or company agreement, which would be an explicit productivity bargain which if '... properly used, [could] contribute to much higher productivity...' It was however pointed out that the oil companies, for example Esso, Shell, Mobile, which did not have an employers association had implemented productivity agreements. Those companies that did belong to an employers association had to negotiate special agreements with them in order to make productivity agreements with their workforce. The attitude of employers associations to productivity agreements had to change thought the Commission. The report stated that productivity agreements and their proliferation would give more and more managements greater influence of assigning worker job roles.[16]

The Labour government's reaction to Donovan

After the Donovan report was published, Minister Castle held a conference at the government's civil defence college Sunningdale on what to do about the Donovan recommendations. They all, so far as Castle was concerned, agreed that intervention was required. For Castle the most controversial part of the Donovan report was the recommendation that section three of the 1906 Trades Disputes Act should only apply to trade unions, unofficial strikes which by definition did not have trade union sanction could therefore be subject to legal action. Castle also wanted to see unions merge and felt that unions should be compelled to merge if they would not do so at the advice of the TUC. She also thought that one union per industry was a good way forward for British trade unionism (Castle 1984: 46, 477, 550, 604).

Castle stimulated by what she perceived as the success of the Sunningdale conference held other weekend discussions on prices and incomes policy with representatives from unions, industry, economists, and administrators. At one such conference Derek Robinson proposed a scheme for capital sharing to ensure that workers who accepted restrained wage increases also gained a portion of any increased profitability. This fits in with Eichengreen's model but what actually came of this proposal is unknown, probably nothing. Meanwhile the widely reported Girling brake strike had convinced Castle that reform of the unions was urgently needed. The Girling strike in Cheshire in November 1968 where 22 operatives engaged in an inter-union dispute led to the lay off of over 5000 workers in motor factories, again highlighted the union problem in the public's mind (Pelling 1992: 256) and in the mind of Ministers such as Castle who felt that few men were inflicting massive damage to highly integrated industries (Castle 1984: 508).

Castle produced the white paper *In Place of Strife*,[17] which was based on the discussions at Sunningdale. The first move was to be the establishment of the IRC, with one of its key functions to arbitrate on union recognition. The white paper was as Castle saw it a charter for trade unions, she thought their rights should be strengthened with a statutory right to belong to a trade union and provisions against unfair dismissal. She also wanted clearer legal immunities for sympathetic strikes and safeguards for the closed shop, and an intention by companies to increase worker participation in management, with the statutory right to gain information from management and that trade unions should be required to register with the IRC. However *In Place of Strife* went further than Donovan in that it also contained provision for the Secretary of Sate to order a strike ballot, where the strike was held to threaten the national interest. It proposed fining unions that refused to register. It contained provisions for trying to force unions to comply with the IRC findings on union-recognition disputes, by fining unions which tried to coerce employers not to follow its conclusions, and fining employers who would not recognise trade unions. The IRC was launched on the 6 March 1969 with George Woodcock as its head. The Secretary of State was to be given power to impose a 28-day 'cooling off' period to deal with strikes which breached procedure. According to Castle her package was a philosophical whole and not an instrument by which to bash the unions. Castle thought that the 'cooling off' period was the most controversial proposal of the white paper. Some senior trade union leaders did not like the suggested 'cooling off' period. In order to get the proposals through and solve the union problem particularly the problem of unofficial shrikes, some cabinet members were in favour of an interim bill, particularly Roy Jenkins although Castle was not (Castle 1984: 550–1, 560–2, 571, 583, 589, 593, 612).

Castle's proposals for the Minster to be able to compel a union to hold a strike ballot before going on strike, and to impose a 28-day 'Conciliation Pause' before a strike could begin, with a government minister able to impose a settlement in cases where unofficial strikes where the result of inter-union disputes, and with an Industrial Board which had the power to impose fines on unions, went in Stewart's judgement far beyond Donovan (Stewart 1978). Despite much strenuous effort Castle's white paper *In Place of Strife* though it went through much tortuous discussion in cabinet and was hotly debated by union leaders, the TUC, and within the parliamentary labour party, ultimately never became law.

The unions and many Labour MPs saw these proposals as a threat to trade union freedom of action. In March 1969, 53 Labour MPs voted against the white paper and another 40 abstained from the vote on it. Later in the month the Labour Party's National Executive Committee rejected *In Place of Strife*. Prime Minister Wilson had described the proposals in *In Place of Strife* as essential to Britain's economic recovery but was left isolated in cabinet along with Barbara Castle (Stewart 1978: 92–5). The TUC attempted to bridge the impasse by drafting the statement *Programme for Action*, which laid out how far the major union leaders were prepared to compromise. The TUC was prepared to give unions advice and opinion on unofficial strikes and promised to expel unions from the TUC if they did not abide by decisions on inter-union disputes. The TUC would undertake a campaign to popularise the report's findings within the unions and to organise the implementation of some of its more palatable suggestions. However, Wilson found these proposals inadequate and talks between the TUC and the government (Wilson and Castle had six meetings with the TUC council between May and June 1969) broke down in June 1969 (Gourevitch *et al.* 1984: 38; Middlemas 1979: 440–1; Pelling 1992: 255–8). In June 1969, the government was told by its chief whip Robert Mellish that it would not have enough support to get the Bill through the select Committee stage of the House of Commons, there would be a massive revolt of labour MPs and the government would be defeated (Nevin 1983: 53–7). The government did not press the Bill. Instead the government accepted the TUCs 'solemn and binding agreement' in its *Programme for Action*. This was according to Pelling and other authors a major defeat for the government. All the same, the TUC had moved a long way (Pelling 1992: 255–8). Ministers genuinely doubted whether the General Council could without statutory powers discipline their member unions as the state expected of a privileged institution. The 'solemn and binding' agreement was based on nothing more than the 30-years-old Bridlington agreement (Middlemas 1979: 440–1). Not only was the agreement useless as the number of working days lost through strikes increased in the late 1960s, wages also rapidly increased destroying the governments attempts at wage moderation and their incomes policy (Nevin 1983: 53–7; Pelling 1992: 255–8). However, this was not exceptional, because the increase in the number of unofficial strikes during 1968–70 was the British version of a Europe-wide unofficial strike wave at the end of the 1960s (Flanagan *et al.* 1983: 371).

Judgements over the impact of Donovan and the Commission's analysis differ. According to Coopey and Woodward 'Donovan turned out to be extremely influential' (Coopey and Woodward 1996: 21–2). Certainly for Castle it seems to have been, she thought many of its proposals useful and wanted to implement legislation in tune with its guidance. However in Nevin's analysis the policies of the Labour government were promoting (exactly the opposite of what Donovan and *In Place of Strife* had recommended) the growth of informal shop-floor bargaining, because the government was using the official trade union structure as an instrument to help them regulate and implement incomes policy. But this left shop-floor trade union members to either accept the wage rates negotiated on their behalf and see the real purchasing power of their earnings be eroded by inflation or try to maintain their real income by bargaining for higher wages at shop-floor level through their shop stewards and the mechanisms of piecework and productivity bargaining. So far as Nevin is concerned, the conclusion to be drawn from Donovan was that the government should have left the labour market alone instead of trying to regulate it. To borrow his analogy, by trying to regulate wage settlements all the government was doing was squeezing one end of a balloon only to see the result of the squeeze appear at another point on the balloon's surface (Nevin 1983: 53–7). Dell has written that the conclusion of the Donovan report that the solution to the problems with industrial relations lay with employers and employees was a disappointing one because this was precisely why the Commission had been set up, because employees and employers had failed to find common ground (Dell 1999: 385–9).

Panitch's analysis of the Donovan report points out some of its most salient flaws. The report tried to make itself acceptable to unions and employers and was thus a comprised piece of work recommending little that was radical or new. It did not advocate legal sanctions against unofficial strikers, nor did it want a 'cooling off' period in circumstances of dispute, or compulsory strike ballots before strike action. The report was inconsistent in advocating penal sanctions for breaches of incomes policy but it did not advocate penal sanctions for unofficial strikes though. As we have seen, there was substantial disagreement with five of the Commission writing supplementary notes that appeared at the end of the report, of these Shonfield's notes were the most critical (Panitch 1976: 165–84).

Judged from the viewpoint of Calmfors and Driffill the government or more precisely Minister Castle was undoubtedly on the right lines in trying to get unions to merge, and lessen inter-union disputes but it is unlikely they had any or only little effect on the long-term trend of union amalgamations begun in 1945 and continued up to 1989 as shown in Figure 5.1. Both the Donovan report and Castle and her sympathisers judged from Eichengreen's model were also on the right lines in trying to get managers to give more information and a share in profits to employees. The first promotes trust in managers by employees and the second gives employees the incentive to commit to a long-run growth pact. The failure of the proposals, however, lay not so much in what was being advocated but the method by which it was hoped to be achieved, that is, within the voluntaristic tradition of British industrial relations.

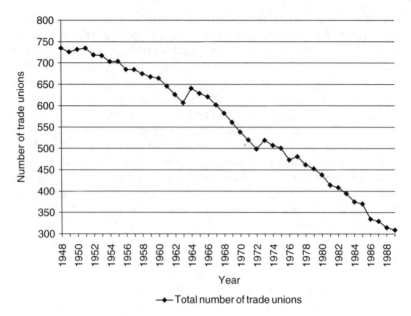

Figure 5.1   Long-term decline in number of British trade unions
Source: Derived from Pelling (1992: 304–5).

British peak associations and Donovan

Donovan made recommendations about trade union structure and the most outstanding was that there existed the informal formal divide and that the two systems conflicted and that unions should merge in order to reduce multi-unionism and consider ways of co-operating for bargaining purposes. The Labour Research Department issued in 1968 a slim pamphlet for trade union members in which although at times critical of the report overall its remarks were benign. It did not think that the most important conclusion of the Commission's findings, that the problem was the, informal–formal divide in British industrial relations was proved. This was because strikes, particularly unofficial, which were one of the most destructive effects of the informal–formal divide, were not so problematic for management's plans as the Commission asserted. Donovan had according to the LRD vindicated shop stewards because of their intimate knowledge of circumstances on the shop floor. Donovan's assertion that restrictive practices were not the fault of labour and the best way to get rid of them was through productivity bargaining was, as one might expect welcomed by the LRD. As to the reform of collective bargaining Donovan proposed, the LRD supported this (Parsons 1968).

TUC president George Woodcock was not unfavourable to the proposals but leaders of the big unions such as Frank Cousins immediately opposed the proposals and so did Hugh Scanlon, President of the Engineers and Foundry Workers (Pelling 1992). In March 1969 the TUC had organised a series of conferences at which ideas were discussed on how to voluntarily implement some of the Donovan recommendations and published 'Action on Donovan', it later in the year also discussed Donovan with the CBI and held a special conference on Donovan. The TUC agreed that rationalisation was needed and noted that trade unions were amalgamating and reconsidering their 'structural' agreements, which was according to the TUC 'without precedent in recent years' (Castle 1984: 634 fn; TUC 1968: 37).

In the Calmfors Driffill model and to a lesser extent in the Eichengreen model it is important to have strong and encompassing peak association for industry and capital. This is particularly true with respect to centralised and co-ordinated wage bargaining. Although Britain has never had legally binding wage contracts for whole branches of industry and has always been firmly within the voluntary tradition, it did until 1965 have two influential organisations (and other more specialised groups) which campaigned for macroeconomic policies favourable to their members and exerted some influence over them. However, in 1965 the Confederation of British Industries was born as an amalgamation of the Federation of British Industries, the British Employers Confederation, and the National Association of British Manufacturers (NABM). The idea that BEC and FBI should merge had been mooted for a long time. Blank saw the merger of the three as the realisation of the aspirations of the FBI's founder Dudley Docker who founded the FBI in 1916. Sir Norman Kipping the Director General of the FBI for 20 years from 1945 to 1965 said in his autobiography that it had been his aim to merge the FBI with the BEC from his earliest days as Director General of the FBI. On Kipping's reminiscences, both the BEC and the FBI wanted amalgamation so they would 'talk' with one voice. The crucial year was 1963 and the FBI and BEC were experiencing difficulty coming to grips with the NEDC because the BEC dealt more with labour issues, that is, wages and the FBI was more concerned with manufacturers costs and prices. In other words, industry had two, sometimes cross-cutting, voices. Kipping compared this with the position of the TUC which spoke with one voice at such forums and it was therefore important that the FBI and BEC could also present a united front, hence the importance of the merger (Kipping 1972: 223–31).

As Grant and Marsh point out in the context of the early 1960s amongst the enthusiasm for planning for economic growth there was a need for more effective representation of industry to government. If government or indeed anybody else provides an interest group with officials or low-cost accommodation then it reduces the operating costs of that interest group and thereby the cost of membership the government had provided the CBI with cheap accomodation. From an Olsonian point of view, this should increase the incentive to be a member of the group and reduce those who try to free ride on the interest group. Secretary of State, George Brown who was the Minister of State for the new department of Economic Affairs was keen that to execute his productivity policy the three should merge as he wanted to be able to talk to one organisation representing a wide range of business interests not three representing diverse and possible conflicting interests. This was a radical change from the mid-1950s when the Conservative government had played off the FBI against the BEC over profits and prices (Grant and Marsh 1977: 15–30).

The reaction of the newly formed CBI to Castle's white paper was one of alarm. They thought the government was going to ram trade unionism down their throat for British industry had according to the CBI director John Davies quite adequate arrangements for collective bargaining that did not need altering. Davies wanted the IRC to take an approach that looked at recognition more from the industrial efficiency point of view. Davies also wanted rationalisation of the trade union movement and thought that the biggest problem for industry was the multiplicity of trade unions; he wanted some provision that a firm should not have to deal with more than three unions in any plant. Castle wanted to bring the CBI and TUC 'together', as she put it, so that the CBI who concede the status quo in appropriate cases, presumably she meant that de jure recognition would be given to unions were it already existed de facto, and in return the TUC would take effective action against unconstitutional strikes. The CBI however did not like the idea because they thought the TUCs idea of the status quo was a very far reaching one. The CBI also thought that little positive would come from the government encouraging trade unionism, what was really bothering the CBI was unconstitutional strikes. The CBI did not like the TUC's alternative and were distressed by the thought that the government were giving up on the legislation (Castle 1984: 446, 613, 651, 671).

Prices, incomes and productivity: the Cohen Council, the NIC, the NBPI, and the NEDC

If there were two pillars to the perceived problem with the British economy during the Long Boom and one was trade union behaviour and reform then the other pillar was excessive wage growth. In 1948 the

Labour government issued its forthright *Statement on Personal Incomes, Costs and Prices* arguing that there was no reason for increases in wages. Companies were successfully exhorted not to increase dividends but the exhortation had no effect on prices. However the policy was a success and as a measure of its success, from the beginning of 1948 to the middle of 1950 prices rose by 8 per cent but bargained wage rates rose by 5 per cent (Fels 1972: 5–6). Trade union leaders (particularly Arthur Deakin) pledged themselves to the policy and successfully tried to suppress wage claims. Dow argued that the success of the incomes policy owed much to the co-operation of the unions, but their co-operation ended in October 1950 when the TGWU pressed a wage claim for its members (Dow 1970: 35).

In August 1957 the Prime Minister established a three-member council on prices, productivity, and incomes under the Chairmanship of Lord Justice Cohen which was supposed to examine wage claims, productivity, and prices and make impartial judgements on whether their impact on the national economy was detrimental or otherwise.[18] The Macmillan government did not seek TUC support and the TUC said that it was biased as the government chose all members. The Council issued its first report which welcomed Thorneycroft's (the Chancellor) 1957 measures and asserted that a little dose of unemployment was healthy for the economy and that inflation was being caused by excess demand resulting from excessive wage rises caused by unions exploiting their bargaining power. It then recommended a wage freeze and the TUC thereafter boycotted it. The TUC's boycott also rested on the fact that the Council would not as the TUC had suggested make recommendations about prices and dividends levels (Cairncross 1994: 61–2; Dell 1996: 230–1; Knowles 1952: 511–6; Panitch 1976: 44). The Council ceased in July 1961 and in the judgement of Worswick the Council's '... main achievement was to push the unions into a position of aggressive hostility towards government economic policy, when, if a wages policy was to be evolved, what was wanted was an atmosphere of co-operation' (Worswick 1962: 59). Words that underscore Eichengreen's emphasis upon the need for the co-operation of labour in securing wage moderation for faster growth and the fact that the Council would not pronounce on dividends also according to the Eichengreen framework undermines industrial co-operation between labour and capital.

In 1962 the government had issued the White Paper, *Incomes policy: the Next Step* and set up the National Incomes Commission (NIC). Wage rises should be kept within the so-called 'guiding light' figure of 2–2.5 per cent (Fels 1972: 13). The function of NIC[19] was to provide impartial and authoritative advice on incomes although the NIC had no powers to speak of and the government put in place no mechanism to enforce its conclusions. The TUC did not co-operate with NIC enquiries during the NIC's short three-year life span, although employers and most employer associations did and government departments supplied information on wage rates, profits, and productivity. Its aims were to appraise pay settlements in the private and public sectors with regard to what was vaguely referred as the 'national interest'. The NIC decided that a pay 'norm' of 3–3.5 per cent was in the national interest possibly because this was the rate of productivity growth predicted by the NEDC. The NIC examined numerous wage agreements and was severely critical of those in the engineering and shipbuilding industry, a Scottish builders agreement, and an agreement of the heating, ventilation, and domestic engineering industry. However, it could do nothing about them and the NIC achieved very little.

The early 1960s saw the creation of the National Economic Development Council supported by the National Economic Development Office. The NEDC was established in 1962 and according to the then Chancellor of the Exchequer its function was to seek agreed ways to improve economic performance. It was as with so many of the productivity initiatives a product of perceived economic decline – the British disease. NEDC was also founded with an eye on the French Commissariat du Plan. It was composed of the CBI, TUC and the government and was firmly in the tripartite tradition so solidified by the Second World War. It had a council and an office and sub-committees. It also had Sector Working Parties or Economic Development Committees, which undertook investigations that covered 60 per cent of manufacturing industry. However with the election of the Conservative government of Edward Heath and its programme of disengagement from industry the NEDC was demoted and Prime Minister Heath stopped chairing its monthly meetings, the Heath government also stopped helping finance the operations of the BPC (Taylor 1996: 149). The disengagement programme was however short-lived and when the government retreated from this course Heath turned back to engaging with the NEDC. In 1983 NEDO was composed of 210 people – half graduates – trying to change British industry by voluntarist methods. The Thatcher years were to prove very difficult for the NEDC with the early 1980s recession causing the TUC temporarily to resign from the NEDC. In Middlemas's judgement one of the problems for the NEDC was that it lacked the resources to do a thorough job unlike the Japanese Ministry of Industry and Technology (MITI) or the Dutch MEHA which had teams of government and managerial consultants working in industry. The NEDC also had no role in wage bargaining (Middlemas 1983: 132, 152, 181, 184, 188, 193).

When the NIC finished, the NBPI took over its role with its foundation first put forward in the February 1965 white paper *Machinery of Prices and Incomes Policy*. Like the NIC, it would function by making enquiries (investigations) about pay settlements and price rises, and producing reports and making recommendations, which were thought by the NBPI to be in the national interest. For Mitchell the core of the NBPI agenda was that wage rises must be financed out of increased productivity (Mitchell 1972: 142). On Fels' account the productivity prices and incomes policy was an essential part of the overall governmental aim of raising the long-run growth rate of the British economy. The main aim of the NBPI was to stimulate long-term efficiency gains and influence the industries and firms it investigated to this end. It conducted detailed investigations of particular areas of the economy in order to gain the knowledge to make recommendations to achieve this. According to the NBPI's conclusions it was the British economy's failure at industrial modernisation, which significantly caused its slow growth (Fels 1972: 249). The NBPI was initially constituted as a Royal Commission but was made statutory in 1966 (so that no minority reports could be issued) with the Prices and Incomes Act of that year which also gave power to impose a standstill on any price or wage rise referred to the NBPI and included the requirement that the NBPI should be given early warning of rises in dividends (Mitchell 1972: 13, 39).[20]

The NBPI had its own staff divided up into small groups (Mitchell 1972: 40). As with the NIC, when it came to what constituted the national interest in terms of annual wage growth it was defined as around 3–3.5 per cent based on the expected rate of productivity growth. However, no 'norm' figure was specified for the annual rate of growth of prices except that price stability should prevail. In order to facilitate these aims the government established an 'early warning' system in November 1965 whereby it would be informed of all significant wage and price increases so that it could decide (if it thought the increases too high) to refer them to the NBPI for analysis. Unlike the NIC, the NBPI enjoyed the voluntary co-operation of both the TUC and the CBI. The NBPI had no formal powers and needed the government to refer a price and wage investigation to it before it could begin making a report on a particular industry or commerce. However, it made 170 reports in its six years, amongst them 79 on wages and 67 on prices. The NBPI recommended rejecting seven cases of price increases and smaller increases in 20 cases. It recommended rejecting 17 pay increases and smaller increases in 24 cases. Most of the NBPI's pricing activities were concentrated on the public sector and in Mitchell's eyes a baffling bunch of sectors at that. The NBPI promoted two forms of pricing: extra cost pricing and pricing in order to finance future capital investment. The NBPI was wound up in March 1971 (Fels 1972: 1, 2, 24–5, 28, 46; Mitchell 1972: 248).

The NBPI undertook pioneering 'technical' work with its earnings surveys which shed light and knowledge on what earnings where in particular industries. The NBPI gathered its own information and so to some extent it could act independently, but it did not wish to become just another arbitrator. During its time the NBPI made numerous findings some novel some not. In 1967, four million workers or one-sixth of total employees were covered by PBR schemes and the NBPI survey confirmed that these schemes were helping to cause wage drift. The NBPI found that PBR systems were an important cause of wage drift because of bonuses, extra hours worked, learning curve effects (workers become better at job over time) and 'piecework creep' or the 'ratchet effect' – the assumption that when jobs changed new rates should be better than old. Here then the institution of PBR was helping to cause inflation through pushing up wages. The NBPI was of the view that productivity agreements provided a better link between pay and productivity (Mitchell 1972: 153, 154–5, 158). Like the Donovan commission the NBPI found that regular overtime of 14 hours per week was usual among bakery workers as a way of maintaining their earnings and commercial drivers had to make up for low basic earnings by long overtime. The NBPI also, similar to Donovan, found that one of the biggest obstacles to pay control was the inability of employers associations to influence and or guide productivity agreements at company or industry level (Mitchell 1972: 38, 43, 54, 56, 63, 106, 168–89, 244).

During the 1960s and 1970s Labour and Conservative governments were to try in vein to restrain wage and price growth by legislative and voluntary means but with little success. Table 5.1 shows the attempts.

Mid-1967 also saw the second prices and incomes act, which gave the government statutory powers to 'freeze' wages and prices for seven months, the existing exceptions were continued and where one or more groups of workers had fallen significantly below other comparable pay levels then catch-up was allowed. Importantly dividend restraint was dropped from this act. This would of course from the vantage of Eichengreen's model make it more difficult to 'sell' the idea of wage restraint to organised labour. In the third prices and incomes act of 1968 a 3.5 per cent limit was imposed on prices and wage increases, again with exceptions for very low paid workers and where more labour in an

Table 5.1 Incomes policies 1966–78

July 1966–December 1966	Freeze on pay increases, exception being made for increases in pay resulting from increased output
January 1967–June 1967	('Severe restraint') standstill continued, but with exceptions for increases: (a) on productivity and efficiency grounds; (b) for the lowest paid as defined by the NBPI; (c) to attract and retain labour power; and (d) to eliminate anomalies in pay
July 1967–March 1968	Prices and Incomes Act 1967 came into effect giving the government statutory powers for a further period of seven months. Exceptions (a) to (c) of the previous policy were retained, and exception might also be made where pay for a particular group had fallen seriously out of line
April 1968–December 1969	Statutory 3.5 per cent ceiling imposed on increases and special exceptions for pay increases: (a) to attract or retain labour power; (b) low pay; and (c) productivity exceptions bound by the general rule that some benefits to the community should be felt in the form of lower prices
January 1970–June 1970	Government guidelines with a norm of 2.5–4.5 per cent for most settlements. Exceptional increases permitted after study by NBPI for the low paid and for efficiency arrangements. Restructuring extreme labour power needs and moves towards equal pay for women were also grounds for exceptional increase
June 1970–November 1972	No formal policies, but the aim was a progressive and substantial reduction in the general level of pay settlements (*n* minus one)
November 1972–April 1973	Statutory stage one – freeze on all pay increases
April 1973–November 1973	Statutory stage two – one pound per week plus 4 per cent limit on increases in average pay bill per head, £250 limit on individual rises. Increases to implement equal pay for women up to one-third of the remaining differential allowable outside limit. Settlements prior to stage two allowed to be implemented in full

Table 5.1   Continued

November 1973–July 1974	Statutory stage three – limits of £2.25 per week or 7 per cent on increases in average pay bill per head. One per cent flexibility margin plus threshold payments. $350-a-year limit on increases. Increases to implement equal pay for women up to one-half remaining difference allowable outside limit. Exceptional increases allowable for new efficiency schemes and unsocial hours. London allowances, cases meeting Pay Board criteria for anomalies and in special cases receiving ministerial consent
July 1974–July 1975	No formal policy, but TUC guidelines allowed increases to maintain real incomes. There was also a TUC low-pay target of £30 a week. Elimination of pay discrimination against women
August 1975–July 1976	Non-statutory policy with six-pound limit for those earning less than £8500 a year, and no increases for those earning more
July 1976–July 1977	Non-statutory policy with maximum increases for £2.50 a week on earnings up to £50 a week, 5 per cent on earnings (£50–80 a week) and four pounds a week on earnings of £80 or more peer week
August 1977–July 1978	Non-statutory policy without the consent of the TUC. General level of pay settlements to ensure national earnings increases of no more that 10 per cent. A 12-month interval between settlements upheld by the TUC
August 1978–Dceemeber 1979	Non-statutory policy, opposed by the TUC. Guideline of 5 per cent for increases. Special case treatment, where government approved. Higher percentage rise for lower paid where resulting earnings are no more than $44.50 a week. Productivity deals as long as self-financing

Source: Taylor (1980: 241–2).

industry was needed. Though the Conservative government elected in 1970 dismantled the NBPI it still tried to restrain wages through income and prices policies. During 1970–72 it tried to gradually reduce prices through informal polices, but in 1972–73 reverted to statutory ceilings on wage increases. In 1973–74 the statutory policies continued with a 7 per cent limit on pay increases with similar exceptions as before. Mid-1974 saw the end of statutory policies but attempts at wage restraint continued until 1979 with informal TUC agreements to try and hold down wage rises (Mitchell 1972: 8–25; Taylor 1980: 241–2). Only when Margaret Thatcher became prime minister were all attempts at collective wage and price restraint completely abandoned.

In Fels' judgement the limited success of the NBPI was because the government's reference policy impeded the control of wage and price increase, only few of the multiplicity of agreements were referred to the NBPI; and the short-lived Department of Employment and Productivity was lax in its attitude towards productivity bargaining and did not seriously try to control PBR schemes. Fels argues that the NBPI had success in inserting productivity considerations into pay bargaining, and thereby it may have had a modest effect on raising national pro-ductivity, it also had limited success in deterring price increases and thereby had a little effect on cutting profit rates (Fels 1972: 245, 250). The most serious impediment the NBPI faced was that it was the only agency of its type without the authority to initiate investigations. The Canadian Prices and Incomes Commission could initiate its own prices and incomes investigations and in New Zealand and Australia similar agencies had similar if not more freedom and powers. In the Nether-lands an independent agency inspected wage agreements and policed incomes policy. Even the United States not a country renowned for inter-fering with the free market, during the Korean war, had an independent agency, which was free from government to administer national wage policy (Fels 1972: 246).

Conclusion

Ultimately the Donovan initiative and the prices and incomes pro-grammes were failures. In their magisterial and comparative nine-country study Flanagan *et al.* said that 'The United Kingdom is unique in our sample of countries[21] (apart from Italy in the 1970s) for the importance of the shop, plant, or company bargaining role of shop stewards' (1983: 364). Moreover it is arguable that they could not be otherwise for that would have fallen foul of the voluntarist tradition of British industrial relations and the liberal conception of the state when it came to business and industry as we saw in the previous chapter. When it came to wage restraint and reducing strike incidence it was unrealistic of the government to expect the TUC to be capable of fulfilling a hypothetical corporatist obligation to discipline large numbers of unions and their members. 'Britain was not Sweden or West Germany' (Middlemas 1990: 224). Indeed Prais in his productivity study which we discussed in Chapter 2 concluded that the 'voluntary approach' to industrial relations with its absence of binding legal contracts between employees and management was an important factor in making very large-scale (for example, car making) production uncompetitive in the UK (Prais 1981: 262–3). Nevertheless from the theoretical advances of Calmfors and Driffill, and Eichengreen the Labour government was on the right lines in trying to reduce multi-unionism and give greater incentives to the workforce with an explicit productivity–pay relationship. The problem was that with such a large number of weakly co-ordinated unions each will try to achieve the maximum real wage they can, thinking that if other unions do not exercise real wage restraint and say x union does then it will be left in the worst outcome therefore the dominant strategy for all unions is to renege on the incomes policy (Carlin and Soskice 1990: 213–15). The problem is in essence the prisoner's dilemma that we reviewed in Chapter 1 in relation to Eichengreen's framework.

In the 1950s Michael Shanks argued for a National Income and Prices forum and in the re-issue of his book was glad to see that the NBPI had come into being (Shanks 1972: 265–7). But in retrospect Shank's enthusiasm looks widely misplaced and it has been easy for scholars to simply right off prices and incomes policies and their accompanying instrumentation as hopeless attempts to control the uncontrollable. Barnett has written of attempts by British governments in the 1960s and 1970s to centrally control wage and price rises through prices and incomes boards as 'applying feeble brakes in the hope of slowing a powerfully engined car with the accelerator pressed to the floor' (Barnett 2002: 576 endnote 79). But this is a harsh judgement given the voluntarist tradition which critically weakened the attempts at incomes policies, and made no way to ensure implementation of the policy through to the shop floor; and as Mitchell has surmised the problem was not that the incomes policy failed, more than that, it was never really tried (Mitchell 1972: 273). Possibly the only quantitative assessment of the NBPI comes from its own assessment of its effectiveness. It concluded that prices and incomes rose by 1 per cent less, or measured in the balance of payments there was a 100 million pound a year improvement, or measured in jobs 1,00,000 more than there would otherwise have been if the NBPI and not been in operation (Mitchell 1972: 267). Fels concluded that the NBPI had a 'modest effect' on increasing Britain's productivity and 'some deterrent' effect on price increases and thereby on company profits, against an unfavourable economic background. Importantly we must remember as Fels has pointed out that the NBPI was the only initiative of its kind not to have power to initiate investigations. This was unlike the Canadian Prices and Incomes Commission, or similar bodies in Australia, the Netherlands and New Zealand. Fels cites the reference policy of the Wilson governments as a handicap on the ability of the NBPI to hold down wage and price increases (Fels 1972: 250).

Barbara Castle thought prices and incomes policies and Donovan 'inseparable' (Castle 1984: 550). Indeed they were, and both failed because of the modus operandi by which they were expected to be made workable. So while the Wilson and Heath governments may have pushed the existing and accepted policy apparatus and framework of British industrial relations to the limit, the governments were unwilling to try and change the rubric of British political economy and industrial relations and give the legally binding powers such initiatives as Donovan and the NBPI needed in order to be effective. But if one woman Castle did not change the framework of British industrial relations to try and improve British economic performance then another surely did, Margaret Thatcher, however her attempt at trade union behavioural reform was not to be achieved in one fell swoop, as Castle had sought, but more by an incremental approach.

6

Employers, Managers, and Britain's Relative Economic Decline

Introduction: the British management question and the function of management

It is important to look at the role of British management in Britain's economic performance for, '...it is management that takes the major decisions which are central to a company's health' (Meyer *et al*. 1970: 139). A range of writers have implicated management in Britain's relatively poor economic performance. Alford has noted, 'Major shortcomings in company organisation and management have been at the centre of Britain's unsatisfactory economic performance' (Alford 1988: 66). Eltis has asserted that lower UK labour productivity and lower company profitability have in part been the result of weaknesses in UK management (Eltis 1996: 192).

If the trade unions came under increasing criticism during the 1950s and 1960s for their perceived role in Britain's increasingly noticeable poor economic performance, British employers and managers also started to receive criticism for their role in relative economic decline. Journalist, executive, and adviser to the former Department of Economic Affairs Michael Shanks said in his widely circulated *Stagnant Society* that Britain's economic problem in 1971 was timid management which lacked vision and was often grossly incompetent (Shanks 1972: 266). Although the criticism was probably not as extensive as that which was given to the unions, nevertheless as Crockett and Elias said, 'Together with the traditional scapegoat of trade unionism, managerial incompetence has been blamed as a source of the "British Disease"...' (Crockett and Elias 1984: 34). Keeble has also recently remarked, 'An accusing finger has been pointed almost permanently at British leaders of industry and their aides since Britain's industrialisation first got under way.' She has also pointed out that no similar question mark has ever hung over the American manager (Keeble 1992: 1, 23). Crafts has written that amongst the persistent themes on Britain's relative economic decline, inadequate management stands out (Crafts 1993c: 331).

Contemporary evidence shows UK managers still comparing badly with their continental counterparts. Although the methodology used to obtain the data in the Table 6.1 may be said to be weak, it is difficult to obtain methodologically robust information on managerial ability because of the very intractability of what is being measured. We can see that UK managers compare poorly in a number of abilities when compared with major competitor countries. In Table 6.1 the closer the score to 100 the better management ranks on the scale, British management fares poorly and the authors note that managers have poor initiative and drive, are poor at delegating authority and taking a long-term view. There are of course obvious problems in using such surveys as accurate measures of performance and ability. The comparatively low ranking of British management may however be more significant.

If we are to make judgements about managerial performance and behaviour then we should at the outset attempt to define what the manager's role is and precisely what it is that management is supposed to achieve. Locke informs us that the 'classic' definition of management's

Table 6.1   Measures of managerial ability

Managers' sense of drive and responsibility	Score	Extent to which leaders delegate responsibility	Score	Capacity of leaders and corporations to take long-term view	Score
USA	74	Japan	70	Japan	89
Japan	72	USA	66	Germany	79
France	65	Canada	64	France	60
Italy	62	Germany	61	Italy	54
Canada	62	UK	59	UK	52
UK	58	France	54	Canada	52
Germany	NA	Italy	47	USA	41

Note: Hampden-Turner and Trompenaars' database for their assertions and construction of the table came from a questionnaire given to 15,000 managers around the world. Managers surveyed were those who presented themselves at seminars from 1986 to 1993. This of course necessitates a self-selection bias. Most were of the upper-middle ranks. Questionnaires were distributed before the seminars took place so as to avoid influencing the content.
Source: Adapted from Hampden-Turner and Trompenaars (1993: 251).

function is to plan, organise, co-ordinate, and control, in order to optimise. Yet Locke quoting the work of others also notes that there may be
more to it than this. In fact management's function may be to inspire
and rationalise after the fact; the manager's job is as a 'fire fighter'
dealing with incomplete information and an ambiguous job role, thus
the manager is not primarily a decision maker. Hence the manager needs
both inherent talent and acquired skill, although in what proportions is
debatable (Locke 1989: 40–1). Lupton's definition of the manager's role
is similar, 'In fact the skill of the manager is very largely a matter of
solving non-routine, sometimes quite novel problems, in non-routine
and novel ways', and further states 'The responsibility of management,
so the argument goes, is to manage, which means to make the best possible
use of the resources at its disposal to achieve the objectives set' (Lupton
1971: 101–3). We see from Locke and Lupton that the manager's objective
is to optimise.

However Williams *et al.* place emphasis upon maximisation, 'One basic
managerial target is to secure the greatest net output from the smallest
input of resources'. In pursuit of this end and, 'In abstract economic
terms, the task of management is to adjust inputs (of labour and of
fixed and working capital) to produce the largest output and to realize a
surplus for capital' (Williams *et al.* 1990: 659, 665). Clearly both definitions embody much of the manager's role and it would be pedantic to
strictly separate the two, and for our purposes we shall see the two as
similar. Other definitions stress the leadership function of management,
'. . . that is, inspiring a willingness to cooperate, to take risks, to innovate,
to go beyond the level of effort that narrow, self-interested analysis
of . . . incentives would summon' (Miller 1992: 2).

Finally at a more abstract and theoretical remove it could strictly be
claimed that management's role is to achieve both technical (productive)
and economic (Pareto/allocative) efficiency. In pursuing these aims
managers will reach the point of profit maximisation. Technical or productive efficiency can be defined when an enterprise is attaining maximum
output by the best use of available resources. Economic, Pareto, or allocative efficiency may be defined when the enterprise is using the most
appropriate combination of resources, say labour and capital. Greatest
overall efficiency is thus achieved when both the optimal combination
of inputs are chosen and when that combination is used optimally and
therefore gives maximum output.

We saw that the writings of Locke, Lupton, and Williams *et al.* point
out that optimisation and maximisation are integral to the definition of
the manager's role. An implication of this is that management pursues

enterprise profitability and possibly profit maximisation. Although this would seem a reasonable assertion about the function of management in any capitalist system it is not without criticism. Coleman notes that any analysis of business behaviour should not automatically assume profitability let alone profit maximisation. Those in charge of the business enterprise may see it as a way to power, prestige, and social status. To this end profits may be pursued but it is by no means assured that profit maximisation is guaranteed (Coleman 1973: 95–6). Here we enter the realm of the motivation of the manager and or entrepreneur. As Meyer *et al.* claim in economic theory little is known about the motivations of the entrepreneur. One motive could of course be profit maximisation but so could sales maximisation or enterprise growth. Alternatively the manager-cum-entrepreneur may not aim to maximise but simply to satisfy, where emphasis is placed not upon securing a maximum but a satisfactory performance (Meyer *et al.* 1970: 122).

Whatever may be the motivation of managements and entrepreneurs it is surely not unreasonable to assert that they will almost have to ensure that their enterprises are profitable if not at the locus of profit maximisation. In attempting to achieve these criteria technical choice is obviously critical. Of course technology changes and here we come to another measure of managerial ability: the ability to adapt to the latest and most technically efficient techniques of production. As Granick points out managers are constantly faced with advantageous or disadvantageous possibilities for change. Modern economies are constantly faced with a changing-world transformation curve with regard to both production processes (including organisational change) and product innovation.[1] The quality of management may therefore be said to rest on its ability to respond to opportunities. This takes two forms, management's ability to take specific decisions related to change and the actions which managements take to carry out these decisions, that is, implementation. This view of management is exemplified particularly well by Carlsson and Taymaz. They say that economic growth is generated through the exploitation of new business opportunities and at any given time, the opportunity set is so large as to be practically infinite therefore the identification and successful exploitation of business opportunities must be one of the primary functions of business management (Carlsson and Taymaz 1995: 359).

Therefore management's role is not only to pursue the objectives we set out above but also and in so doing, to adapt the enterprise to change (Granick 1972: 21). Here Granick has proposed that British managers and British workers resist rapid change (Granick 1972: 42).[2] This has been pointed out most forcefully by Barnett's remark on managerial performance during the Second World War, 'Management for its part stubbornly resisted new methods of building such as prefabrication or flow-production of standard ships' (Barnett 1986: 120).

We should ask, however, whether managers and entrepreneurs are the same, for the dividing line between the two is not clear and it is not easy to draw limits to the role of the manager. The concepts of the manager and entrepreneur may change as the structure of industry changes. Pollard provides a useful working distinction between the two. Managers may be seen as taking decisions within the enterprise, attempting to ensure the efficient use of its resources and creating a '...proper institutional and human framework to make this happen'; whereas the entrepreneur may be said to make those decisions relating to the kind of business to be operated and the goods and services to be offered. To draw more distinct but cruder definitions of the two, we can note that the manager makes tactical decisions and the entrepreneur strategic ones (Pollard 1968: 12–14; 1994: 63).

There has of course been in economic history a vigorous debate concerning the role of British entrepreneurs and managers that relates to the mid- and late Victorian period. This concerns whether they adapted optimally to changing production possibilities. Much of this debate turns on the definitions of manager and entrepreneur, and to what extent they are distinct or similar, or overlap. The New Economic Historians argued that there were good reasons why entrepreneurs of the late nineteenth century did not take up new methods of production.[3] New methods were ignored because they would not have increased profitability given prevailing factor supply conditions.

The New Economic Historians' argument however has received criticism from numerous quarters.[4] It is precisely the functions of the entrepreneur underlying their arguments, which has come in for attack. Coleman and Macleod argue that the analysis given by the New Economic Historians does not take account of the longer run, the dynamic implications of not adopting new techniques. It assumes that entrepreneurs deliberately decided to stay with the old techniques on economic grounds and that their information was sufficient to make such choices; in essence the New Economic Historians' view of the entrepreneur is a rather constrained one. Consequently such an analysis does not distinguish between rationality, ignorance, or complacency. Coleman and Macleod document a whole range of industries, not just the often cited metal industries, to highlight the extent of the problem.[5] They assert that after roughly 1860, '...a mountain of apparently damning evidence on the British

businessman can be built up. He can be presented as sliding into incompetence, displaying all the while an attitude to new techniques which
combined ignorance, indifference, hostility, prejudice and complacency
in a dosage which ranged from the damaging to the lethal' (Coleman
and Macleod 1986: 588).

Ackrill while acknowledging the importance and relevance of the
arguments put forward by the New Economic Historians wrote, 'But
these able (and numerate) defenders of British business performance
perhaps went too far...' (Ackrill 1988: 61). Aldcroft has documented
the slow adoption of modern methods of manufacture in machine tools
around the turn of the century when Britain suffered from, '...a very
large number of relatively small and inefficient firms...producing a
multiplicity of articles...' Machine-shop layout was also poor. What is
particularly interesting in Aldcroft's argument is that he has reported an
impressive amount of evidence which shows that not only may British
manufactures have been slow to modernise but that even when no
modernisation was undertaken they still invested relatively little in trying
to sell and market their products. This is important because even if the
New Economic Historians are correct it is still curious as to why British
producers should have approached selling and marketing with little
enthusiasm. For irrespective of what they produced, presumably the more
they sold the greater their overhead costs would be spread across production runs and therefore the greater their profits (Aldcroft 1964: 122).

The point of discussing this debate is to show that judging the manager's
or entrepreneur's performance is an exacting task. More especially one
must take into account both the short and the long run and investigate
not only if managers and entrepreneurs respond to market signals but
equally one must ask to what extent do they attempt to shape the markets
they operate in. Making judgements about managerial and entrepreneurial performance is a highly contingent and empirical matter, it depends
upon the conditions under which the entrepreneur operates, for instance
labour, resource, and product markets. We must also try to take account
of the dynamic or longer-run implications, and in what way the market
and the production technology evolve.

There are a number of ways in which we may judge the historical
evidence concerning the behaviour of businessmen. First, we could ask
whether the evidence shows that entrepreneurs pursued profit maximisation or optimal use of resources in the light of present knowledge.
Secondly, we might use a criterion involving the use of externalities
and take account therefore of social costs and benefits, but externalities
being difficult to assess and quantify might make judgement by such

criteria very difficult to reach. Finally, we could make decisions on contemporary standards, known at the time, '...i.e. we may try to purge our minds as far as possible of current teachings, and consider our evidence in the light of what contemporaries saw as the relevant criteria'. According to Coleman in the perfect world all three criteria would be used (Coleman 1973: 95). We shall wherever applicable attempt to use all three criterion when assessing performance, keeping in mind that the first and second criteria are easy to make with hindsight, and that the last is more sympathetic and possibly more astute measure.

Managers might respond to technical and organisational change in three principal ways. Managers might approach it with over-confidence, and introduce it under the premise that the gains from it will be so great as to outweigh any social resistance and costs. Alternatively they might simply lack any awareness that there could be social costs from technical or organisational change. A third possible alternative is that managers could so overestimate the difficulties or lack the means to anticipate it that they abandon innovation altogether (Lupton 1971: 109–10). Again we will attempt to detect where possible whichever approach seems to be discernible.

When undertaking an examination of the business response to the productivity campaign it will be necessary to take into account both of Coleman's criteria and Lupton's three types of approach at two levels, by looking at both how individual firms and collective business organisations, such as the FBI and BEC reacted (Zeitlin 1998: 111). We have rehearsed this debate because we will have to bear in mind these factors for the next chapter. In this chapter we will look at the responses of both managers and entrepreneurs, without however attempting to draw a sharp distinction between the two, for as we have seen it is unlikely that one can at the margin. Suffice to note that each has a different focus, one strategic and long term the other tactical and short term, but of course the long term and strategic is to a certain degree a function and product of the short term and tactical.

Managerial control of the labour process

The issue of managerial control over labour has figured in the alleged causes of Britain's relative economic decline. Coleman, for example, has observed, 'Too many managements exhibited a hidebound, or at best unimaginative attitude in industrial relations generally and, in particular, in their dealings with another equally hidebound power group, British trade unions' (Coleman 1987: 6).[6] Other scholars have highlighted the importance of institutions in this situation, 'Recent research has placed considerable emphasis on the strength in Britain of institutions as a barrier to management initiatives in the field of industrial relations, as elsewhere in the economy' (Ackrill 1988: 68).

In contrast to the wealth of argument on the adverse impact of workers and their unions on productivity growth and economic performance, there is relatively much less on how one aspect of the manager's function has retarded growth, that of managing labour (Gospel 1992: 11). Yet as Lazonick has pointedly noted, if British workers and their bargaining power has been the cause of Britain's relative economic decline, then why and how was it that British workers managed to gain so much bargaining power over the production process? (Lazonick 1994: 91) Power has not only to be taken but, given. Some would define the managerial direction of labour as crucial to management's role, 'If management is not accepting responsibility for the control of labour then it is not managing' (Anthony 1986: 1). Others would however dispute this. The legendary Austrian management 'guru' Peter F. Drucker wrote, '...the main function and purpose of the enterprise is the production of goods, not the governance of men' (Drucker 1951: 81).

Clegg in the early 1960s criticised British management for allowing the widespread underemployment of labour, saying that underemployment of labour was one of the major scandals of the British economy. He claimed there were throughout British industry hundreds of thousands of workers who were paid to do nothing for a considerable part of their working time. Clegg placed most of the blame for this underemployment on management, arguing that the re-negotiation of labour restrictive practices would help boost the UK's economic growth.[7] Clegg argued that British employers were ill-equipped to re-negotiate with labour. Moreover they had allowed restrictive practices to grow up and continued to tolerate them for many years. Management were ignorant of workers' attitudes to restrictive practices and they belittled and misunderstood workers' interests. Management was also responsible for such restrictive practices as the banking of job tickets, because management could not guarantee a speedy supply of materials. The spreading of work by workers to work overtime is also given by Clegg as an example of poor management because of the unwillingness to give more than meagre rates of pay (Clegg 1964: 10).

A number of academics now trace the inability of British managers to exercise control over the shop floor back to the nineteenth century. For instance, Lazonick has stressed how limited managerial capabilities of small firms in nineteenth-century Britain in highly competitive and atomistic markets left control of the technical division of labour in the hands of groups of adult male workers. Firms opted for collective accommodation rather than damage their profits through industrial conflict with workers, and shop-floor control therefore remained with workers into the second half of the twentieth century (Lazonick 1990). In this respect Lazonick has written, 'The root cause of Britain's inferior economic performance was the failure of British enterprises to invest in modern managerial structures that could plan and coordinate shop-floor work' (Lazonick 1994: 92).

According to Tolliday and Zeitlin, British employers were different from their continental counterparts in three respects concerning labour control. First they did not establish direct control over the production process on the shop floor; secondly they failed to develop complex managerial and supervisory hierarchies; thirdly they did not construct effective associations for collective action (Tolliday and Zeitlin 1991). For instance, during the period 1870–1950, in the shipbuilding industry employees retained effective workplace autonomy and employers made no attempts to increase their effective control (Reid 1991). Zeitlin notes that engineering employees also retained high levels of workplace autonomy with employers again making no attempts to increase their degree of control (Zeitlin 1991).

Anthony argues that British management has been engaged in a long retreat from the responsibility for the control and direction of labour. Employers have abdicated their responsibility for engaging the co-operation of labour. This began with the emergence of agents who acted as contractors for the hiring and firing of workers. Foremen then emerged as the real controllers of labour, but they were not really managers (Anthony 1986). Pollard places the origins of subcontracting back to eighteenth century and highlights its impact upon management, noting that as the size of the typical productive unit in different industries began to grow this strained managerial abilities. One method management used to cope with this was to subcontract work. 'This method survived into the factory age, to become if not a method of management, then a method of escaping management' (Pollard 1968: 51–2, 222). For example, contracting out occurred in the iron and steel industries, shipbuilding, and the docks in the nineteenth century, and continued into the twentieth century. Managers in these industries ceded control over production by contracting it out to skilled workers who organised production and employed and paid their own charge hands (Mankelow and Wilkinson 1998: 233). Here it seems then that management has failed to exercise a degree of control over labour that according to some authors was culpable. A factor related to managerial control of the labour process is corporate structure. As Gospel has noted corporate structure is an important intervening variable explaining certain aspects of labour management (Gospel 1988: 107). Moreover, it has also been asserted that corporate structure has itself been a drag on the performance of the British economy. So it is to this that we will proceed.

Managers and institutional aspects of firm structure

The failure to adopt the M-Form or multi-divisional structure has led to a situation where in the words of one author, 'Next to technical innovation, it is in the organisation of his business that the British entrepreneur has had to suffer much adverse criticism' (Pollard 1994: 70). Alford states that the multi-divisional company form was well established in the USA before the Second World War but did not really become established in the UK until the 1960s (Alford 1988: 64). This new form of company structure had according to Chandler two basic features – distinct operating units and a management cadre consisting of a hierarchy of full-time salaried executives. The modern M-Form firm has both a production function and a governance structure. The M-Form firm consists of many units, each unit whether it be sales, purchasing, or research has its own administrative office with its own managers, staff, and resources to carry out its specific task. Therefore each unit could, according to Chandler, theoretically act as an independent business enterprise. In the M-Form enterprise managers are monitored by their immediate superiors and this chain of supervision continues up to the top of the hierarchy (Chandler 1990: 14–5).

Chandler proposes that the reason why Britain adopted the M-Form much later than America and Germany was because of the preference for personal over professional management, which he terms 'personal capitalism'. In order to exploit the new technologies of the 'Second Industrial Revolution' with their economies of scale and scope and reduced transaction costs, entrepreneurs had to invest in three interrelated factors. First they had to invest in large production facilities to reap the economies of scale and scope, second they had to invest in national and international marketing and distribution networks, and thirdly they had to invest in management.[8] British entrepreneurs failed to invest in these three factors sufficiently early and hence Britain industrialised late in the new industries (electrical equipment, industrial chemicals, heavy machinery, aluminium, copper, and steel) of the 'Second Industrial

Revolution'. British family-owned firms with their boards of sons and fathers opted instead for the gentlemanly life, the company was a source of assured income, profits were not ploughed back to make the long-term investments necessary for the new products. Chandler has written that 'This commitment to personal rather than professional management characterised British industrial capitalism. It was also this commitment that made industrial capitalism less dynamic in Britain than in the United States and Germany, in terms of the development of new products and processes and of the growth and competitiveness of enterprises and industries' (Chandler 1990: 8, 12, 145, 249, 286, 292, 323, 354, 374, 379, 390, 393, 497, 500, 592, 595). Gospel also subscribes to the Chandler thesis, arguing that Britain's small firms were slower to develop strong internal management hierarchies because of the persistence of family ownership, where families were keen to retain control. The nature of the British market is also brought forth as explanation. British markets were smaller and less 'dynamic' than those in the USA (Gospel 1988: 105–6; 1992: 5–6).

However by the interwar period some British firms were beginning to take up the multi-divisional form, such as ICI, Spillers (flour milling), Turner and Newall (asbestos product manufacturers), and possibly Dunlop (the rubber company), but there were problems. Companies expanding at the turn of the century such as the Calico Printers' Association had experienced formidable barriers in amalgamating, such as achieving full integration and overall management control. These problems had signalled a warning about the difficulties involved to those firms wishing to expand by merger. The recognition of these difficulties spawned a number of specialist institutions. The Institute of Costs and Works Accountants (founded 1919), the Institute of Industrial Administration (founded 1921), and the Works Managers' Association (founded in the 1930s), highlight the way industrial society was attempting to grapple with these problems. Some large companies belonged to Management Research Group No. 1 (founded 1926) which provided seminars on specialised topics to which members could send their staff. Hannah draws from these trends the conclusion that, '...within their varied management structures of the 1920s and 1930s, British manufacturing companies were directing a good deal more resources to management problems than previously'. Despite the formation of a small number of M-Form companies in interwar Britain, the growth of the multi-divisional firm had to await the post-1945 period (Hannah 1983: Ch. 6, 86).

Yet even Hannah's documentation of a small number of M-Form companies has been contested. Gourvish sees the merger that created ICI as defensive rather than inspirational, and asserts that ICI '...fell short of the full multidivisional form'. Gourvish directly places the blame for what he refers to as 'corporate lag' on the persistence of traditional attitudes in top management, irrespective of whether the management was owned or salaried. The 'club' atmosphere of most boardrooms was the principal factor impacting on attitudes to organisational change (Gourvish 1987: 34). Channon has also estimated that in 1950 only 12 per cent of major UK companies had a multi-divisional structure, but by 1970 this had risen to 72 per cent (Channon 1973: 67). The above writers have all noted the lag in adoption of this new business institution and its corollaries for the British economy – poorer industrial performance.

This argument is not without its criticisms. Pollard for instance notes that smaller firms can be more innovative than the larger ones, and questions whether the M-Form organisational structure suited to the mass-production of standardised products was appropriate for the more diversified markets of the British economy. Pollard also notes that UK business led the world in establishing overseas branches that formed multinationals (Pollard 1994: 71). Williams *et al.* drawing on the work of Channon also criticise Chandler's argument boldly stating that, '...there is no universal link between performance and, for example, the adoption of particular organisational structures' (Williams *et al.* 1983: 90). Whatever the merits or demerits of Chandlerian M-Form companies it could be argued that the premise of Chandler's thesis is weakly founded. Most manufacturing employment and possibly pro-duction in the USA at the beginning of the twentieth century was not by large M-Form companies but by small specialty producers. Scranton has singled out USA machine tool production as a business where there was high market product differentiation and little price competition – M-Form was not the dominant mode of business (Scranton 1997).

Therefore, while it is beyond reasonable doubt that UK business was slow in adopting the M-Form large corporate structure it is not certain that this lag was wholly bad for the UK economy. But, it may not be that corporate structure was so much the problem as governance structure. Bowden *et al.* have shown in their study of the abysmal performance of British Motor Corporation's Cowley plant at Oxford in the 1960s, that the problem was an inability to rid the plant of woeful management. Management at the plant were unwilling to tackle the wage-setting system and structure whereby 43 per cent of the plant's workforce had their wages linked to another 29 per cent of the workforce whose wages were determined solely on a piecework basis. One of the damaging outcomes of this complex linkage was that when productivity in the piecework group went up (and thereby so did their wages) by reducing the number of workers in the piecework group, the wages of the other 43 per cent of the workforce went up, but with no necessary gain in their productivity. The Donovan Commission after extensive investigation in the 1960s also found in the motor industry that 'Employers [had] failed to develop adequate management policies, and in particular [had] not tackled effectively the problem of devising national wage structures' (Cmnd 1968 3628: 107). Management were unwilling to tackle this problem not only because of union power but also more importantly because of the professional culture and production ethos that had been passed onto the company by Lord Nuffield and his successors. This ethos and culture led to a weakly co-ordinated and sprawling company structure with no reporting and control systems and no corporate plan. The problem in a nutshell was that the ineffective management could not be easily identified and removed and there was no effective non-executive control. The principal shareholders in this public quoted company exercised poor supervisory oversight and only when dividends fell very sharply in 1967 did they start selling their shares. Government policy of encouraging mergers particularly with the foundation of the Industrial Reorganisation Company in 1967 did not help the situation by creating the impression that shareholders did not have to monitor the performance of their holdings because the government was doing that (Bowden *et al.* 2001). Management at Cowley was woefully inadequate but it was difficult to remove. British companies may not have suffered from structural inadequacy *per se* but a particular form of structural inadequacy, that of governance structure.

Management style and the institutions of marketing, sales, and design

Tiratsoo in his case study of the Standard motorcar company in Coventry just after the War highlights a number of failings in the areas of design, marketing, and sales. Standard was expected to perform well after the War because of its supposed innovative director John Black and its modern plant. However by 1954 Standard was performing badly and his colleagues removed Black from his post. Standard had a number of failings which according to Tiratsoo where widespread across British management. Black like many managers in the 1950s ignored questions of design. Tiratsoo asserts that few companies engaged in market research; managing directors would simply call in their engineers and production staff and tell them what type of product they wanted rather than actively conduct research to find out what the customer wanted. For instance the Vanguard,

Standard's principal motorcar in the early 1950s, did not sell well because of design weakness. Black had planned this car around a tractor engine that he was producing following a rather poor deal he had agreed with Harry Ferguson. The Vanguard's poor design was revealed in the inability of the suspension and body shell to cope with the cobbled roads of Belgium and the dusty roads of South Africa. In the late 1940s Black decided that his company needed a smaller car that would sell well in the USA. Black therefore commissioned the Mayflower. Yet according to Tiratsoo the car was designed without any market research, and its design reflected more Black's whims than anything else. The car sold very poorly in the USA (Tiratsoo 1995: 91–2, 99).

Barnett has placed considerable emphasis upon the role of design in Britain's relative economic decline, writing, '...poor design–old-fashioned, dowdy, crudely amateurish – was to play a major role in the rout from 1960 onwards of British industries from machine tools to textiles and motor vehicles, while disconsolate British designers of high talent either went abroad, or, staying at home, designed for foreign companies' (Barnett 1986: 295). Thus in this sphere British firms were at a disadvantage to foreign competitors. Yet here too others would dispute this claim. Mant for instance wrote, '...one can say that the British have performed *prodigies* of salesmanship in continuing to shift poorly designed and over-priced products in increasingly fierce international markets. Arguably, the British genius, aside from making money, *is* marketing', although Mant may have an unusual view of the function of marketing and clearly sees sales and marketing as virtually synonymous (Mant 1977: 58). The importance of marketing, particularly the key technique of marketing, market research, is that it enables companies in theory at least to produce what the customer requires, thus promoting allocative efficiency. Yet as the Political and Economic Planing (hereafter PEP) Report noted in the mid-1960s, '...in many British firms production is still carried on with small regard for marketing' (PEP 1966: 162).

Although many British goods after the War were of poor design, collectively British industrialists had little zest to rectify this and little desire to acknowledge it either. Although the FBI had originally supported the establishment of a design centre, it would not help finance the Council of Industrial Design, a state sponsored body established by the government in 1944 whose aim was 'to raise the standard of design of British products' (Grove 1962: 229–30). Very few companies donated any money to it either. Indeed one Treasury official thought that '...the Council would not make any headway with industry until it gets it'. In 1952 a member of the Council of Industrial Design told the Treasury and Board of Trade that '...The greater part of industry still had to be converted to the importance of design.' Many reports in the immediate post-War period spoke of the reluctance of British industrialists to accept the importance of good design. For instance, a report by the Council of Art and Industry declared, 'The attitude of many Birmingham manufactures towards design is still, without doubt, conditioned by years of catering for a market where goods were expected to be ornate and shoddy...' The Machine Tool Manufacturers' Association response to criticisms of British exhibits at the Paris Fair of 1947 was that either foreigners exhibiting were cheating by producing special demonstration models that were not part of their normal manufacturing range or the War and post-War restrictions had temporarily made British goods inferior (Maguire 1991: 19–20, 24, 27). It is perhaps fitting to conclude these issues with the words of two established economists, Thirlwall and Gibson. Their remarks are written in the context of the UK's relatively poor export performance and periodic balance of payments problems, 'Management cannot escape responsibility for poor quality, inferior design, lack of reliability, delivery delays and lack of interest in marketing abroad' (Thirlwall and Gibson 1992: 358).

One of the conclusions that Tiratsoo drew from his study of Standard was the authoritarian management style of Sir John Black was characteristic of British management practice and thought.[9] Managers were seen as, '...classic generals of antiquity, leading their armies into battle' (Tiratsoo 1995: 93, 96). Millar made similar findings in his mid-1970s study of a privately owned, medium-sized (4000 employees in the Federal Republic and 1350 abroad) German company that manufactured electronic switching gear. The company had plants in both the UK and Germany. Millar conducted structured interviews with various members of staff in the two selected plants, one in the UK and one in Germany. In the UK plant, according to Millar, '...one top manager stated, "everyone is given the opportunity to express his opinion – we may then take the decision we intended to take anyway"'. One more example should suffice, 'There is still a more personalised view of leadership in the UK and a "them and us" attitude. This seemed typified by such comments as: "subordinates can make decisions within limits, but when they go outside their field we've got to bring them back in"' (Millar 1979: 58, 28).

Management experience and the institutions of education, training, reward, and selection

One of the reasons often advanced to support the assertion that UK management is by comparative standards relatively weak is the paucity of its education and training at all levels. This of course assumes that educational attainment and training can be seen as a rough proxy for managerial ability. Gospel and Palmer have argued that British management has tended to be less well educated and trained especially in technical and production areas than management in the USA, Germany, and Japan (Gospel and Palmer 1993: 71). Barnett complained, 'British coal management with its narrow day-to-day outlook and inadequate professional education, failed to grasp that it was not enough simply to slot new machinery into the existing system of operating the pit, but that the system had to be redesigned as a whole round the machinery.' In the shipbuilding industry Barnett lamented at the shipyard owners who were practical men with minimal technical education. These '... "practical men" in management lacked the new skills of flow-production planning and detailed cost-control developed abroad' (Barnett 1986: 83, 109, 111). According to Keeble in the late 1950s only one in five managers of large firms were graduates (Keeble 1992: 51). However Germany and Japan had surpassed this ratio in the 1930s. According to Hannah in the 1950s only a third of top British businessmen (presumably Hannah is referring to executive level) had been to university, this was poor compared to Germany, France, America, and Japan which had surpassed this ratio prior to 1914 (Hannah 1992: 49). Moreover graduate recruitment by businesses really began only in the 1950s with the 'milkround'.

Crockett and Elias using a subset of data from the National Training Survey of 1975–76 found that over 20 per cent of those whose occupational status within the survey was that of manager had no formal schooling beyond elementary education. For top managers the proportion without a secondary education was 13 per cent. Amongst general management those with a university education constituted just 11 per cent. It should be noted that 82 per cent of all managers were men. Crockett and Elias therefore assert that as far as formal education is concerned British managers are only marginally more qualified than the general population (Crockett and Elias 1984).[10]

Keeble outlines three approaches to management education and training: corporate, academic, and professional; and has claimed that the UK has been poor at all three compared to the USA, Germany, and Japan. Anthony on the other hand separates management education, training, and development. Anthony claims that management education is preparatory to a career in management and takes place in university business schools, polytechnics, and colleges. Education provides managements with theoretical, conceptual, and analytical skills. Management training is provided within the employing organisation and is concerned with the provision of skills and techniques that the employing organisation's appraisal programmes have identified as relevant. Management development involves making judgements of managers' potential and the requirement for planned experience or training, and the assessment of the needs of the organisation that the manager might be developed to fulfil (Anthony 1986: 103–4). However one may conceptualise management learning, most authors concur that the UK has been relatively poor at management education, training, and development.

In the USA in 1881 the University of Pennsylvania established the now famous Wharton School for formal business education and although initially American business was not particularly interested, by 1900 it was. The Harvard Graduate School of Business was founded in 1908 and by the First World War the USA had 30 business schools and in 1920, 65. In 1925 American general managers established the American Management Association, which quickly became the leading professional organisation for top managers. In Germany by the mid-ninetieth century there were in some states polytechnics and the prestigious technical schools (*technische hochschulen*) and they prospered with the support of industrialists and the engineering profession with which they had strong links. The first business school in Germany was founded in Leipzig in 1898 and then two more were established in 1901 in Cologne and Fankfurt am Main, numerous others then followed and, 'By 1920 it was possible to acquire the full range of undergraduate and graduate degrees in business economics' (Locke 1985: 234). By 1928, 16,638 diplomas had been issued by the business schools in Germany (Locke 1989: 74–6; Matthews *et al.* 1997: 424).

University affiliated business schools did not become established in the UK until 1964–65 with the university business schools of London and Manchester, although individuals had been able to take degrees and diplomas in commerce many years prior to 1964 (Keeble 1992: 93; Locke 1989: 98). In 1902 Birmingham University introduced a degree in Commerce as did the University of Manchester in 1904 and so did the University of London in 1920. Yet the uptake of these commerce degrees was poor. Birmingham businessmen were not keen on taking the graduates of the school. Manchester's commerce students were told in 1944 that they had wasted their time (Keeble 1992: 101–6). In 1945, the Henley Administrative Staff College was established and in 1947 the government founded the British Institute of Management (hereafter BIM). Henley Staff College offered short courses in management and between 1946 and 1958 almost 2000 people were trained there. Even here however some of these training colleges have been referred to as more like managerial finishing schools than centres for the provision of management education and training (Anthony 1986: 121; Keeble 1992: 86; Locke 1989: 155–6).

Swords-Isherwood has shown that British management has lacked engineers amongst its members as compared to the USA and the Continent, particularly Germany. She argues that the educational system has favoured non-industrial pursuits with its emphasis upon the liberal arts (Swords-Isherwood 1980: 94). Mant documents that the largest single grouping of university educated managers within German industry is that of the engineers and in Sweden, Mant notes that, '...engineers form the effective backbone of industrial management'. Another comparative factor that he points out is that in Britain those in management with an engineering background have a lower probability of being promoted to executive management than those of other backgrounds (Mant 1977: 61–2). Mant's observations concur with those of Millar. In one interview with a top German manager working in the UK, the manger stated, 'Engineers are not much valued in British companies. The people who have the say are almost exclusively the finance and sales people' (Millar 1979: 46).

The importance of those with engineering qualifications succeeding in management may lie in the fact that without such a qualification managers may retard the implementation of technical progress within their firms. In the late 1970s a Parliamentary Committee of Inquiry was held on the British engineering profession that received evidence from 500 individuals and 200 organisations and institutions involved in engineering. This comprehensive report concluded not only were Britain's industrial leaders often trained in finance and general administration but that a lack of technical understanding among top managers had retarded the capability of many companies to devise and implement new technologies in response to new market opportunities (Cmnd 1980: 36–7). More recent research starkly confirms how this lack of understanding may operate in practice. Daly *et al.* conducted 45 interviews with both management and shop-floor workers in 45 matched plants in West Germany and Britain during 1983 and 1984. The plants were small to medium size (50–500 hundred employees) and they were located in the metal working sector producing such items as screws, drills, and motor parts. The aim of the study was to examine how different types of machinery and differences in skills and qualifications of the shop-floor workers affected productivity, they said:

we were told at several interviews, non-engineers are less receptive to technological innovation; their lack of technical understanding leads to delays in installing technologically complex equipment because they are afraid to 'chance their arm'. For example, a British mainten- ance foreman told us he could not persuade his management to buy electronic equipment which would reduce their heavy repair costs, because – so he thought – they did not understand the technical potential of the equipment; the management were primarily salesmen and were suspicious that the equipment manufactures were 'trying to pull a fast one' (Daly *et al.* 1985: 56).

The percentages reported in Table 6.2 do suggest that those with engin- eering qualifications have been in short supply in British management. Moreover the table highlights another aspect of controversy surrounding Britain's managers: the proportion of accountants who are managers.

As is obvious from the table the proportion of managers who were qualified accountants rose nearly five times from 1931 to 1951 and nearly doubled between 1951 and 1971. Moreover in 1951 and 1971 managers with accountancy qualifications outnumber the other categories. Unfortu- nately the table does not contain comparative figures from other countries but it does show accountant managers in the ascendancy.

The implementation of financial accounting is an area where British enterprises are said to have been slow to develop. For instance, it has been alleged that the diffusion of cost accounting was retarded in Britain because management had poor cost consciousness, in part because labour had been a relatively cheap factor of production in Britain since the nineteenth century (Alford 1988: 72). Mid-century writings seem to bear out this point. For example, in 1948 the *Accountants Journal* suggested:

A much neglected aspect of possible improvement in overall British production efficiency is the wider application of up-to-date costing and financial accounting methods...

Table 6.2 Academic qualifications of company directors for selected years, 1931–71

Year	Total directors in sample	Engineering qualification %	Lawyers %	Accountants %
1931	1653	1.8	0.7	1.7
1951	1592	4.9	0.6	7.4
1971	1870	6.9	1.8	12.1

Source: Adapted from Matthews *et al.* (1997: 413).

It is a view commonly held – and to a great extent confirmed – that in the medium-or small size manufacturing units in the United King-dom the accountancy methods used are often elementary and proper costing, in most instances, is totally absent.[11]

Even where accounting did exist it is argued that it was no more than 'lowly book-keeping' or the drawing-up of balance sheets, whereas cost accounting (the monitoring of costing for parts of production and indi-vidual projects) was limited to a few large multinationals. It has been argued for example that Britain's aircraft industry on the eve of the Second World War totally lacked qualified cost accountants and qualified production engineers as compared to the American and German industries (Barnett 1986: 130, 293). The fascinating study of management at the British Motor Corporation's Cowley plant at Oxford in the 1960s also highlights the low status of company financing. The first finance director was not appointed until 1967 and accountants were given low status within the company (Bowden *et al.* 2001: 66–7). Yet like other areas of the role, nature, and composition of management in British industry even these judgements cannot pass without discordant views. Take for example the blunt assertions of a former manager, Alaster Mant, 'There are simply too many accountants in high places in British industry.' So far as Mant is concerned the culture of British business seems to be at fault with what he terms the 'laundering of money' preponderant, with too little emphasis placed upon the culture of actual production (Mant 1977: 56).

Even if we give sympathy to many of the above caveats on the discussion over the role of engineers and accountants in management in Britain's relative economic decline, it is hard not to be persuaded by the detailed argument of Matthews. Matthews has persuasively stated that the problem rests with lawyers and more so engineers in management than account-ants for the following reasons. In the late nineteenth century, accountants in their early training had more emphasis placed on performance in examinations, thus their route to becoming an accountant was based more on meritocracy than many of the other professions and this has left a strong meritocratic legacy. Accountant examinations are more broadly based than supposed, covering such subjects as economics and banking and were broader than those of engineering or law; their text-books also taught the importance of having a broad view of the business. The training of the accountant involves covering many aspects of a business including the founding and winding up of enterprises, including in many cases bankruptcy. Although there are degrees in accountancy, many if not most accountants have not taken a degree in accountancy but in other subjects unlike engineers who have usually taken degrees in engineering before entering the profession, hence accountants have wider knowledge bases. Accountants as part of their training may gain knowledge of different types of business of all shapes and sizes, in transport, finance, or retailing for example. Accountants particularly those involved in the higher stages of auditing are involved in large amounts of complex negotiations thus they need to develop good communication skills. Although British management has a reputation for secrecy under the Companies Acts auditors have access to information, which is denied to others. Accountants also gain a trans-departmental view of companies. Engineers also lack communication skills, are arrogant towards management functions, do not have such broad business experience, and are often poor team players. In sum accountants, make better managers and executives. Matthews argues that engineers often focus too much upon technical excellence at the expense of profit and loss considerations, consider the case of the RB211 aero engine made when the engineer Sir Denning Pearson led Rolls Royce. This technically excellent engine put Rolls Royce into receivership because development costs had been allowed to spiral out of control (Matthews 1999). In sum UK management has suffered more from lack of accountancy and finance skills than those of engineering.

Granick's findings concerning British management are illuminating. First, we should note Granick's assertion that at all levels UK managers have been poorly paid compared to their continental and US counterparts except possibly at the very top. The industrial relations expert Hugh Clegg contemporaneously noted this commenting that 'International firms find that British managers transferred to the continent must be given large salary increases to put them on a par with their new colleagues' (Clegg 1971: 78). Table 6.3 below gives a schematic breakdown of Granick's findings on comparative salary levels.

Although as we can see from the table the UK is at the bottom of the four, British managers received compensation in much reduced work pressure and did not normally have sanctions imposed on them for incompetence. Granick recorded that British top executives took a lax attitude towards managers and factory floor workers, asserting that UK top management was poor because in the UK the low prestige of industrial management did not attract the highly talented. Granick also pointed out that British managers compensated for their relatively low incomes by taking considerable leisure on the job. At the time of entrance into the firm there was also very little pre-selection of those

Table 6.3 Comparisons of middle management remuneration in four industrial countries

France	Four to six times the income of male manual workers
United States	Four times the income of all manual workers and three and one-half times the income of male manual workers
Soviet Union	Two to three times the income of all manual workers
Britain	Two to three times the income of male manual workers

Note: The table does not take account of income tax, but when this is accounted for only the Soviet Union moves up in the table and inequalities between the other countries are accentuated. Granick's information was gathered from 1963 to 1967.
Source: Adapted from Granick (1972: 264).

persons who would go on in the future to become the middle and top management. Strikingly Granick noted the, '. . . early age at which most managers begin work, and the concomitant feature of their starting in a position which is neither managerial nor even that of a management trainee'. We should also be aware that British top managers unlike American ones have a fairly narrow and concentrated range of experience, say in marketing or sales, and tend to see themselves as specialists in one particular function (Granick 1972: 370). On these measures then UK management does indeed appear to have been at a disadvantage to its rivals.

Conclusion

We have reviewed in this chapter an array of aspects concerning management and British business and its effects on Britain's economic performance. We have seen how the manager and entrepreneur cannot be sharply differentiated and the arguments over exactly what attributes they are supposed to have. While their goals may be the pursuit of profit it may not be the case that profit maximisation is their only pursuit. British management is also documented as being poorly educated, exercising poor control over the labour process, and retarding the introduction of the multi-divisional firm in the UK. Yet it is not clear that these factors have had the detrimental impact on the UK's economy that many authors have alleged, particularly with respect to company structure. British management has also been relatively poorly paid and selected very young.

These assertions when examined in detail present an equivocal picture of how the British employer and manager has impacted upon institutional and organisational change, but the broad thrust does seem to present a more depressing picture of how British managers have retarded economic performance. More to the point one analyst has gone so far as to say, '...the problem with much of British industry in the immediate post-war years was not labour intransigence but management malaise. Too few of those at the top in business really knew their jobs...the country was being pulled down the slope of industrial decline by its managers, not by obstructive workers' (Tiratsoo 1995: 101).

We saw in the introduction that several authors took management as the primary determinant of company performance. However there are those such as Caves who would most strongly disagree, 'The hypothesis that poor management causes low productivity is essentially unsatisfying. It leaves the entrepreneur to carry the residual burden of opprobrium after everyone else has either been absolved or stuck with some share of the guilt.'[12] Cave's remark is a salutary reminder and it is an assertion that we will look at in the next chapter just as we explored in Chapter 3 the question of workers. We shall therefore look at managers from the perspective of the way in which the productivity agencies and initiatives tried to improve management. How did British management respond to the institutional and organisational changes brought about by the productivity drive?

7
British Capital and the Productivity Drive: A Comparative Perspective

Introduction: management and the productivity drive

The productivity agencies consistently drew attention to the importance of management in increasing productivity in Western Europe and the UK. Naturally the first criticisms came from the AACP. The *Management Accounting* productivity team report stressed the importance of management; after, '...very careful consideration, the greatest single factor in American industrial supremacy is the effectiveness of its management at all levels' and, 'Good management is a fundamental requirement of efficient business' (AACP 1950a: 6, 64).[1] The AACP team on education for management also stressed the importance of good management. In Appendix I of their report they quoted from 25 AACP productivity team reports which all emphasised the role that American executives and managers played in the quest for a higher productivity growth rate. The Report stated that virtually all productivity teams up to that point in time had claimed that productivity per labour year was higher than in the UK. Two principal reasons were cited, first the climate of opinion which regarded maximum effort by all workers as a prerequisite to a good material standard of living and secondly the quality of management (AACP 1951a: app. I, 1).

In 1954 an EPA report gave the opinions of over 40 American managers who had toured Western Europe, studying its management. The American managers took the view that the single most important problem confronting European management was a required change in attitude. More specifically they made five detailed criticisms concerning 'top' management. These were that 'top' management resisted constructive change; they failed to realise their primary function was to plan, the ability to plan was something that as we saw in Chapter 6 Locke considers integral to the function of management; top managers concerned themselves too much with day-to-day operations of the firm; they failed to delegate responsibilities to their subordinates; finally, they failed to give their subordinates adequate authority to carry out such responsibilities as were delegated. Other criticisms included the need for European managers to explain much more to their workers the reasons behind the decisions their firms took (EPA 1954: 14, 39). Strong evidence that management was seen as the principal obstacle to production reform during the productivity drive comes from the fact that after its first year of operation the ECA switched from targeting organised labour to management as the organisation that most needed to be reformed. The ECA noted in one report that, 'The problem of increasing productivity is getting management to take action...' (McGlade 1995: 405).

R. W. Mann, the Managing Director of Victor Products Ltd and Chairman of Tyneside LPC voiced the same opinion at a BPC meeting in 1958; at which he had been asked to talk about the problems of introducing 'productivity' to an industrial area. Mann should be in a good position to know as his LPC had run over 20 Circuit Schemes. He complained that 'top' management thought increasing productivity could be talked into being rather than actually taking active steps to achieve rising productivity.[2] Chairs of other productivity associations felt the same way. Hodgetts, chairman of the Action Committee of the Birmingham LPA said the feeling there was that top management had to be convinced of the need for productivity (Carew 1991).[3] The BPC thought that ideas about productivity were slow to penetrate medium and small firms because of managerial resistance for various reasons.[4] Tiratsoo and Tomlinson have said the War revealed that many '...small capitalists were indifferent to technical innovation...'(Tiratsoo and Tomlinson 1993: 46, 62).

These views gain strength and resonance from other evidence. Individuals unconnected with the productivity agencies such as the experienced works manager A. P. Young concluded, 'For a given set of conditions, however, the productivity depends largely on the quality of the management, especially that of works management.'[5] He also observed, '...some of the best organised establishments in Britain compare favourably with the best in the United States'.[6] In 1952 C. A. Peachey a works manager of Northern Electric Canada toured a number of telephone manufacturing plants in France, Belgium, and England and wrote to Kipping at the FBI. He observed that little had changed in British plants since the last time he visited them in 1939, and he believed that operating managers might have caused the slow pace of change. Peachey held that productivity in UK plants could be as high as that in North American firms, because where North American firms had plants in the UK operating with American management, then the productivity of those plants was as high as their American counterparts.[7] In reply, Kipping expressed the view that British firms had not made a sufficient attack on the problems of work simplification.[8]

An important aspect that the above commentaries elucidate is that both middle and top management is considered to be better in the USA and that both tiers are important to efficient production. However despite much of the above evidence there is dispute over where the emphasis of the AACP reports lay. For instance, Carew has tended to underline the emphasis in the AACP reports on the role of organised labour in restricting the growth of productivity, whereas Tomlinson has pointed to the criticisms of management in the AACP reports (Tomlinson 1991b: 46; 1993: 4; 1994b: 180). Lastly, we should note, as with the case of the EPA report, criticisms by the productivity agencies did not just apply to British management.

As part of the productivity drive American politicians and company executives initiated four international conferences by which Americans could 'reach out' to European business leaders and imbue them with the 'gospel of productivity'. The first conducted under the code name 'Operation Impact' was held in 1951 in New York. There were to be three more of these conferences held in 1954 (Paris), 1956 (New York) and we shall return to this one further on in the chapter, and the last one was held in 1960 (London). From 17 European countries 300 business leaders attended the 'Operation Impact' conference and the British delegation were considered to be the most sceptical regarding the applicability of American methods to Europe. Indeed according to a US source, the National Management Council, the FBI had to be 'reinspired' to co-operate more fully (Kipping 1998: 55–6, 69).

Employers where on many occasions less than enthusiastic about the productivity agencies and some campaigned against EPA projects, for instance those projects concerning the trade unions. The European Employers' Association sent a circular to their members asking them to request their respective governments to oppose the development of trade union schemes in the 1955–57 EPA programmes. One scheme included that on automation.[9] There is strong evidence that the BEC and FBI were in the beginning openly hostile to the EPA. In 1954 the Deputy Director of the EPA, Grégoire, told a meeting of the Council of European Industrial Federations (hereafter CEIF) in Paris of the objectives and work of the EPA and asked for their support of EPA projects.[10] Those attending except for Pollock, the recently appointed director of the BEC, enthusiastically heard Grégoire's speech. The Deputy Director of the EPA reported that Pollock, '... seems to have stated quite bluntly that our [EPA] kind of work was of no use whatsoever ... and maintained this attitude throughout the meeting', though Grégoire had some success in convincing both Pollock and Kipping of the FBI of the usefulness of such an agency.[11] In 1959 the BEC believed that from the '... employers' point of view the Agency was of little use', and ten years later a Confederation of British Industries (hereafter CBI) Memorandum questioned whether it was worth the government continuing to support the BPC as there were so many other bodies such as the National Economic Development Office and the Industrial Society which sought to promote efficiency.[12]

It is justifiable then, to see the employers as, and unlike the trade unions, somewhat sceptical to the promoters of the productivity drive. Tomlinson wrote that the FBI accepted the idea of the AACP for mostly defensive reasons, and that they largely resisted government initiatives to boost productivity (Tomlinson 1992: 48–50; 1994c: 175). Certainly the material above does convey the impression that the employers were somewhat dubious about the merits of the productivity agencies.

The quality of management was seen as essential to the success of the productivity drive and productivity improvement more generally. In the rest of this chapter we will focus in detail on some of the projects which explicitly involved management; exploring in the process one project concerning machine tools. Other topics we will look at are those of investment, taxation, producer collusion, managerial education, the distribution of productivity gains, management and employment, managerial control over the labour process, and joint consultation. Henceforth we will explore how managements reacted to the productivity drive, more especially the British, beginning with the AACP's and Melman's fascinating exploration of the machine tool industries of Western Europe.

British industrialists and Americanisation

The primary function of the AACP along with those of the other Western European agencies was: '... to increase British productivity through the study of U.S. manufacturing methods' (AACP 1953a: 1). More generally the US after the Second World War sought to 'nudge' as Berghahn phrases it, Western European industry away from its deeply ingrained organisational habits towards American ones. Berghahn has noted that, 'No doubt the Americans were well ahead of Europe in terms of technology and production organisation. This was also true of standardisation' (Berghahn 1986: 112, 248). Others have remarked that the ERP '... aimed at improving the productivity of European industry through the transfer of American technology and managerial know-how' (Bjarnar and Kipping 1998: 1). While Mercer points out that the Americans also sought to promote greater competition through the enactment of anti-trust laws and notes that while these processes have come to be labelled 'Americanisation' there is no crisp and succinct definition of what it constitutes (Mercer 1995: 90–1). Despite this it is clear that many authors have identified within 'Americanisation' a number of overriding components. One was mass production or 'Fordism'. Mass production with its resultant high productivity was seen as constituting three basic techniques or the so-called three charmed 'S's of American production: standardisation, specialisation, and simplification. Production was also to take place using predominantly unskilled labour and involve 'scientific management' (Zeitlin 1998: 101). Scientific management was a composite term used to refer to managerial methods such as work study, accounting, marketing, stock control, and production planning (Tiratsoo and Gourvish 1996: 208, 211).

One of the first people to advocate the 'Americanisation' of the UK economy was James Silberman. James Silberman – Head of the Productivity Section of the US Department of Labour – spent one month touring UK factories in 1948 and formed a very pessimistic view of British employers. Silberman complained that in comparison to the US where buyers were encouraged to give identical orders and accept a measure of standardisation, British producers failed to accumulate orders in advance so that average production runs could be bigger. This led to British producers experiencing poor utilisation of jigs and fixtures and resulted in less practice for each batch produced. Silberman also believed that British manufacturers were poor at 'job production'.[13]

There followed a number of AACP team reports that were to recommend the adoption of American techniques and to criticise management. In 1953 the AACP *Metal working Machine Tools* productivity report told of how US businessmen were more eager and willing to take what it called 'reasonable' risk in the pursuit of greater productivity and that they engaged in high-pressure selling techniques with the facility of hire-purchase. It also complained that there were too many small firms in the industry, each individualistic and '...too jealous of its...independence to pay much more than lip service to any idea of industry wide standardisation and rationalisation'. Other complaints were that executives within the industry were recruited from within its own ranks and thus lacked a broad range of experience, and would be remedied by the recruitment of university-trained individuals. It is worth noting here that these criticisms are of course similar to the assertions and findings of Miller, Aldcroft, and Granick that we surveyed in Chapter 6.

The AACP report also criticised what it referred to as the production of 'compromise' all-embracing general purpose machine tools – according to the Report the industry's defence of this practice was that it gave the benefits of standardisation, and customers bought them. Other criticisms were that designs were built with a view to covering the widest possible range of applications and this gave customers' suggestions little influence on design. The *Metal Working Machine Tools* report concluded that there was very little evidence that the industry as a whole has made any real attempt at application. The results from a ruthless application of a simplification, standardisation and specialisation programme, not only to each individual firm but also to the industry as a whole would be of tremendous benefit to the nation (AACP 1953b: 48). The AACP 'reverse flow' team from the USA, the *British Pressed Metal Team* report, was like the *Metal Working Machines Tools* report critical of production techniques, 'On the part of management there is the need for cost-consciousness, recognition and adoption of improved methods handling, line production methods, improved plant layout, greater standardization, and better cooperation between safety engineers and production personnel' (AACP 1953a: 28–9).[14]

The quote from the *Metal Working Machine Tools* report indicates that British management did little to implement the recommendations of the AACP. The AACP's judgement has been confirmed by Gospel for example who remarked, '... the main ambivalence towards the findings was on the part of British management, who either did not read the [AACP] reports or who did not believe what they read' (Gospel 1988: 91). However there is a large degree of ambiguity here. Gospel's claim stands uneasily with the many examples of companies which in various industries adopted the techniques they had read in the reports or had been informed of by AACP teams touring the country on return from their visits to America. Intriguingly while some AACP reports like those above may have reported a poor response from management others reported quite the opposite. As another AACP report stated 'Since the team's [Drop Forging] visit a clear effort has been made in the industry to increase the utilisation of the machine. Firms have approached this task in various ways...'[15] In the steel founding industry the AACP remarked that, 'Since the war a younger generation of managers has begun to come to the fore and the productivity report has given added weight to their case for new methods and fresh enthusiasm to their efforts. Increasing productivity is now widely accepted in the industry as predominantly a managerial responsibility...'[16] In 1951 the AACP carried out a survey of firms in various industries to see how much the recommendations of the AACP's various reports had been implemented. At the beginning it noted that those most likely to implement them were already keen to see firm efficiency increased. Numerous firms undertook innovation such as K&L Steelfounders, or Lake and Elliot that in 1951 installed an electric furnace. The clothing manufacturers Clifford Williams experimented with new layouts and methods and its managing director maintained contact with the US.[17] This is of course not to claim that the firms we have mentioned or indeed the plethora cited in the various reports would not have undertaken innovation without the AACP and its reports, but merely to make the weaker claim that managers may have been encouraged to innovate faster than they usually would, and to show that many responded to the dissemination of best practice techniques.

Whatever may have been the level of adoption of American techniques by British managers an equally pressing question is: just how much notice should managers have taken of the AACP's findings? As we saw in Chapter 6 particularly with reference to the debate on the mid- and late Victorian entrepreneur it may not always be optimal to switch production techniques if it is uncertain or unclear that short and possibly long-run profit levels are going to be less or no greater than present profit levels.

Indeed scholars such as Burnham have argued that the recommendations of the AACP team reports were not applicable to the UK economy. Burnham has argued that the whole theoretical basis in which the AACP was grounded did not form an appropriate solution to the UK's economic problems. This was because US Fordist techniques of accumulation were not suitable for the UK economy (Burnham 1990: 96–100). Broadberry like Burnham has also argued that US Fordist methods of mass production were not suitable for the British economy. He wrote, '...after the second World War British manufacturing pursued a relatively unsuccessful policy of Americanisation...', Americanisation was the copying of machine intensive, heavily resource using, mass production methods with emphasis upon the production of standardised goods. Broadberry proposes that British skilled craft workers resisted these labour saving techniques of production and American technology was unpopular with British managers, and that resource costs were higher in the UK; thus Britain was unsuited for mass production methods. It would have been far better for it to focus upon flexible production (Broadberry 1997a: 14–15, 77–8, 89, 105, 127, 229–33, 248, 391; 1997b: 413). There is contemporary evidence that supports the idea that Americanisation might have been of limited use in the UK. The British pressed metal team report commented, 'It was a common complaint of British executives that their customers would not let them standardize...' (AACP 1953a: 4).

The action of British managers towards the AACPs' findings, if judged by the arguments of Burnham and Broadberry and the remarks of the British pressed metal team, would then appear to have been quite sensible. The argument that American production institutions were not suitable for the UK economy and therefore that British managers should not have adopted them is however open to challenge. Tiratsoo and Gourvish for example have claimed that '... the Americans were emphatically not trying to sell one production system, but rather a multiplicity of existing processes' (Tiratsoo and Gourvish 1996: 214).[18] From this perspective Broadberry and Burnham may have – to some degree at least – misread the nature of the productivity drive. Although of course it is difficult to believe that the arguments of Broadberry and Burnham are without foundation it is more probably the case that the truth lies somewhere in between. The key point is as Tiratsoo and Tomlinson have proposed, '... "Americanisation" was differentially applicable to industries in Britain. In some cases markets could have been exploited with standardised products, in other cases this might have been a problem. In particular, standardisation of components would seem to have offered a much more fertile field for economies of scale than standardisation of some final products.' Tiratsoo and Tomlinson offer the example of an engineering firm which produced 20,000 different types of bearing arguing that such firms would almost certainly have benefited from a portion of the three 'S's (Tiratsoo and Tomlinson 1993: 151). A similar perspective is gleaned from the case of West Germany where in 1953 the Standardisation Committee of German Industry calculated that a reduction from about 20,000 piston rings to 2000 in one factory would have saved capital assets of 1.2 million Deustch Marks (Berghahn 1986: 248).

Yet in some respects at least it is not wholly clear that British managers should have opted for a strategy of standardisation. As Zeitlin argues, 'Although this apparently promised to reconcile production economy with product diversity, standardisation of components raised nearly as many problems as it resolved. It increased production and inventory costs in the short run; it could also inhibit the development of new models because of the interdependence among their constituent parts', in essence it was not easily compatible with design changes and technical innovation. Zeitlin also claims contrary to the recommendations of Silberman that batch production involved high levels of stocks and was unsuitable to meet changing patterns of demand and that British producers were aware of these problems in the application of American techniques. British employers organisations did go some way towards examining the applicability of this particular 'S'. According to a 1950 AACP report they set up six 'Production Efficiency' panels that were spread throughout the country and discussions on simplification figured prominently in their agendas (AACP 1949: 9). Thus given how highly uncertain it was as to whether British manufactures should have pursued standardisation this cautious and tentative approach looks justified.

We need not only assess the response of British managers to the productivity campaign via the AACP and its reports, as there is another project which sheds light on managerial behaviour: Melman's EPA project on machine tools. In the late 1950s the British machine tool industry was coming under increasing criticism from academics, trade unionists, financial analysts, politicians, and domestic users. The TUC for instance questioned the structure and small size of some producers in the industry. They were also irritated by the Machine Tool Trades Association's attempts at preventing government intervention in the industry, on the grounds that the industry was already performing as best as it could.[19]

Seymour Melman, a noted US professor of engineering and commentator on the US machine tool industry was invited by the EPA to look at the economic and technical factors that influenced productivity in the European machine tool industry. Melman's study was structured along the general lines of other studies conducted for the EPA. It was envisaged that it would look at the economic and technical factors that influenced productivity in the machine tool industries of the member countries of the EPA. In 1959 Melman spent three months visiting 15 of the most technically progressive and large machine tool makers in Western Europe and the USSR, where he also saw some technical institutes.

Melman began his preliminary report with, 'The technological efficiency of operations of the Western European machine tool industry can be improved at many critical points.' He argued that although the quality of machine tool products in the industry was high, production was based upon the handicraft system. This entailed a skilled work force that formed the basis of production and, whilst being able to operate general purpose machines and assemble various types, resulted in low productivity. He also argued that managers did not carry out careful analysis of alternative possibilities of production and had little interest in doing so. Melman said in a British radio broadcast that the Western machine tool industry had a mythology that only people with a long handicraft tradition were capable of designing new machines and building them. Melman thought this was contradicted by the systematic research and design operations on a large scale in the Soviet machine tool industry.[20]

Melman believed that the way to rapidly increase the technical efficiency of the machine tool industry in Western Europe was to introduce mass production methods as quickly as possible. This would entail and be aided by standardisation of components, design of products to allow for large as opposed to small quantity production, re-design of machines to permit assembly of modular and building-block units, and concentration of production in specialised plants. Melman's Report, although compiled for the EPA, was not necessarily a reflection of the EPA's views. His Report was allowed by the Secretary General of the OEEC to be circulated to a number of groups, this was to allow for open and critical discussion.[21] At the end of his Report, Melman compared the recommendations with those made by the 1953 AACP Report *Metal Working Machine Tools* which were similar to those of his own Report, and complained that from 1953 to 1959 those recommendations had been largely ignored.[22]

Melman's Report however does appear to contain inconsistencies, for he argued that in the main, the reason for the much higher productivity of machine tool production in the USA was the tighter system of production which was of the small-batch type. Melman's Report may also have been out of step with the strategy European NPCs were to urge after 1953, that is, 'creative adaptation' of manufacturing operations rather than slavishly copy the Soviet model as Melman suggested. A prime example is that of the Norwegian Productivity Institute that promoted networking and co-operation between those firms involved in batch production, the overall aim was to secure greater rationalisation in Norwegian industry.[23]

Melman's Report was received by the interested parties with both criticism and disdain. The European Committee for Co-operation in the Machine Tool Industry was very critical, arguing that Melman had brought discredit upon the industry. The Chairman of the Committee (Fischer) derided Melman's assertions saying that he had failed to take account of the essential character of the machine tool industry. Fischer said that he had been authorised by the trade associations in the countries that were members of the European Committee to pass on the collective opinion that the Melman Report was unacceptable. Fischer went on, '...to request, that the Melman Report be buried as quickly and discreetly as possible: to inform you that, whenever your committee has any points to discuss concerning the machine-tool industry, we will always be most willing to help, but we would ask you not to bring the press into these matters'. Another member (Deletaille) thought that Melman's ideas had brought the machine tool industry into disrepute. Deletaille even argued that while productivity in the machine tool industry suffered as a consequence of its emphasis upon specialised production this was not important, Melman was wrong to argue for increased productivity via mass production. In the discussion of the Report others argued that the Report was prejudicial to the industry and dissemination of the Report should be stopped.[24]

In the UK the DSIR and the Machine Tool Trades Association were also critical of the Melman Report. In 1959 representatives of the Machine Tool Trades Association argued that Melman had seen on his visit to the USSR an unrepresentative sample of production and that from this it was wrong to generalise, moreover the industry was already thinking along Melman's lines. Individual employers said Melman's study on the USSR was outside his terms of reference and it failed to take account of the effects of a centrally planned economy on machine tool production. So far as one of them was concerned a detailed examination of the Melman Report would be of no practical use to the industry.[25] Other machine tool associations in Western Europe did not like the Melman Report. The German Engineering Association, the *Verein Deutscher Ingenieure* (hereafter VDI), was strongly critical.

The DSIR, accused Melman of generalisations based upon limited evidence, unrepresentative sampling, and ignoring demand factors. It did however admit that Melman was right on some issues, such as the need for increased standardisation of components and more extensive use of modularisation. The Machine Tool Advisory Council established a sub-committee which reported on Melman's ideas in 1960 and while rejecting Melman's main argument, that the Western European machine tool makers should introduce mass production as quickly as possible, did agree with Melman on some points and was far less hostile to it than the OEEC committee.[26] The sub-committee argued that demand was too low for mass production methods to be justified. They did however accept that there was scope as Melman had said for rationalisation within the industry. They also believed that with a high and stable level of demand mass production methods could be introduced quickly. They further accepted that greater standardisation could be achieved in the assembly and location of machine tool manufacturing. They agreed manufacturers were too slow in recognising the advantages of using more complex forms of electronic control of machine tools. It was also noted that the UK industry suffered from over-concentration on the production of universal machine tools, this was due to, in their opinion, a lack of intensive development effort, which led in turn to an over-dependency upon licensing agreements to manufacture machine tools of a foreign design. The sub-committee stated that the greatest single factor impeding the machine tool industry in the UK was the difficulty in recruiting skilled labour, qualified technical staff, and engineers.[27]

Therefore what may we deduce from this evidence. In Chapter 6 we saw that Aldcroft had drawn attention to the weakness of the British machine tool industry around the turn of the twentieth century and these criticisms have reappeared here. Certainly, while the machine tool industry may have taken a great dislike to the criticisms of Melman and those of the AACP reports criticisms, and recommendations, it slowly came to accept many of them. As the PEP report pointed out, managers in the machine tool industry gradually came to accept the sub-committee report as a useful document with many worthwhile prescriptions, but asserted that it would have been far better for the industry if they had accepted and acted on these prescriptions much earlier when conditions where more favourable to change (PEP 1966: 317). One study in the early 1960s reported that firms were still slow in innovating, 'In most small batch industries some rationalisation to give bigger batches is necessary before major increases in productivity will be possible.' The report also spoke of the need for more production planning with many firms under-utilising their data-processing equipment for this purpose, the handling of light materials also needed to be improved.[28] What reaffirms the validity of many of the Melman, Silberman, and AACP findings is that when companies implemented their recommendations they could make impressive productivity gains. For instance, around 1950 it was reported that an unnamed machine tool shop in Halifax which started employing the methods of sub-assembly, line production, increased use of jigs, fixtures, and special tools, experienced a 23 per cent increase in productivity. These methods were employed as part of a through reorganisation of the machinery and a new wage system that included an individual merit award scheme.[29]

However as we have also cared to mention it would have been imprudent for British managers to try and rapidly and uncritically assimilate American techniques into UK production methods.

Zeitlin has remarked, 'Despite its enormous ideological influence, the practical impact of the Americanisation drive on British engineering remained limited during the first post-war decade', but then went on to note that a significant stratum of British engineering firms responded positively to the potentialities of Americanisation in the furtherance of productivity growth. He has however gone further and argued that British manufacturers adopted American production techniques only when economically viable, and that they fully realised the unsuitability of American methods to many applications. For instance, British metal working firms were cautious and instrumental in their approach to American techniques and 'selectively grafted' them on to native production practices (Zeitlin 1998: 105, 108, 114, 119). Yet from our evidence this seems a slightly over-optimistic view of British managers and their associations who as with the case of the Melman Report, in the first instance rejected it outright without taking a more pragmatic and less ideologically dogmatic approach. As to whether a similar scenario evolved in the machine tool industries of other Western European countries, for example Germany, is unknown.

Thus in the light of present-day knowledge and the evidence of the period, the actions of British managers seem rational in many cases but somewhat hidebound. Judging by the three yardsticks of Coleman's criteria that we mentioned earlier, British mangers are performing well in the light of what is now known and they were wise not to easily embrace some aspects of Americanisation. This is of course the most testing yardstick, thus under this guise the behaviour of British managers looks impressive. But they were also unwise in rejecting the Melman Report out of hand, but here of course so did other European machine tool associations, in this respect they were not unusual. In this sense British and European managers were attached firmly to the managerial prerogative, and their fault may have been that they let industry pride come before productivity efficiency.

The distribution of productivity gains, investment, producer collusion, and co-operation

In the previous section we reviewed British industrialists' response to the adoption of American techniques primarily with reference to the

AACP's and Melman's report. But, of course not all the agencies specifically sought to transplant American methods into the UK. The BPC sought to disseminate those most efficient techniques which were already in use in the UK and these may have had little or nothing to do with American techniques, and therefore here the criticisms of Broadberry and Burnham about the inappropriateness of American methods in reducing Britain's productivity shortfall do not completely apply.

According to evidence before a parliamentary select committee the task of the BPC was, '...to spread more widely knowledge of the best methods and practices, as they exist in progressive firms. The means used may include inter-factory visits [Circuit Schemes], discussion groups, lectures, conferences, film shows and appreciation courses and seminars in work study and other techniques'.[30] To begin with, employers who undertook to set up BPC Circuit Schemes could find it tremendously difficult to get other employers to co-operate. Co-operation between workers and managers in the Eichengreen framework is of course paramount to the building of a promising and viable productivity pact, but we can also see co-operation amongst managers themselves as important to enhancing efficiency. The Watford Circuit Scheme provides a good example of how difficult it could be to engender co-operation, for the chairman (a manufacturer himself) of Watford LPC complained that he had to put in tremendous effort to get 60–70 firms in his area to co-operate with the Circuit Scheme.

Although it might have been difficult to get employers involved in the promotion of productivity, such participation could prove beneficial to them. For instance, as far as Circuit Schemes were concerned, the same manufacturer who found it so difficult to establish the Watford Circuit Scheme commented:

> There was one point made, and that was that the reports were extremely critical. Indeed, I have a whole batch of them here and the whole of them show that when a man goes down and sees how other people do very different jobs they can find all sorts of ways of criticising. One friend of mine told me "When I read the report on my firm I nearly burst a blood vessel. There were 12 items criticising our work. However, I went to bed and slept on it and next day I decided that the criticisms were useful and changed my mind about blowing these people up".[31]

While employers may have found criticism hard to bear there is an obvious reason as to why they may have lacked a desire to co-operate as expressed in the words of the chairman of Taunton LPC, '...industries tend to be competitive – boots and shoes, gloves and so forth – and the attitude has been "I am not having these people in my works. They might find out about our processes" '.[32] Indeed Middlemas has implied that despite full support from the FBI the LPCs encountered secretiveness and suspicion from firms competing with each other.[33] Tiratsoo and Tomlinson also note that British firms were secretive about their production methods and that they feared the EPA might make known to European competitors their production operations (Tiratsoo and Tomlinson 1997: 74).

Compare the above however to the situation in other countries. In Norway there was also a form of inter-factory visits but which began in 1966 and appeared equivalent in method to the BPC's Circuit Scheme technique. Norwegian firms took part in *Bedriftsanalyser* (analyses of a firm) where managerial teams from local enterprises visited and studied each other's firms, after which there were conferences to discuss what had been gleaned. The Norwegian Productivity Institute declared that these exchange visits had met with enthusiasm, and that firms had learned from each other (Amdam and Bjarnar 1998: 100). In the USA motor manufactures showed competitors around their plants so that they could learn of the latest techniques and were aware that competitors could learn of their process, but thought that innovation was so rapid that little competitive advantage would be lost (Bright 1958: 90–1). Hutton in his 'propaganda' work for the productivity drive also emphasised this aspect saying that American firms had a greater willingness to share their experiences and 'know-how', saying that firms, '...circularize each other with results; representatives meet at conferences and other places to pool their experience' (Hutton 1953: 46–7).

As to co-operation between the countries of Western European, some British businessmen were equally reluctant to co-operate with the EPA on similar dissemination initiatives. The British government had failed on many occasions to get British industry to receive missions from other European countries. The government thought this was because they did not want to admit, what were in effect competitors, into their factories and thereby learn their methods and trade secrets. This was particularly true of the best firms who would not want to share their techniques with less productive ones. Only where there were 'tight' monopolies would research results be shared or in co-operation over management techniques did the government think enthusiasm might prevail.[34]

However the government paper did say that this attitude was not universally held by businesses and could sometimes be overcome.

It was also probably the larger firms that were more willing to co-operate.[35] Although industries with tight monopolies might be willing to share knowledge this may have done little to aid rapid increases in efficiency. As a contemporary American observer spoke of the effects that collusion might have on productivity, James McGraw, president of McGraw Hill Publishing, noted in 1947 that British businessmen should accept a share of the blame for Britain's technical lag during the past 30 years. By draining off exorbitant profits, they had lived well but kept their own industries from deriving full benefit from modern technical advances. British capitalism had committed the fatal error of building cartel walls around itself, which had meant easy profits but also atrophy.[36] McGraw was not the only one in the USA to hold these opinions. McGlade says that 'According to U.S. officials, ongoing obsolescence, not wartime dislocation and destruction, stood as the cause of British and European economic and industrial woes' (McGlade 1995: 18). Senator William Benton also criticised European management of complacency and for being so interested in secure returns by avoiding competition by cartel building.

Others argued that Western European businessmen were restrictive. According to one high ranking French official just after the War, 'American officials will have to realize that there is no sector of the French economy not covered by private agreements among producers and these providing services, setting prices, limiting output and regulating competitive practices.' He went on, 'Trade and professional associations are all in league against the consumer...' In Italy restrictive practices were so significant to Italian business leaders that they violently opposed even attempts at documenting their existence.[37] The EPA had designs on conducting a study of Western European restrictive practices, but the CEIF thought the worth of such a study doubtful and asserted that if such a study were carried out then it should also include the restrictive practices of trade unions.[38] European employers perceived this as one-sidedness in the EPA's programme and it aroused strong hostility from the CEIF which claimed that the 'EPA obstinately refuses to deal with trade unionist restrictive practices and only wants to deal with the employers' RBP [restrictive business practices]' (Boel 1998: 43–4).[39] The fighting of restrictive business practices was supposed to be central to the EPA's mission since this was one of the main elements in the Moody Amendment which combined with the Benton Amendment was the legislative statute that allowed the EPA to receive technical assistance funds from the USA.

So far therefore the picture is somewhat bleak with British and Western European employers heavily criticised by the Americans for restrictive practices and the employers acting defensively to protect their historically entrenched organisational mode. However according to Senator Benton, Geoffrey Crowther of the BPC had told him that at a recent meeting of the leaders of 70 AACP productivity team tours, there had been a vigorous demand to breakaway from cartels and trade associations. Most leaders of AACP productivity team tours would have been middle managers.[40]

As is evident from the opinions of McGraw and to a lesser extent Senator Benton, collusion might lead to lower investment and thereby stagnating production technology, and as we remarked in Chapter 1, the relatively low level of investment and poor returns to investment figure prominently in the literature on Britain's relative economic decline. American members of the AACP thought that some sections of British industry were 'running down' their equipment, and that this policy would ultimately lead to disaster as the backlog of re-investment would become so big that markets would be permanently lost.[41] This was a sentiment shared by some in the trade union movement, as the secretary of the Manchester and Salford Trades Council noted, '...much of the backwardness in many of our Industries has been due to the policy of the Employers and their failure over the last 30 years or more, to Re-Capitalise and Re-Equip our Industries'.[42] The FBI was well aware that expenditure by private industry on plant and machinery – investment – was '...unquestionable in the long-term interest of increased production and improved productivity...'[43] Moreover in 1955 readers of the BPC Bulletin were made acutely aware of the serious problems facing British industry, 'All this time [since 1938] our rate of capital investment per worker has been lower, dangerously lower, than that of any of our serious competitors.'[44] Data from the era does indeed show lower investment as reported in Figures 7.1 and 7.2.

As the two bar charts show, levels of investment in UK industry certainly are poor by Western European standards. According to Sir Greville Maginess, President of the BEC, the principal explanation lay in problems with capital depreciation and taxation.[45] At an FBI meeting in 1948 one eminent member complained that the 'profits tax' was unjustifiable and called for its abolition.[46] This supports the thesis of Cooley and Ohanian we precised in Chapter 4, that ex post capital income taxation acted as a drag on British growth. The contemporary observer Goodman commented that depreciation and tax allowances in America appeared to be more generous than in the UK, and that US

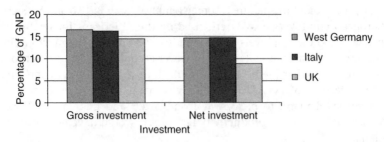

Figure 7.1   Investment ratios in West Germany, Italy, and the UK, 1953–60

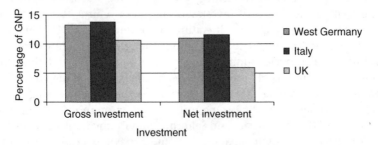

Figure 7.2   Investment ratios for manufacturing industry only in West Germany, Italy, and the UK, 1953–60
Source: Adapted from Pollard (1982: 25).

industry did not bear the same level of taxation as British industry. He therefore called for depreciation allowances on machinery to be more generous to permit increased rates of technical change.[47] But it is not so clear-cut because Britain compared to major competitors such as Germany did not suffer from excessive company taxation, for data from the Board of Trade showed that German corporate taxation was higher than that of the UK.[48] Yet, would large amounts of investment have been the only way in which to achieve a lower incremental capital to output ratio, that is, higher productivity? According to the judgements Silberman made after his tour he was able to give examples of factories operating in the UK which could increase their productivity by as much as 20 per cent with little capital expenditure and that in many industrial processes in the UK twice or four times as much labour was used as in America.[49] In 1952 Peachey made a similar judgement. Pachey the works manager we mentioned earlier who had toured a number of telephone manufacturing plants in France, Belgium, and England concluded, 'The point that struck me the most forcibly was that British operating management are not doing all they could, with what they have. This is not a question of capital investment.'[50] If British management were not doing all they could with what they had then why was this the case?

There is a plausible reason why British industrialists and managers might not have been doing all they could to invest. In Eichengreen or Lancaster terms they might have feared that the gains from investment would go primarily to labour. The AACP was to stress investment as a key to productivity growth and both the FBI and TUC accepted this to a degree (Tomlinson 1991a: 87). Industry fears are reflected in one particular letter to Burton of the BEC in 1956, relating employer's reactions to the BEC's Automation Committee Report where the writer said he felt the lower ranks in trade unions were using their usual techniques to raise wages regardless of economic conditions.[51]

James McGraw, claimed that he had talked to many top businessmen and government leaders in the UK, most of them agreed that the pace of recovery was too slow in the UK. As a result of rising labour costs which flowed from the full employment policy, which had '... encouraged trade union leaders to insist on higher wages without guaranteeing higher output'.[52] As the Political and Economic Planing Report of 1965 on attitudes in British management pointed out, wages are the most obvious source of conflict between the two 'sides' of industry (PEP 1966: 70). One managing director who it was claimed had succeeded in his factory in bringing the workers into close liaison with managers took the view that workers and unions simply did not appreciate the harsh underlying economic reality of life.[53] The FBI he thought was and could be in the forefront of convincing workers of the need for efficiency and the economic reality, although it is not quite clear what he meant by this.[54] The request to the FBI was unusual, given the FBI's division of responsibility with the BEC (which nominally, at least, was responsible for all wages questions).[55]

A discussion between Harle of the TUC and R. W. Mann of Victor Products illustrates the problems over distributing the 'fruits' of productivity growth. Harle in the AEU *Monthly Journal* had attacked Mann for using time study in his Wallsend works to increase productivity but with no corresponding increase in the rewards, particularly in the form of wages which went to labour. He asked of Mann whether he would recommend to management that they share the gains from productivity. Considering the rate at which new methods were introduced into the Wallsend factory the increases in productivity would be considerable he assumed. However, because of the way jobs were timed no contribution as far as he could discern was made to wages.[56]

In his reply, Mann revealed that after taxation profits were split on the principle of a third to increase the size of the company, a third to shareholders, and a third to a non-contributory pension scheme for all employees. Mann's profit sharing scheme and the distribution of profits on a one-third basis fits in part the Eichengreen architecture for a successful long-run productivity settlement. It also nicely mirrors and supports the assertions we drew in Chapter 3 from the examples of Chamberlains and Shield Engineering. It was argued that such schemes could be highly efficacious, but later evidence from the experiments at Esso's Fawley refinery and other such productivity bargains had raised the suspicion that such agreements gave little benefit to management. Here though we have an example where management is strongly supporting such schemes, moreover Mann pointedly asserted in his reply that his firm received over 200 productivity enhancing suggestions a year from the workers.[57] It therefore seems inconceivable that Mann's enterprise is on the losing end. Now compare the financial strategy of Mann's Victor Products with the attitudes of some German employers who argued that profit sharing was unsuitable for the German economy because of the German tax structure amongst other factors. Indeed in 1951, the first company which attempted to introduced profit sharing in Germany after the War, *Didier-Werke* of Wiesbaden, also held this view (Link 1991: 318–9).

France was the first of the early industrialising countries and probably the first country in the world to introduce profit sharing but gave quite a cool reception to profit sharing, which was an integral part in promoting the productivity drive. In 1842 Edme-Jean Leclaire with his house-painting firm – Maison Leclaire – in Paris launched what became a highly successful profit-sharing plan for his 200 workers (Park 1987: 39–44). Given this comparatively longer tradition of profit sharing it is slightly surprising and or ironic that roughly 100 years later one ECA report accused French managers of resistance to production reform and commented: 'Basically, the French managers postulate their operations on the highest possible profit on a low volume of business and do not share with the workforce whatever benefits accrue to a given production organisation through technological improvements' (McGlade 1995: 405). Pilot plant projects where the Americans showcased production reforms in few factories, which resulted in spectacular productivity gains, were also impeded by French employers' unwillingness to share the benefits of productivity increases with the workers. In 1952, disputes arose in the French foundry industry over this issue and the non-communist trade union FO withdrew from the initiative (Kipping and Nioche 1998: 58).

In Chapter 3 we mentioned the Italian Vicenza Productivity Centre and the derisory rewards given to workers for making useful productivity enhancing suggestions. Eleven medium-sized firms were involved with the productivity enhancing experiments, began in 1952 in Vicneza, and these experiments had two strands – profit sharing and mixed (comprised of workers and employers) firm advisory boards. However the Italian Confederation of Industrialists – Confindustria – were extremely concerned over the prospect that employees should receive a share of the profits rendered by increased productivity and were critical of the mixed advisory boards (Segreto 1998: 87–9). Viewed from this light Mann strikes as being a highly progressive and efficient British entrepreneur.

As we have seen in Eichengreen's analysis high levels of investment were crucial to the Golden Age. In order for high investment to occur however, we saw that not only must the level of wages be fixed to an agreed growth path but so must dividend growth. However the FBI were reluctant to accept dividend restraint in the early post-War period but nevertheless did because they found it difficult to oppose the Attlee government's calls for limitation.[58] The FBI accepted voluntary dividend restraint from 1948 to December 1950 and Kipping has said that 97 per cent of all companies in the FBI observed the dividend freeze but it broke down thereafter because industry thought that it prohibited the movement of capital from declining to growing businesses and because of the Attlee government's nationalisation at below market prices of steel (Jones 1987: 37, 155; Kipping 1972: 78–81). Some producer associations such as the National Association of Drop Forgers and Stampers were reluctant to accept dividend limitation. They stated in 1951 that while acknowledging that they had much to learn from American methods doubted, '...whether the investor is at present benefiting adequately from the profits of industry due to the limitation of Dividends'.[59] In order to induce firms into restraining dividend growth post-War governments offered what Eichengreen refers to as bonds which would be lost if firms did not keep an agreed level of dividend growth. For instance, in Norway the government introduced in 1953–54 price, profit, and dividend controls in order to ensure that capital would keep to an agreed bargain. This was after an American Mutual Security Agency Mission report in 1952 had criticised the system of centralised collective bargaining in Norway for being rigid, un-dynamic, and preventing workers from sharing in productivity gains (Amdam and Yttri 1998: 125–6). In Sweden in the late 1940s the government limited the payment of dividends by public companies and firms were encouraged to deposit 40 per cent of their annual profits into a state account in which their profits would be subject to only minimal taxation (Eichengreen 1996b: 46–9).

In the late 1940s the FBI also called for reductions in government expenditure, corporate and personal taxation. They felt the last factor was a contributory cause to the calls for higher wages by workers.[60] Kipping believed at one FBI meeting that there was general agreement on the necessity for cuts in national capital expenditure and in the process claimed that industry could not embark upon the necessary investment because of their overwhelming need to purchase food and raw materials.[61] Middlemas has gone as far as to say that, 'The FBI's Home Economic Policy Committee complained regularly about the dead hand of state bureaucracy and the way public industries and welfare services soaked up limited investment allocations and supply of raw materials...' (Middlemas 1986: 161). But, as we saw in Figure 4.1 in Chapter 4, government expenditure was not comparatively excessive. Moreover in Eichengreen's model, government expenditure on social welfare is a necessary prerequisite to secure workers' adherence to wage moderation. For instance, the first post-War Belgian government implemented a social security scheme and in Germany post-War governments indexed pensions to living standards rather than inflation in an effort to ensure organised labour's commitment to wage moderation. The other institutional mechanism that helped to bond capital into high levels of investment was government subsidies of firms and raw material inputs. In Germany the steel and aircraft industries received subsidies. In Austria government provided firms with guaranteed raw materials and semi-finished products at significantly below market prices, it also threatened to levy tax penalties on those which failed to keep an agreed investment wages pledge (Eichengreen 1996b: 46–9).

We have already explored the issues of unions and workers' alleged retarding effects on the utilisation of machinery and we have seen in this chapter with the examples of Melman and the AACP that British managers were slow or unenthusiastic in exploiting innovation in some cases but in others they may have had good reason to be sceptical. But why might managers be cautious or unwilling to adopt innovations, could it be due to, and as we commented in Chapter 6 to their low level of training and education in comparison to their rivals?

Technical change and the institutions of education, training, selection, and reward

After the Second World War the USA had firmly become established as the world's most advanced country in the teaching of the latest management techniques or what Locke has referred to as the 'new paradigm'; 'Immediately after World War II, the gap between U.S. and European business education was greater than ever before' (Locke 1985: 240). The USA had become the world's leading country in business education for four reasons. The First World War had spurred the American administration into passing the 1920 National Defence Act that created the Service Corps, which were heavily trained in management science. The Cold War also pushed forward the application of scientific management techniques such as linear programming and acted as a spur to the development of computers. The economic dislocation caused by the Second World War was also far less severe in the USA then in the countries of Western Europe and other belligerent nations. These factors left the USA at the very frontier of management education and its rivals significantly behind. The 'new paradigm' in business education was promoted in Western Europe by American businesses through the ERP, the productivity team tours, conferences and symposiums. At this time France, Belgium, and to a lesser extent Britain sent many students to the American business schools to learn the new techniques and then teach them to their own management communities on their return. Germany was an exception to this exchange because of the pre-War tradition of management education in Germany, it was involved in this transatlantic knowledge transference programme to a far lesser degree, and its post-Second World War management training was to a great extent a continuation of what had occurred pre-War (Locke 1985: 240–1; 1989: 113–21).

In 1950 the ECA had concluded that management training had to be increased and it set up two programmes to help achieve this. First, there were Jobs Method Training (a component of Training Within Industry (hereafter TWI)) classes to be undertaken by the NPCs and secondly there was its Pilot Plants programme. The Pilot Plants programme enabled European management to retrain and re-equip their factories from ECA funds if they implemented American-style business strategies, and tried to secure labour–management co-operation, collective bargaining, increased profit margins, and company sales. TWI was composed of three branches: Job Relations, Job Instruction, and Job Methods.

The EPA was also to embark heavily upon programmes to try and increase the level and quantity of management education in Western Europe. The leaders of the EPA subscribed to the view that deficiencies in management education were partly the cause of relatively low European productivity compared to the USA. Moreover the EPA thought that deficiencies in Western European management education were partly caused by the Western European view that managers were 'born and not bred', hence little management education was undertaken. Whereas in the USA, management was better because there was less emphasis upon this aspect and more upon the ability to make good managers by training and education. The EPA wanted to counteract the opinion that they thought common in Western Europe (unlike America) that leaders were indeed 'born and not made'. The EPA's stance is partly at odds with the material we reviewed in the previous chapter where Locke had claimed that the good manager is a product of both factors. Here the EPA would seem then to have taken an over-optimistic view of their ability to change European management. Nevertheless between 1953 and 1957, 15,000 managers of medium and small firms participated in various short training courses organised by the EPA, which were designed to disseminate American management techniques (Boel 1994).

The BIM suggested that the AACP should send a specialist team to the USA to study management education. It spent 40 days in the USA and its Report *Education for Management* contained a number of important observations. First, it reported that there was in the UK a lack of management courses as compared to the USA; secondly, that management was recognised as a genuine profession in the USA; thirdly, that US businesses were willing to release executives for formal management education and that executives were 'management-education-conscious'. It also noted that there was strong competition in recruiting by businesses for the best university-educated graduates, and that a lot of attention was paid by American business to the selection of men suitable for university training in administrative studies. At the end of its report the team emphatically stated that they believed that there was a close link between productivity and management education and that it was vital that British industry recognised this link (AACP 1951a).[62]

Another AACP team looked into management education with its main brief to examine management accounting practices in the USA. It visited 59 firms in states such as Chicago, Kentucky, and New York, and 12 government departments, and educational and professional bodies. The team concluded that, 'American industrialists have for many years appreciated the need for training men to undertake the functions of administration and management and, with the increasing tempo and complexity of industrial life, they have increased their support and given more attention to this important aspect of their business economy' (AACP 1950a: 64).[63] In 1951 the BIM hosted a three-day management training seminar which was attended by 750 of Britain's top businessmen and trade unionists, which made it according to the ECA *Productivity Bulletin* the largest gathering in pursuit of the productivity effort of its kind in the UK (McGlade 1995: 475–6). Yet as we saw in Chapter 6 it was not until the 1960s that business schools in the UK were founded and prior to this many industrialists remained unimpressed of the merits of trained managers. Tiratsoo and Tomlinson for instance found that in the mid- and late 1960s many businessmen were ambivalent towards their own professional development and the recruitment of graduates to their companies (Tiratsoo and Tomlinson 1997: 54–5).

We saw in the previous chapter with the work of Granick and Clegg that British higher managers and executives were underpaid relative to their continental and Atlantic counterparts, this however is no longer so. During the 1980s top managerial or executive pay rose rapidly and continues to do so. From 1979 to 1986 the top tenth of male white-collar pay in the private sector increased by 28.5 per cent (MacInnes 1987: 127). British executives now seem to have swung the pendulum the other way with too much pay for too little performance. If British executives have been playing remunerative catch-up with their continental and Atlantic counterparts then the game has gone too far. David Higgs who undertook research for the British government on the recruitment of non-executive directors has rightly recommended that the sphere of recruitment from which they are drawn needs to be greatly widened.

Thatcherism was successful at raising the incentives to managers and executives by rectifying the poor comparative pay of British managers, but it was far less successful at opening up the boardroom world to fresh faces, particularly at the non-executive level. In Chapter 6 the findings of Bowden and colleagues showed that at Cowley there was no effective method for removing poor management. The governance structure of British business is still very much a hot issue and one where it does not fare well, with the 'pale, male and stale' composition of non-executive directors who determine who the executive directors are and oversee the decisions of the board. There is evidence of self-serving multiplication of non-executive and executive salaries and interlocking non-executive directorships where non-executives hold four or five non-executive posts at the same time, with only 1 per cent of non-executive directorships advertised and only 4 per cent of the posts where a formal interview takes place.[64]

Consultation, communication, and the managerial prerogative

Lupton defines joint consultation as, '. . . the formal machinery through which the managers and the workers in a firm, or their elected or appointed representatives, discuss their common problems, decide about them and exchange information'. One thing that we should not do is to equate the machinery of joint consultation with the machinery of collective bargaining. There are a number of reasons advanced as to why joint consultation may enhance enterprise performance. First, it is argued that if individuals are given the opportunity to participate in the decisions which affect their jobs, or at least are informed about them, then they will 'feel better' about working for the firm. Second, joint consultation provides a mechanism by which workers can air their minor grievances and put forward their ideas for improvement, thus helping to keep employees satisfied. Third, joint consultation helps to solidify common ground and the common interests between workers and managers. Fourth, joint consultation allows workers an opportunity to exercise their organising talents in matters of administration, in such things as sports clubs, profit sharing, bonus schemes and the like, it is assumed of course that these organising talents cannot find vent in the normal course of work. Fifth, joint consultation allows workers and managers to meet in circumstances where the relationship of subordinate to superior is played down, and their common role of employees of the firm is played up. This is argued to be good for morale. In these effects joint consultation, it is said, will lower labour turnover and absence rates, reduce conflict, and help to promote a feeling of loyalty, belonging, and a greater will to work (Lupton 1971: 88–90). Given that workers' resistance to changes in production techniques partly depends upon the extent of communication between management and labour, then consultation appears an important area of investigation (PEP 1966: 80).

A strict definition of the managerial prerogative is difficult to locate and in any case an all-embracing definition could be controversial. It may be said however to include a number of factors; such as the right to decide who should operate new machines, how much overtime should be worked, how many apprentices should be employed, and how workers should be paid (Wigham 1973: 5). The managerial prerogative may be said to rest upon four pillars. One is that property ownership is said to give its owners the right to control the assets that they own. It is also held that the right to manage in companies with a share capital is said to devolve from statute law, that is, the manager manages by virtue of responsibility to the shareholders. It is argued that in the interests of economic efficiency management must be allowed to manage, for management is a specialised and expert activity. In part this claim rests upon the general assertion found in most economic textbooks that specialisation and the division of labour leads to greater productive efficiency.[65] Finally, support for the managerial prerogative comes from the belief in natural leaders and in this respect we may borrow the hallowed phrase 'leaders are born not made' (derived from Anthony 1986: 43).

As we saw from Chapter 3 joint consultation did not really become commonplace after the Second World War in Britain when compared to its extent in other Western European countries, indeed, Clegg has asserted after the fall of the first post-War government joint consultation went into decline (Clegg 1970: 192). Dartmann notes that employers regarded JPCs with suspicion, as a threat to the 'right to manage', and were therefore reluctant to set them up (Dartmann 1996a: 72). As Tiratsoo and Tomlinson have argued, many businessmen (as distinct from managers) were not really in favour of joint consultation, because they either feared it would open the way to union agitators or it would compromise the managers' ability to manage (Tiratsoo and Tomlinson 1993: 95, 167). British employers and their collective representatives such as the Engineering Employers Federation felt JC could interfere with the managerial prerogative (Wigham 1973: 157). For example, the trade unions in the woollen textile industry saw the employers approach to joint consultation in their industry as 'diffident' and thought that no 'real headway' had been made in their request for greater representation.[66] In Germany on the other hand employers had JC imposed upon them. So while German employers may have been against the introduction of co-determination, it has been beneficial to them because it has given rise to superior performance in their manu-facturing industries and has contributed to an environment of higher trust (Streeck 1992: 4).

Not only did British employers not like joint consultation they even objected to attempts by the EPA to run management courses for trade unionists because of the underlying assumption that organised labour had a proper place in the management of the enterprise. Pollock director of the BEC had a fairly negative attitude towards this aspect of the EPA's activities and thought that a careful watch should be kept on them. The

BEC were also not prepared to have the EPA's trade union programme made into a joint employer–trade union scheme.[67]

The EPA Report, *Joint Consultation in Practice*, somewhat ambiguously in the light of BEC attitudes noted above, proposed, 'Support for joint consultation was keenest at the top and progressively weakened down the scale of management (EPA *Joint Consultation in Practice*, 31).' Why we might ask would the enthusiasm for JC decline still further as we progress down the managerial hierarchy? Given that middle managers or floor supervisors are a critical factor in implementing change in the workplace this is very important. Middle managers may be resistant to changes in management styles because the burden of carrying out the changes falls mainly on them. Joint consultation could have appeared to middle managers as requiring them to give up some of their power and status or to put more graphically, 'Many middle managers feel that "participative" management styles may mean that they will participate themselves right out of their job' (Smith 1990: 15; Yankelovich and Immerwahr 1985: 162–3; Yankelovich *et al.* 1985a: 73).

The importance of an institutional mechanism such as joint consultation in the context of the Eichengreen framework is that it allows workers knowledge of management behaviour and an input into firms' investment decisions (Eichengreen 1994: 885–6; 1996b: 47–8). If employees know little or nothing of what management is planning, and they have no say in a firm's investment strategy, but they perceive management to be poor, then it is difficult to see why they should make immediate short-run or first-period wage restraint and trust and co-operate with managers to make wise investments in the first period, to lead in the longer run to wage and output growth (Hargreaves Heap 1991: 40). As we saw in Chapter 3 British and German unions were seeking reassurance concerning employment and wage growth so that first-period restraint would result in second-period benefits.

Joint consultation is not without its problems though, because allowing workers an input into the decision-making process could be destabilising. Kenneth Arrow has conclusively proved in his 'impossibility theorem' that no social choice function can guarantee Pareto optimality because it is impossible to align the preferences of individuals in an organisation so that they are transitive, independent of irrelevant alternatives, and fulfil the criteria of 'universal domain'. Therefore to quote Miller, 'The Arrow theorem suggests that a firm's manager who permits other employees to share in the decision making of the firm could create organisational instability, indecisiveness, inefficiency, or manipulability' (Miller 1992: 64).[68] Any one of these problems could lead to decision cycling, something which under a productivity drive where managers are constantly faced with successive waves of innovation one would think could be highly damaging to enterprise performance.[69] British managers under the productivity drive may have opted for an unchecked managerial hierarchy with its superiority in efficiency, coherence, and consistency compared to participative management; although dictatorial managers have an incentive to behave opportunistically by appropriating worker ideas for improved firm performance and managers are fallible in their decision making (Smith 1990: 25).

If British industrialists might not have wanted to concede to workers any input into the firm's decision-making process what was their attitude towards simply sharing information with the labour force? One particularly important type of information sharing in the Eichengreen framework is of course financial. Recently Tiratsoo and Tomlinson have conveyed the impression that British managers were hostile to this particular aspect of the 'human relations' side of Americanisation. They use varying types of evidence collected from the 1950s and 1960s that recorded British industrialists as unwilling to share financial information with their employees. One survey at the end of the 1950s revealed that only one in five British firms shared financial information with their workers, while most firms considered providing such information a novelty. Indeed they quote one British manager who starkly told an American academic visiting the UK as part of the productivity drive that if a trade union representative wanted to see the firm's balance sheet, 'he would kick him out of the office' (Tiratsoo and Tomlinson 1997: 55, 73).

However the findings of Tiratsoo and Tomlinson on this matter cannot be accepted without some qualification. The General Manager of the British Oxygen Corporation, Seaman, argued that it was essential that workers were made aware of their effectiveness in the 'general picture'. Company boards must take every step to ensure that every member of the organisation knows how the firm works and each individual's part in it. Seaman also made a point which bears upon the Eichengreen thesis, that Boards of a company must satisfactorily demonstrate to the workers that capital was being set aside for development and that satisfactory capital development ratios could occur without threatening the 'sharing out of the cake'. It was thus imperative that senior management make the 'capital transition period clear', an unclear concept but presumably indicating that in order for increasing investment in the future, workers will have to be assured of increasing wages.[70] Seaman's recommendations to British managers look most apposite given that at least two AACP reports noted that British employers failed to set out before their workers the likely impact of new techniques on the work force and how much they stood to gain (Coleman and Macleod 1986: 609).

Seaman and the AACP were not the only ones to recommend an information flow from managers to workers. In 1957 the director of the Federation of Master Cotton Spinners Associations advised his members to, '...pay a little more recognition to the moral obligation to do everything possible to avoid unnecessary redundancy when new technical methods or automation in any form [were] introduced'. Employers should give a warning as early as possible and they should plan in such a way so as to avoid the 'savage' effects of redundancy.[71] The longer the time span managers and workers had to adjust to the idea of technical change, the more easily it could be adopted and the less 'friction' there would be (PEP 1966: 294). The DSIR Report considered that if management made manpower an integral part of forward planning then a '...sharp clash of interest over redundancy...', could be avoided. For good management could do much to soften the impact upon labour (DSIR 1956). The BEC's automation committee also thought that employers should give a warning as early as possible to employees whom they intended to make redundant, particularly for those whom they had employed for a long time. But it argued ultimately that the decision to introduce automation must rest with the employer.[72]

Similar views were expressed by Sir Hugh Beaver of the BIM at a conference of international manufactures held in 1956 under the auspices of the USTAP programme. Beaver believed that in the long run inventions and mechanisation had had the effect of increasing the numbers employed. But serious problems were possible in the short run, with the risk of '...serious disorganisation and periods of widespread mass unemployment intermediately'.[73] Here there seems to have been widespread agreement amongst British business for Garrett of the BEC was particularly pleased with this reference to the human problems of automation; if the human problems of automation were not kept in perspective then, '...the new tools that are coming into our hands may end in disaster rather than a higher standard of living'.[74] Others simply believed that new thinking was required on the issue of redundancy.[75] In the above material we have examples of managers and employers who in Coleman's schema were attempting to include in their decision matrix the social or external costs of unemployment. As employers' associations were attempting to reassure workers about employment to facilitate reform of production methods.

Conclusion

In Chapter 6 we noted that the broad thrust of much of the literature on Britain's post-War relative economic decline has placed a heavy emphasis upon the failings of management and its consequent negative impact upon economic performance. But we also took care to record that in many cases the basic analytical supports upon which this critical literature rests are contested. How does this survey of managerial performance during successive initiatives to improve productivity between 1950s and 1980s contribute to the long- standing debates about British managerial inadequacy?

First, we should be clear that Americanisation did not simply imply rapid increases in investment through the accumulation of narrow capital or machinery, as we saw from the comments of Silberman for example. It did not imply either a wholesale implementation of what has come to be referred to as the three 'S's (simplification, standardisation, and specialisation). As others have rightly observed the Americans were not simply trying to entice European countries into adopting a self-contained and entire model of production, such as Fordism (Tiratsoo and Tomlinson 1998b: 115–17). The productivity drive also involved promoting British and indeed European best practice more widely, as is evident in the work of the BPC and in the Soviet system of manufacture, which informed Melman's report on the machine tool industry. But here too methods such as standardisation and specialisation were in evidence and given that this was a period of intense antagonism between two great military and economic powers, it should not seem surprising that agents should recommend adopting Soviet techniques.

However what is of critical concern and surely the point of greatest significance is to what extent British managers and entrepreneurs identified and adopted those American techniques which were suited to the structural characteristics of the UK economy and to manager's abilities; more especially their ability to discriminate against those which would have been beyond their grasp and unsuited to the UK. Moreover how quickly did they not only select but also graft and assimilate onto their own methods those techniques that were applicable? As we saw from the work of economic historians such as Broadberry it has been argued that British industrialists would have been unwise to blindly follow US methods because these methods were unsuited to the British economy with its different factor and product markets and resource endowments. As Bjarnar and Kipping have asserted Americanisation was most successful when it resulted from the selective and partial adaptation of the American management model not wholesale adoption (Bjarnar and Kipping 1998: 14). The extent and speed to which the competitive advantages offered by the US economy were absorbed and translated into the UK economy were primarily questions of entrepreneurial motivation, management ability, and organisational structure and strategy (Dunning 1998: 78). The ability of economic agents to adopt the latest technical innovations is more generally a function of the quality of their human capital which would form part of what Abramovitz (following Ohkawa and Rosovsky) called the 'social capability' for catch-up to the lead country, in this case of course the USA. Social capability, although difficult to define and measure, is composed of a number of institutional elements. Most important is probably education, which is taken as a proxy for technical competence (Abramovitz 1986: 387–9). Social capability for catch-up however embodies other institutions, such as competition policy and enforcement, political, commercial, financial, and industrial organisations. In so far as competition policy is concerned we noted its relative weakness until the mid-1950s, and the failure of British policy makers to absorb this aspect of the American system.

More specifically we should take care to define what exactly are the factors that determine the adoption of new techniques and here we may borrow the taxonomy of Carlsson and Eliasson. According to Carlsson and Eliasson adoption of new techniques will be determined by the level of economic competence within the firm and of managers more generally. Economic competence is defined as the ability to identify, expand, and exploit the opportunity set and is determined by the following factors: the selective or strategic capability of the firm, its ability to make innovative choices of markets, products, technologies, and organisational structure; the ability to select key personnel and acquire new resources. Secondly, organisational capability, which is the ability to co-ordinate and integrate and thirdly technical ability which relates to functions which include, production, marketing, engineering, research and development, as well as product-specific capabilities. Finally we may note the ability to learn (Carlsson and Eliasson 1995: 65–6). From the evidence and discussion in the proceeding chapter it should be obvious that British managers would perform badly in some of the functions of Carlsson's and Eliasson's list. As we noted in Chapter 6 British managers were comparatively poorly educated and trained, poor at marketing and sales and had low technical ability. These inability's may have prevented British management in their ability to adopt some aspects of American techniques, such as automated mass production because, '. . . automation puts a great premium on managerial planning', it also requires that management through its sales and marketing department is able to sell the large amounts of homogenous products (Bright 1958: 12, 214–15).[76] In these aspects British managers would be unsuited to Americanisation. Yet in Chapter 6 we also took note of the fact that British management style is relatively authoritarian and personalised, in this sense they would have been suited to the close supervision of effort that assembly line mass production requires. The conclusions of Broadberry and Burnham are pertinent in that it would have been unwise for British managers to unquestioningly adopt assembly line mass production, but it would have been useful to adopt sub-assembly, line production, and widespread use of jigs and fixtures, as exemplified by the unidentified machine tool shop in Halifax.

As we saw from the productivity agencies even when techniques where applicable they were not always adopted. More up-to-date evidence shows that British manufacturers are still in some ways slow to respond to opportunities for advancement. In Chapter 6 the findings of the Parliamentary Inquiry into British engineering were discussed. This committee also reported that they were impressed with the way the VDI assembles teams of experts to draw up and publish codes of practice and recommend techniques. Some of the VDI's best codes of practice were translated into English and published, '...but few British companies showed any interest in them' (Cmnd. 1980: 7794, 140–1). Despite this there clearly were positive responses from British managers as the evidence presented above showed and here Tiratsoo and Tomlinson's conclusions look somewhat overdrawn. As we saw with firms such as Lake and Elliot and Clifford Williams, firms could be eager to adapt. This evidence is highly important given that the ultimate test for the real extent of the Americanisation of European business must be sought in the implementation of American practices at company level (Bjarnar and Kipping 1998: 13).

Tomlinson's assertion that the FBI was important in shaping responses also looks in need of qualification, given the comparative abundance of archival material of responses of individual firms to proposals for reform of production methods. Individual firms and employer associations seem to have behaved in a far more decentralised manner compared to organised labour, which remained highly centralised and dependent on the organising and responsive abilities of the TUC. This need not surprise us, as Kipping explained, 'The Federation seeks to lead but not to dictate. It is servant of its members and has no *raison d'être* nor policy apart from them. It helps to form and to express industrial opinion: it cannot, even if it would, enforce industrial action' (Kipping 1954: 16).

In Chapter 3 we investigated how the trade unions responded to the productivity drive, noting that throughout the period the TUC and trade union leaders were, at least publicly, behind the productivity drive and its agencies, although they may have had difficulties convincing some of their members. A similar picture emerges on the employer side. As a trade unionist and employer pointed out, '...the structure of trade unionism is very closely comparable to industry generally and though the FBI and all sorts of other organisations might support our work it was left to individual firms whether they came in or not'.[77] The FBI was concerned not to alienate any sector of its membership, thus this in part ruled out taking strong stands or making bold policy statements on any particular issue though the FBI was until 1965 the leading industrial organisation in the country with the largest and most representative membership both of individual firms and industrial bodies and the 'voice' of British industry (Blank 1973: 51). More pertinently although it did little to promote the productivity drive and the attempt to present the FBI Grand Council as obstructive to the dissemination of new production techniques has obscured the extent to which firms needed to know about new methods in the pursuit of growth, profit, and managerial rewards. The TUC may have been more supportive of the productivity drive than either the FBI or BEC but this does not imply that ordinary employers or managers automatically rejected measures to enhance productivity growth. The response of managers and entrepreneurs to the productivity agencies is not so bleak as painted by Tiratsoo and Tomlinson (1998a).

De Wit has remarked, 'A new technology does not only create uncertainty, it also crates expectations' (Witt de 1994: 170). In Chapter 3 we examined the uncertainties innovation created for labour and their fears of redundancy and exploitation. In this chapter we have documented management's expectations of appropriation by the workers of any increased financial gain from innovation. In our case we have found through exploring managerial attitudes that in some instances they appeared concerned that employees might try to exploit technical change to gain higher rewards and thus alter distributive outcomes in the terms of Knight. More crucially as we outlined in Chapter 1, using the bargaining frameworks of Eichengreen and Lancaster, if management suspects that labour will renege on any multi-period time specified bargain it makes with management then management is unlikely to invest or innovate. In this sense our evidence sits uneasily with the assertions of Lewchuk who as outlined in Chapter 2 asserted that in the post-War period British managers believed they could make 'automation pay' because they thought labour would adopt a co-operative approach to the implementation of the new techniques (Lewchuk 1987).

However management was also reluctant to adopt those new institutional mechanisms that are necessary for some form of monitoring, particularly joint production committees (which in the British case would not have been allowed to monitor investment decisions). To an extent we may see this as others have, as a desire by British management to retain its traditional prerogatives (Tiratsoo and Tomlinson 1997: 74). Campbell Fraser, member of the CBI said in 1973 that although it was probably true that some managers were reluctant to change their methods and attitudes, there was a greater degree of professionalism in management than ever before. A revolution in management training and had taken place and managers were better equipped for their jobs than at any time in the last 30 years.[78]

8
Conclusion

The performance of the British economy since 1945 in comparison to its major industrial rivals has generated an awful lot of smoke and rarely is there so much smoke without some fire. Scholars have fired salvos across each other's bows on the causes of underperformance, explanations abound and there still seems no settled agreement as to the causes of underperformance or its significance (Booth 2003; Broadberry and Crafts 1998; Crafts 2002; Tomlinson 2001; Tomlinson and Tiratsoo 1998).

The productivity drive has left us with a rich historical vein by which to explore Britain's productivity problem and to focus on both public policy at the macroeconomic level, that is, incomes policies and trade union reform, and attempts to alter microeconomic factors, that is, improved management and increased incentives to workers. As noted in Chapter 1, institutions now form a central element in many accounts of economic performance, but they are difficult to define. In this work we have taken them to be structures, which constrain and govern economic activity, although it is not always easy to categorise a particular custom, convention, or pattern of behaviour as an institution. Indeed in some cases the application of the term 'institution' may strain any given definition.

The productivity initiatives should not be seen innocently as unbiased and impartial instruments by which to view Britain's relative economic decline from an untainted light. We ought to acknowledge the possibility that the organisations of labour, capital, and government might have attempted to capture the productivity agencies and either, attenuate their efforts, or try to align the projects and efforts with their own agendas. With both the Donovan Commission and the NBPI the government had to ease the concerns of both trade unionists and employers before they would join these bodies.

In Chapter 2 much of the literature was reviewed on how it is argued that British labour has retarded economic performance and institutional accounts held centre stage. British labour has stood accused of exercising many restrictive practices, which has led to a low effort outcome and poor utilisation of labour and therefore given rise to poor enterprise performance. Leading economic historians such as Crafts for instance have argued that British trade unions with their craft legacy and multi-unionism with its low scope and low sophistication have impeded the productivity growth rate of the British economy. Taking our lead from Crafts we ranged across varying hypotheses as to why British labour had proved to be a check on performance. British industrial relations practices have been seen by many as detrimental to rapid innovation, and the reassertion of the managerial prerogative and the rapid productivity growth in the 1980s are given as evidence that entrenched institutional practices of British labour were the cause of poor performance. British workers were held out as preventing the rapid assimilation of the most productive and efficient techniques, such as Fordism. Empirical studies were also documented as highlighting the problem of British labour in implementing technical change. Authors like Pratten have argued that workers have been restrictive in outlook and intransigent in their attitudes towards organisational and institutional change. Attitudes are important for if employers do take them into account when considering technical and organisational change then negative attitudes by labour may discourage innovation on the part of management. This may be because management thinks that workers will capture the future benefits of innovation or because unionists will simply impede or prevent change. According to some the attitudes of British labour are a significant factor in Britain's slow growth rate.

The attitudes of British labour towards the productivity drive from peak to shop-floor level were heavily explored in Chapter 3 where it was argued that their attitudes were not significantly different from those of American and Western European labour. Moreover we took advantage of EPA investigations concerning technical change, which did not show that the attitudes of British workers were significantly different from those of other European countries. From 1950 onwards, British trade unions were to come under increasing pressure to change their practices, and we saw that many union leaders were aware of their need to change. Within the productivity drive itself labour productivity was seen as the central and most important component of fast productivity growth. However both peak and shop-floor labour saw the promotion of higher productivity in their own instrumental terms. This proved difficult because British labour still saw themselves as having to fight for their right to share in the distribution of output gains, as was exemplified by the words of Patrick Fisher. This attitude manifested itself and was investigated through a set of issues of central concern to workers, such as unemployment and wages. All these issues were of keen interest to trade unionists and through them it emerged that the political economy of the productivity drive was fundamentally flawed. British trade union leaders however tried to push workers into embracing the productivity drive and alter their ideological outlook on structural economic change but this proved difficult in a number of instances.

Economic growth and adjustment is a political as well as an economic process as it involves the redistribution of wealth, esteem, and power. Eichengreen's institutional arrangements were only weakly present and workers had few mechanisms by which to ensure that they would gain from willing co-operation in innovation. If losers such as workers think that they will in no way be compensated then it is not difficult to see why they might resist the loss of their livelihoods. British unions were however no different from their continental or Atlantic counterparts who were just as keen to seek protection from the ravages of the market.

However Western European unions may have been at an advantage over their British counterparts. They had in many cases Eichengreen-type arrangements to help alleviate their fears concerning the effects of innovation. Chapter 3 closely documented how the issue of distributive justice is paramount in the minds of the workers when approaching change and why it cannot be evaded. In an increasingly competitive world and in the environment of what is now so often referred to as the 'international' shop floor, distributive conflict could well be harmful to economic growth.

But we must recognise that in some cases differing interpretations can be taken as to why wage moderation occurred and here a possible inadequacy of the Eichengreen model becomes evident. Eichhengreen's framework has difficulty in grappling with the balances of power between economic organisations. In Chapter 3 for example we discussed the fact that post-War wage moderation in Germany may have had more to do with the weakness of organised labour vis-à-vis capital than the effects of Eichengreen-type institutional mechanisms.

In Chapters 4 and 5 we probed the state and governments' role as a cause of Britain's relative economic decline. Given that industrial activity is so heavily influenced by wider government policy it proved useful to take up those prominent themes which have continually reappeared as causes of decline in the secondary literature. British economic policy has been held responsible for severe cyclical swings in the economy thus deterring employers from investing; but this argument was seen to be weak, the 'stop-go' cycles were no bigger than the cycles experienced by the economies of Britain's major international competitors. One of the most frequent criticisms of government policy has been that it focused on the needs of the City and the wider financial community and not on industry. The dominance of the so-called financial nexus in British economic policy making is alleged to have blocked the formation of a developmental state in Britain and by preventing this it forestalled the government and its ministries taking an active stance in industrial modernisation. The liberal view of the state characterised much of this literature but there were exceptions.

More generally British governments, particularly Attlee's, were seen as implicitly unwilling to alter the inherited institutional framework by which the British economy functioned. Indeed as Middlemas informs us, '...the Second World War experience encouraged a somewhat complacent and very insular belief in the value of British institutions and recent traditions, especially when these were compared with those of other European nations' (Middlemas 1986: 114). Others are more explicit about the aftermath of the War, 'One of the fruits of victory in 1945 was the survival of Britain's cultural and institutional heritage' (Cain and Hopkins 1993: 266). So while Britain emerged as a victor from the War there was consequently little impetus to implement the kind of radical reform that the speeding-up of economic growth required. Compounding this inertia was the relatively high level of living standards in Britain up until the 1960s; only since then did Western European competitors begin to supersede the UK (Tomlinson 1996a: 753). Certainly as far as the productivity campaign reveals there is little institutional change of many production processes.

Labour however is not the most important factor in production; management is, as the remarks of those who study it and the productivity agencies attested. Accordingly we took up the many accusations levelled against British management in Chapter 6. To begin with we had to take account of two important problems when analysing management, how do we define the manager's role and in what ways is it separate and distinct from that of the entrepreneur. For definitions of their respective roles will affect how any analysis is deployed. Given this it was discovered that their functions cannot be wholly separated and it is therefore prudent not to draw sharp distinctions between the two. British management, it is said, has exercised poor control of the labour process, been inadequately educated and poorly trained, took little interest in product innovation such as better design and saw management as an authoritarian and dictatorial occupation. However some of these criticisms may not be as valid as is often supposed.

With these criticisms in mind we took up the response of British management towards the productivity drive in Chapter 7. Immediately we saw that the productivity agencies placed great importance upon executive and middle management in the achievement of higher productivity. Secondly, when compared to the response of British trade unions British manufacturers appeared less enthusiastic towards the efforts of the productivity agencies to change and inform the behaviour of management. The reactions of the two primary leaders of British industry – Pollock and Kipping – towards the initial efforts of the EPA were examples of this. But their reactions towards the productivity agencies look to have had little effect on the response of British firms towards these agencies. This decentralised reaction stands in contrast to the highly concerted attempt on the part of union leaders to rally support for the productivity drive amongst those in the lower ranks of the trade union movement. An interesting asymmetry, that other authors on the productivity drive, such as Tiratsoo and Tomlinson have not called attention to.

In Chapter 7 we presented some AACP findings and the Melman initiative, which aimed to boost the productivity of the machine tool industries of Western Europe. Melman and his recommendations received extensive criticism and rejection from the many manufacturing peak associations of Western Europe. Melman however was not calling for the adoption of American techniques, but those in use in the USSR and the best practices in Western Europe. Nevertheless in the case of Britain it was visibly obvious that although Melman's recommendations for enhanced productivity may not have all been applicable, many were. Thus the high-handed rejection of his report by British manufacture associations was unwise.

The unquestioning adoption of AACP and EPA recommendations by British industrialists and managers could have impacted negatively on performance. It has been argued that American techniques such as mass production with its consequent standardisation could well have been inappropriate for the UK economy. Here we attempted to 'short circuit' the problem that American methods may have been inappropriate by focusing on the activities of the BPC, such as its Circuit Schemes. The focus showed that not only could those at the peak of British industry exhibit hostility towards the productivity campaign. We noted the reaction of one British manufacturer who expressed great dislike at having to accept the many criticisms made of his firm by those participating in the BPC's Circuit Scheme. Here we must exercise caution. It is understandable if not entirely rational that British employers and managers did worry that by participating in such activities as inter-firm visits they could give competitors knowledge of their own techniques which would then be used in competition against them. We detailed this not only at the national but pan-Western European level.

Throughout Chapters 3 and 7 we examined primarily although not exclusively the attitudes of unions and managers towards technical and organisation change and its impact upon production institutions. Attitudes are important, as Nichols remarked in Chapter 2 economists tend to explain lower British productivity by invoking attitudes towards change. Here however we must exercise care, for attitudes are not always good predictors of behaviour (Nichols 1986: 42, 50). Yet if attitudes do count then here we have seen that British trade union attitudes towards productivity were no different from those of other nations in Western Europe. As concerns management although those at the top of employer representation bodies showed in some cases negative attitudes, the approach of individual firms could be a lot different and more pragmatic. A number of individual firms and employers responded in a positive way to the productivity drive. It was therefore argued that blanket condemnations of British managers were unjustified although this does not warrant exoneration either. The point must surely be that numerous employers did appear to accept new ways and new styles of management, which did not excessively strain their existing practices, and styles.

Although labour and management may have frequently responded well to the productivity agencies' exhortation for higher productivity only moderate reforms were being asked of them. When changes and reforms far more reaching and substantive were asked for, their response to the British governments' initiatives of Donovan and the NBPI and incomes policies, was far less then enthusiastic. Trade union leaders were hostile to the implications of Donovan and unions in combination with employers were continually stretching the boundaries of the pay–productivity linkage. The perspective of Calmfors and Driffill allowed investigation into whether the trade union reforms of post-War governments were on the right lines to promote increased wage centralisation and co-ordination or more decentralisation and less co-ordination. In terms of the Calmfors Driffill model that we began with in the 'Introduction', we may say that many of the productivity initiatives such as NIC, NBPI, the Donovan Commission, and the NEDC, tried with little success to increase the degree of centralised wage bargaining and its co-ordination. British

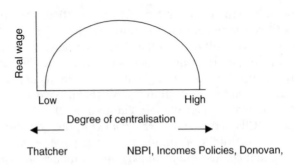

Figure 8.1   The hump-shaped hypothesis of Calmfors and Driffill

industrial relations with their heritage of voluntary agreements were historically unsuited to these types of reform. As Kipping, Director General of the FBI said, 'I continue to have faith in voluntarism in conditions of genuine emergency, but I do not see it as permanent machinery' (Kipping 1972: 81). Whereas, Thatcher attempted with some degree of success to shift the degree of centralisation and co-ordination of wage bargaining to the left of the diagram towards more decentralised and un-coordinated wage bargaining (Figure 8.1) (Calmfors and Driffill 1988: 15). Although the impact on productivity seems to have been confined to a one off 'shake out effect' on labour productivity, there was certainly no productivity miracle. See table 8.1 for the overall growth ranking four years after Thatcher left office. Ironically, this was at a time when British trade unions were continuing the post-Second World War trend of merging.

The failure of the NBPI, incomes policies, and Donovan must be seen not only as an outcome of the inherent weakness of these initiatives but also a lack of political will to implement and make them work. It was also a function of the resistance of these institutions to the changes these initiatives sought. Thatcher in her project seems to have suffered no such lack of political will, although again met with resistance. The slowness of British institutions to embrace modification has long antecedents. Alford comments that the rate of UK economic growth has been slow since the eighteenth century, this rate influenced and was influenced by the institutional and social systems, which both had great depth but were slow to change (Alford 1988: 105). Institutions involve sunk costs and as a result their alteration requires considerable momentum and co-ordination, moreover Britain industrialised with a particular set of institutions. As was highlighted by our discussion of the machine tool industry in Chapter 7, it suffered from too many small

Table 8.1 Levels of real GDP per head for selected years and countries in international dollars of 1990 (purchasing power parity adjusted)

	1870			1913			1950			1973			1994	
Rank	Country	GDP/ P.H.	Rank	Country	GDP/ P.H.	Rank	Country	GDP/ P.H.	Rank	Country	GDP/ P.H.	Rank	Country	GDP/ P.H.
1	Australia	3,801	1	Australia	5,505	1	USA	9,573	1	Switzerland	17,953	1	USA	22,569
2	UK	3,263	2	USA	5,307	2	Switzerland	8,939	2	USA	16,607	2	Switzerland	20,830
3	New Zealand	3,115	3	New Zealand	5,115	3	New Zealand	8,495	3	Canada	13,644	3	Hong Kong	19,592
4	Belgium	2,640	4	UK	5,032	4	Australia	7,218	4	Sweden	13,494	4	Japan	19,505
5	Netherlands	2,640	5	Canada	4,213	5	Canada	7,047	5	Denmark	13,416	5	Denmark	19,305
6	USA	2,457	6	Switzerland	4,207	6	UK	6,847	6	Germany	13,152	6	Germany	19,097
7	Switzerland	2,172	7	Belgium	4,130	7	Sweden	6,738	7	France	12,940	7	Singapore	18,797
8	Denmark	1,927	8	Netherlands	3,950	8	Denmark	6,683	8	Netherlands	12,763	8	Norway	18,372
9	Germany	1,913	9	Germany	3,833	9	Netherlands	5,850	9	New Zealand	12,575	9	Canada	18,350
10	Austria	1,875	10	Denmark	3,764	10	Belgium	5,346	10	Australia	12,485	10	France	17,968
11	France	1,858	11	Austria	3,488	11	France	5,221	11	UK	11,920	11	Austria	17,285
12	Ireland	1,775	12	France	3,452	12	Norway	4,969	12	Belgium	11,905	12	Belgium	17,225
13	Sweden	1,664	13	Sweden	3,096	13	Germany	4,281	13	Austria	11,308	13	Netherlands	17,152
14	Canada	1,620	14	Ireland	2,733	14	Finland	4,131	14	Japan	11,017	14	Australia	17,107
15	Italy	1,467	15	Italy	2,507	15	Austria	3,731	15	Finland	10,768	15	Sweden	16,710
16	Spain	1,376	16	Norway	2,275	16	Ireland	3,518	16	Italy	10,409	16	Italy	16,404
17	Norway	1,303	17	Spain	2,255	17	Italy	3,425	17	Norway	10,229	17	UK	16,371
18	Finland	1,107	18	Finland	2,050	18	Spain	2,397	18	Spain	8,739	18	New Zealand	15,085
19	Portugal	1,085	19	Greece	1,621	19	Portugal	2,132	19	Greece	7,779	19	Finland	14,779
20	Japan	741	20	Portugal	1,354	20	Singapore	2,038	20	Portugal	7,568	20	Taiwan	12,985

Note: P.H. – per head.
Source: Adapted from Crafts (1997: 13–15).

and individualistic producers, with their efforts unco-ordinated; this example amongst others surely reinforces Eichengreen's contention that institutional lock-in is partly responsible for Britain's relative economic decline (Eichengreen 1996a: 216).

Phelps Brown quoting Ronald Dore draws attention to the importance of history, 'The way a country comes to industrialisation can have a lasting effect on the kind of industrial society it becomes. It will be a long time before Britain loses the marks of the pioneer, the scars and stiffness that come from the searing experience of having made the first, most long-drawn-out industrial revolution' (Phelps Brown 1977: 20).[1] Those involved in the productivity drive were not unaware of this. Graham Hutton was explicit, 'We have to recognize the greater rigidity of British and European institutions...' (Hutton 1953: 141). Thirty-seven years after the productivity drive Hutton, one of its greatest prophets and promoters, lamented that British labour and management institutions had indeed been slow to change for the British economy was slipping ever further behind its rivals – the productivity drive had been for him a failure (Hutton 1980). One can only speculate if Hutton would have reached the same conclusion in 1990 after Thatcher's attempts at productivity improvement. Hutton's comments about British institutions have considerable plausibility for the basic features of institutions are that they are static, inherited from the past, past glorifying, psychologically defensible, dictatorial, and creatures of habit. Therefore institutions are resistant to change and do not accept it easily (Wendell 1980: 17). Thus we may concur with Wendell, 'Institutional sanctioned behaviour patterns control the tempo at which the institution will permit new technical knowledge to come into use.' Institutions that resist change will therefore slow down the adoption of new, more efficient techniques (Wendell 1980: 25). The productivity drive has shown us that British economic performance was profoundly affected by the historical legacies of many institutions, particularly the state.

Many economists would agree with the sentiment of Baily, 'Public policy to encourage productivity growth is multidimensional and often indirect, in the sense that it is often better aimed at creating economic conditions and incentives that encourage agents in the economy to increase productivity, rather than having the government seek to increase productivity in any direct way' (Baily 2002: 19). Many economists would also agree with the assertion that macroeconomic policy over the last ten years has been better than at any time since the end of the Second World War particularly because of the foundation of the Bank of England Monetary Policy Committee setting interest rates, rather than politicians, which has helped to dampen cyclical fluctuations. This is surely in part responsible for the fact that from 1992–93 to 2004 the British economy has grown continuously at or near its long-run-trend rate of growth of 2.0–2.2 per cent per annum; a feat not equalled in recorded British economic history. In the light of this and Baily's quote above, the question then arises why it is that studies of Britain's productivity (Mckinsey Global Institute 1998; Porter and Ketels 2003: 9–14) still report that it lags significantly behind its most serious industrial competitors, when many of them have experienced less growth and poorer macroeconomic environments. Though Britain may be the world's oldest industrial economy it sill provides much work for economic historians yet.

Notes

1 Introduction: Institutions and the quest for productivity

1. Booth drew heavily on the findings of Broadberry's *The Productivity Race* to reach his assertion that during the Long Boom '... Britain's manufacturing performance was mildly disappointing' (Booth 2003: 10).
2. The definition belongs to Lynne Zucker quoted in Rowlinson (1997: 82-3).
3. For a very good and succinct survey of the Old and the New institutional economics, see Rutherford (1996; 2001) and Tsuru (1993).
4. Many economists would agree with this assertion, as Oulton says, 'It is now generally agreed that the explanation for differences between countries in long-run growth rates should be sought in institutions...', see Oulton (1995: 53).
5. Transaction costs consist of arranging a contract and monitoring and enforcing it once it has been agreed. Production costs are the costs of executing a contract (Matthews 1986: 906).
6. Crafts sees game theoretical analysis as one of the major advances that has come to economic history from the application of economic analysis and one of a number of profitable ways by which economic historians can hope to give a far more sophisticated view of the past, see Crafts (1991c).
7. 'Time-shape' refers to the path or trajectory that consumption and investment take over time which was agreed by the workers and capitalists at the outset.
8. For examples of extensions and explorations of Lancaster's framework and further interesting discussion, see Elster (1984: 91-2), Grout (1984), Hoel (1978), and Ploeg (1987).
9. For an elucidating and in-depth theoretical perspective similar to that of Eichengreen's on economic growth, which pays particular attention to the impact of differing technologies, see Schott (1984). Hargreaves Heap purports that most economic interactions can be viewed from three angles of game theory; either a prisoner's dilemma, a co-ordination game, or a bargaining game. The outcome of these games is influenced decisively by the institutional context. In connection with Eichengreen, Hargreaves Heap also sees the explanation for the post-War diversity in economic performance between both the European and the other industrialised countries as having new light shed on it by institutional explanations involving the three types of games mentioned, see Hargreaves Heap (1991).
10. A Pareto superior outcome is a situation where one person can be made better-off without anybody being made worse-off. Contrast this with a Pareto optimal outcome where nobody can be made better-off without making somebody else worse-off.
11. This concept is made in greater explanatory detail by Elster (1989: 181-2).
12. A similar and related finding was made by Freeman (1988).
13. Also see in the bibliography the other many writings by Tomlinson on the quest for productivity during this period.

14. Many other writers have noted this fact. For instance, Eltis (1996: 191) and Pelling (1996: Ch. 3). See also Dintenfass (1992: 46) for international comparisons which again stress the poor returns on UK investment.

15. Embodied technical progress is technical improvement which is contained in the net or replacement capital stock. Disembodied technical progress is technical improvement in new capital stock

16. Richard was General Secretary of the *Confédération Génénrale du Travail – Force Ouvière* (hereafter CGT-FO), Vice-Chairman of the AFAP, and a founder-Chairman of the French trade unions centre for the study of productivity.

17. For more evidence, see MRC.MSS.292/552.371/1, 'Anglo-American Council on Productivity, verbatim report of the final meeting of the U.K. specialist team on Mechanical Aids and Material Handling held on Friday, November 4 1949', n.d. p. 3. MRC.MSS.292/552.371/1, 'Anglo-American Council on Productivity, verbatim report of the final meeting of the specialist team on Mechanical Aids and Material Handling held on Friday, November 4 1949', n.d. p. 12. Hutton (1953: 14, 20–1, 25–7, 29, 61, 64). For general evidence that the UK was significantly behind the USA in the application of automation and more generally advanced technology, see Bailey, *Automation in North America*, reported in BPC, Bulletin, No. 50, 29 January 1958, p. 3, in MRC.MSS.292/552.471/3. Bagrit (1966: 53–6), Goodman, *Man and Automation*, p. 70, and Carew (1987: 40).

18. For examples, see Wollard, *What Automation Means*, BPC, Bulletin, Supplement, June 1955. MRC.MSS.292/571.88/1, Colomb S. and Liénart, P., 'About automation', n.d. MRC.MSS.292/571.81/4. Harle, R., 'American trade unions and automation', n.d. MRC.MSS.292/557.371/1a, Southwell, E., 'Application of automation in Europe', n.d. The EPA held an international seminar for trade unionists on automation, see MRC.MSS.292/571.88/1, 'EPA trade union seminar on automation, final report, London 14–17 May 1956', n.d. MRC. MSS. 200/F/5/S2/14/1, Haskins, B. C., 'BPC seminar: low cost automation', 1962.

19. MRC.MSS.292/552.471/5, 'Analysis of team reports', n.d. See also MRC.MSS. 292/552.737/2B, 'Analysis of The Anglo-American productivity team reports', 2 December 1952. See also Carew (1987: 136–7), where Carew notes that in 1950 the AACP's sub-committee on mechanisation was disbanded. Along with mechanical aids was, first, appreciation by work people of the need for higher productivity, the second most important factors were modern methods of costing, production, planning, and control, the third most important factors were the spirit of competition and work study.

20. MRC.MSS.200/F/3/D3/7/43, 'Anglo-American Council on Productivity, digest of reports – Pressed Metal Team (United Kingdom Productivity Team No. 4)', 27 September 1949, p. 1.

21. MRC.MSS.292/552.471/3, BPC Bulletin, No. 26, November 1955, p. 4.

22. Ibid., BPC, Bulletin, No. 59, 27 October 1958, p. 4.

23. Ibid., BPC, Bulletin, No. 41, April 1957, p. 3. MRC.ibid., BPC, Bulletin, No. 19, April 1955, p. 6.

24. MRC.MSS.292/552.436/1, 'British Productivity Council, summary of activities of the local productivity committees and associations, September 1958–April 1959', 21 May 1959. MRC.MSS.292/552.471/3, See for example the BPC, Bulletins, No. 31, June 1956; No. 39, February 1957; No. 50, 29 January

1958; No. 58, 29 September 1958; No. 59, 27 October 1958; No. 60, 27 November 1958; No. 61, 23 December 1958; No. 62, January 1959; No. 63, 26 February 1959; No. 65, 30 April 1959; No. 72, 29 December 1959; TBBPC, No. 1, January 1960; TBBPC, No. 3, March 1960; and TBBPC, No. 6, June 1960.

2 British workers and Britain's relative economic decline

1. Taylor notes that trade unions have suffered long-standing criticism from some quarters, 'From their origins in the nineteenth century, trade unions have been viewed with hostility by economists and employers' (Taylor 1982: 142).
2. Although it should be noted that in such models multiple unionism is assumed, as is that unions bargain independently, are self-interested maximises, and that they are myopic.
3. Strictly speaking, workers are receiving an economic rent when their pay is above their transfer earnings, which is what they could gain in their next best occupation (Creedy 1984: 233–4).
4. See also Brittan (1978) for a similar argument to Olson's but it applies to the UK only.
5. Batstone defines union scope as the proportion of a workforce, which the union has in membership and aspires to have – its relative size – and the nature of its membership, union sophistication is defined by internal organisational arrangements and resources (Batstone and Gourlay 1986: 22–4).
6. Barnett in his widely read and influential work wrote that, '... trade unions, [were] possibly the strongest single factor militating against technical innovation and high productivity'. Barnett also stated that, 'From the very beginning the machine was perceived by British work people as an enemy; technical progress as the destroyer of status and independence' (Barnett 1986: 273–4, 189). Mokyr wrote, '... the resistance to technological change played an important role in the demise of Britain's [economic] leadership', one of the routes by which this occurred was through the system of labour relations, '... in which unions developed mechanisms to short-circuit new technologies', (Mokyr 1992: 336; 2000: 81). Kaplinsky seems to sum up a general perception which must surely reside with many people, and not just some academics, that, '... in the UK, ... through a process of extended struggle, the trade unions have managed to prevent or slow down the introduction of new labour displacing automation technologies' (1984: 147).
7. Knight used three measures of strike activity – days lost, strike frequency, and the median duration of strikes.
8. Addison and Chilton have argued that in the long run unionised workers must have higher productivity than non-unionised ones. If they did not, then unionised firms would go out of business, because the higher wage which is usually associated with unionised workers would make a firm in which they were host less profitable than one where they were not. Eventually due to the increasing cumulative productivity divergence between the two types of firm, all unionised firms would either go bankrupt or be taken over, by non-unionised ones. Thus *a priori* in a long-run competitive market situation unionised firms must exhibit higher productivity. See Addison and Chilton (1993).

9. Machine tools can be considered to be of strategic and paramount importance to an economy because they are the only forms of machinery that are 'self-reproducible'. For more on this see Chapter 7.
10. The technologies were: NCMTs, Machine Centres, Computer Numerically Controlled, Direct Numerical Control, Computer Aided Design and Manufacture, Industrial Robots, and Flexible Manufacturing Systems.
11. MRC.MSS.292/571.88/1, Colomb, S., 'Automation in the Renault works', in 'EPA trade union seminar on automation, final report, London 14–17 May 1956', n.d. p. 42.

3   British workers and the productivity drive: A comparative perspective

1. Taylor writing about the early 1950s says, 'Many union leaders . . . were well aware of Britain's increasingly poor productivity performance . . .' (Taylor 1993: 85). The government in 1955 established a cabinet committee to examine reform of industrial relations practices because of the rising level of unofficial strikes and rising wage settlements (Davis Smith 1990: 120–3).
2. MRC.MSS.292/552.471/3, BPC, Bulletin, No. 41, 25 April 1951, p. 1.
3. MRC.MSS.292/552.471/4, TBBPC, No. 7, July–August 1960, p. 6, letter to the editor from R. W. James. Local productivity committees were also aware of the problem, which endured to the 1960s; in one particular piece of promotional literature, the Tyneside Productivity Committee stated, 'The present rate of increase of our productivity is not so great as our main competitors.' See MRC.MSS.292/552.434/10, 'Tyneside Productivity Committee: draft copy', n.d. but probably early 1950s, p. 2.
4. MRC.MSS.200/C/3/EDU/7/1, TBBPC, No. 1, Vol. 18, January 1965, front cover.
5. Tomlinson also stresses that in the 1940s and 50s productivity was nearly always defined in terms of labour (Tomlinson 1996a: 740).
6. MRC.MSS.292/552.4/2a, letter to Dr Schneider from Secretary, Production Department, 10 December 1953. From 1955–56 Edwin Fletcher was Deputy Director of the EPA.
7. MRC.MSS.292/552.32/3a, 'AACP third session: draft minutes of morning session', 18 October 1952.
8. MRC.MSS.292/552.4/4, 'Notes for Mr. Gaitskell', 10 April 1959, p. 4.
9. MRC.MSS.292B/552.434/7, letter to Mr Poole, Secretary, Cannock and District Trades Council, from Patrick Fisher, Secretary, Production Department, TUC, 31 October 1963.
10. MRC.MSS.292B/552.434/7, letter to J. Whiston, Midland Federation of Trade Councils, from Organisation Department, TUC, 25 May 1964.
11. MRC.MSS.292B/552.434/15, 'Productivity Council a waste of time: cold shoulder for the man from the TUC', *Crawley and District Observer*, 11 September 1964. Letter to Colleague, TUC, from H. Harwood, Secretary, Crawley Trades Council, 19 March 1963 and 'Crawley National Productivity Year Committee: Trades Council to continue boycott of National Productivity Year', 4 April 1963. See also MRC.MSS.292B/552.434/7, 'Productivity Year a failure? Trade unionists to quit' n.d. for Cannock Trade Council's withdrawal from its National Productivity Year Local Committee for similar reasons.

12. Middlemas wrote within the context of the 1940–50s, 'Productivity had always been an important target for the TUC...' (Middlemas 1986: 228).
13. MRC.MSS.292/552.455/3a, TUC interdepartmental correspondence from LM to JAH, 9 April 1957.
14. Ibid., TUC interdepartmental correspondence from L. Murray to R. Harle, 17 November 1955. It is perhaps not surprising that those in the TUC took such a dislike to Hutton's writings, for the editor of the *Economist* in 1951 wrote to Sir Norman Kipping, Director General of the FBI, and told him that he found Hutton's literary style, '...a little confused', see MRC.MSS.200/F/3/D3/7/82, letter to Norman Kipping from Geoffrey Crowther, 16 July 1951. MRC.MSS.292/552.455/3a, TUC interdepartmental correspondence from L. Murray to R. Harle, 17 November 1955.
15. MRC.MSS.200/F/3/S1/36/28, 'The foundations of high productivity: a special report prepared for the Anglo-American Council on Productivity', n.d. p. 1.
16. MRC.MSS.292/552.31/1, 'Trades Union Congress: "The foundations of high productivity": note on the Pleming–Waddell report: 10 October 1950', 6 October 1950, pp. 1–2.
17. MRC.MSS.292/552.434/10, 'Tyneside Productivity Committee', n.d. p. 2.
18. Eric Runacres said of those trade union leaders on the TUC General Council and members of the BPC that they, '...showed a considerable interest, and...often used to go down to LPA meetings and take a hand sometimes'. Interview with Eric Runacres, Deputy Director of the BPC 1959–71, Secretary 1962–71, Vice-Chairman of OECD Committee on National Productivity Centres 1960–66, conducted on 25 March 1997.
19. See for example, Carew (1987: 201, 208), who mentions Hill's attitude towards the TUC position on the productivity drive but does not report the speech in any direct form.
20. MRC.MSS.292/552.471/6, 'Trades Union Congress, statement by Mr E. J. Hill at the British Productivity Council Conference, 19 March 1953', 20 April 1953, p. 2.
21. Ibid., p. 1.
22. MRC.MSS.292/552.471/6, 'British Productivity Council Conference 1953, history of case', n.d. MRC.MSS.292/552.471/6, letter to TUC from Paisley Branch Scotland of the United Society of Boilermakers and Iron and Steel Shipbuilders, 14 April 1953. See the file MRC.MSS.292/552.471/6 for the letters in support.
23. MRC.MSS.292/552.471/6, letters to V. Tewson from the Bromley (Kent) Trades Council, 15 May and 2 July 1953.
24. MRC.MSS.292/552.455/2, letter to the Production Department from Tonbridge Trades Council, 30 September 1953. MRC.MSS.292/552.3/5, letter to Mr Harries TUC, from the Manchester and Salford Trades Council, 19 October 1948. MRC.292/552.3/5, letter to V. Tewson from Croydon Trades Council, 4 September 1948.
25. Public Records Office (hereafter PRO) BT258/1248, 'Second Regional Conference intended mainly for LPCs in the North & North Midland regions of England 17 December 1954', n.d. p. 2.
26. According to Eric Runacres, '...given what you would expect...the trade union support was very good', Runacres was referring to the BPC. Interview with Eric Runacres.

27. MRC.MSS.292/552.436/2, 'Extract from speech made by Sir Vincent Tewson I.C.F.T.U.-E.R.O. Conference of trade union officers', October 1953. See also letter to T. Hutton from V. Tewson, 3 March 1955.
28. MRC.MSS.36 A93(i), Fletcher, E., 'The automatic factory: what does it mean?', 17 June 1955, p. 4.
29. MRC.MSS.200 B/3/3/275 (58), BPC, Bulletin No. 72, 29 December 1959, p. 1.
30. MRC.MSS.292/571.81/5B, 'The National Union of Bank Employees: report on office management conference, report submitted by W. N. Bernard', n.d. p. 2.
31. MRC.MSS.292/552.455/3a, letter to T. Hutton from the General Secretary, 4 March 1955.
32. Ibid.
33. Economic historians also highlight this, Middleton for instance wrote, 'The experience of mass unemployment between the wars acted as the searing influence for a good 25 to 30 years after the war's end' (Middleton 1996: 539).
34. Batstone and Gourlay wrote, 'Unions then, are products of their past and agents of their future: it follows that their futures are to a degree shaped by their past' (1986: 21).
35. MRC.MSS.36 A93 (ii), Wright, L. T., 'Principle speeches and reports of working groups, 8–12 April 1957', n.d. p. 38.
36. Ibid., letter to Sir Vincent Tewson from F. C. Blackburn, 19 May 1955.
37. MRC.MSS.36 A93 (i), Fletcher, E., 'The automatic factory: what does it mean?', 17 June 1955, p. 4. James Crawford, President of the National Union of Boot and Shoe Operatives also thought that, 'In Great Britain because of what we have come to call "over-employment", there have been no immediate evidences of redundancy due to automation. Hence the reaction of the unions – as manifested at the recent Trades Union Congress – has not been as marked as in America.' See MRC.MSS.292/571.81/2, Crawford, J., 'Automation – a boon or a blessing? address to the Midlands TUC, Regional Advisory Committee', forwarded by Crawford to the TUC, 29 November 1955, p. 7.
38. MRC.MSS.36 A93 (i), Goodman, L. L., 'World trends in automation', *Financial Times*, 23 July 1956, p. 56.
39. Dartmann has asserted that co-determination provided German unions with the institution that allayed their fears about increased unemployment resulting from measures that increased the rate of productivity growth (Dartmann 1996a: 336).
40. MRC.MSS.36 A93 (i), 'America's workers shake hands with robots by Noel Clark', *Daily Mail*, 8 May 1956.
41. Ibid., 'Automation: a report to the UAW-CIO economic and collective bargaining conference held in Detroit, Michigan the 12th and 13th of November, 1954: a resolution on automation', n.d. p. 12.
42. MRC.MSS.292/564.1/3, 'The Benton Amendment to the Mutual Security Act: address by Senator William Benton before the Anglo-American Press Association, Paris, 7 November 1951', n.d. p. 11.
43. MRC.MSS.36 A93 (i), *South Wales Echo & Evening Express*, 9 November 1955.
44. MRC.MSS.292/571.81/5B, letter to Sir Vincent Tewson from Sir Thomas Miles, 11 March 1957, p. 2. Williamson in 1951 penned an article for the *Sunday Times* in which he wrote, 'Workers must be taken into closer consultation on all matters affecting the industry in which they are engaged...', and that, 'Management must give up the idea that this would be an interference

with managerial functions.' See MRC.MSS.200/F/3/S1/36/36, Williamson, T., 'Real wages: another view-point on industrial productivity', in 'Unity in industry: a call to labour and management', reprinted from the *Sunday Times*, 16 September 1951, pp. 7–8.

45. MRC.MSS.202/S/C/NM/3/3, 'British Motor Corporation: joint shop stewards' committee: automation conference 24th/25th September, resolutions', n.d.

46. MRC.MSS.36 A93 (I), 'Prelude to automation: shop stewards want full consultation', *Manchester Guardian*, 28 may 1955. Others argued for the wholesale resurrection of Joint Production Committees as a way of significantly improving productivity, see Scarr, A. E., 'Slog harder or work more effectively?', *Amalgamated Engineering Union Journal* (hereafter AEUJ), new ser. No. 17, XIV, May 1947, p. 143. Wilkinson, J. A., 'Joint consultation-key to productivity?', AEUJ, new ser. No. 10, October 1956, p. 310.

47. MRC.MSS.292/557.91/5, 'Trades Union Congress: report of conference of General Council members of the National Production Advisory Council on Industry with representatives of the National Union of Pottery Workers, 16 June 1949', 22 June 1949, p. 2.

48. Tiratsoo and Tomlinson assert that they were only compulsory for enterprises with over 100 workers, and they were essentially consultative covering welfare and production issues, but they were kept out of wages and conditions of work questions – like JPCs in the UK (Tiratsoo and Tomlinson 1993: 105).

49. MRC.MSS.292/571.81/4, Harle, R., 'American trade unions and automation', n.d. pp. 46–7.

50. MRC.MSS.292/557.37/1a, Southwell, E., 'Application of automation in Europe', n.d. pp. 26–7.

51. MRC.MSS.292/552.31/1, 'Anglo-American Council on Productivity, sessions on Friday, 29 October' aide-memoire', 29 October 1948, p. 1.

52. MRC.MSS.292/571.81/5B, 'Meeting between the Production Committee and CSEU: notes for chairman', 15 July 1957. However this remark seems to stand at odds with what Lewis Wright told his audience when he was chairman of the BPC and General Secretary of the AWA:

> On the other hand, you need have no suspicions that the BPC is a device through which trade unions attempt to tell management how to do its job. There is nothing of that. It is common ground to us all that the responsibility for raising productivity rests with management ... [Trade unions] play their part by creating an atmosphere of opinion by which efficient management can do its best.

See MRC.MSS.200B/3/3/270 pt. 1, 'Speech by Lewis T. Wright at B.P.C. Meeting in the T.U.C. Congress Hall', 16 December 1958, p. 2.

53. MRC.MSS.292B/552.434/2, letter to Secretary, S. W. Hert's. Productivity Association from John Branson, Secretary, Watford Trades Council, 20 November 1969. The S. W. Hert's. Productivity Association was to emphatically deny this claim, by asserting that at its last two seminars trade union participation was 50 and 35 per cent respectively, see MRC.ibid., letter to Mr Branson from R. W. Reeves, Chairman, S. W. Hert's. Productivity Association, 27 November 1969.

54. MRC.MSS.292B/552.434/11, letter to G. Woodcock, General Secretary, TUC, from Hon. Secretary, Shirebrook and District Trades Council, 12 June 1962.

55. MRC.MSS.292/571.81/5B, 'Meeting between the Production Committee and CSEU: notes for chairman', 15 July 1957.

56. Conway, J., 'Trade unions and automation', AEUJ, new ser. No. 12, December 1963, p. 426.

57. MRC.MSS.200/F/3/D3/7/102, '140 shop stewards in frank exchanges', *National Productivity Year News, November 1962–November 1963*, No. 11, June 1963.

58. MRC.MSS.200/C/3/EDU/7/1, 'Mr Woodcock on why productivity is also concern of the unions', TBBPC, Vol. 18, No. 1, January 1965.

59. MRC.MSS.292/557.342/10, 'Transatlantic study group to Europe, September–October 1960: report of an American study group to the European Productivity Agency (O.E.E.C.)', n.d. p. 10

60. Ibid., p. 30.

61. MRC.MSS.292/557.342/10, 'Transatlantic study group to Europe, September–October 1960: report of an American study group to the European Productivity Agency (O.E.E.C.)', n.d.

62. At a meeting of the Co-operative Research Sub-Committee of the Productivity and Applied Research Committee of the OEEC, a representative from the European Recovery Programme Trade Union Advisory Committee indicated that the attitude of trade unions towards the extension of automation, would incorporate the desire for the full consultation between managements and trade unions regarding automation's introduction into the firm. According to H. K. Mitchell who compiled the Report for the President of the Confederation of European Industrial Federations the representative of the European Recovery Programme Trades Union Advisory Council appeared to have adopted a sensible attitude to the general question of the introduction of automation. See MRC.MSS.200/B/3/2/C1162 pt. 2, H. K. Mitchell, 'Council of European Industrial Federations, automatic processes in industry, preliminary meeting held in Paris on 10th June 1955, of the ad hoc group of the Co-operative Research Sub-Committee of the Organisation of European Economic Co-operation, report to the president of the C.E.I.F.', 27 June 1955.

63. MRC.MSS.292/557.342/10, 'Transatlantic study group to Europe, September–October, 1960: report of an American study group to the European Productivity Agency (O.E.E.C.)', n.d. p. 11. An example of this was when new machinery was installed in a certain area of cotton manufacture. In the first three weeks the new machine system was experimental and the operatives could go back to the old system if they wished, however they decided not to and their average earnings had risen by 10 per cent. See MRC.MSS.292/552.32/3a, 'Third session: draft minutes of morning session, 18th October', 29 October 1951 p. 2.

64. MRC.MSS.292/557.342/10, 'Transatlantic study group to Europe, September–October, 1960: report of an American study group to the European Productivity Agency (O.E.E.C.)', n.d. p. 12.

65. This is because managers may have strong financial incentives to engage in opportunistic credit-taking and make it appear that they are the originators of innovative ideas rather than their employees (Smith 1990: 6–8).

66. MRC.MSS.292/571.81/5A, 'Trades Union Congress, Sci. Adv. Cttee.' 31 January 1955', see also TUC, *Report*, 1955, pp. 247–9.

67. MRC.MSS.292/557.37/2, Cynog-Jones, T. W., 'Workers investment in industry: follow-up of the investment trade union seminar of the Hague (November

1956)', n.d. pp. 29–30. Cynog-Jones was at the time the Research Director of the USDAW (Carew 1987: 191).

68. MRC.MSS.36 A93 (i) Goodman, L. L., 'World trends in automation', *Financial Times*, 23 July 1956, p. 56.

69. Priest, 'Automation replacing workers in U.S. industry', AEUJ, XXII, new ser. No. 8, July 1955, p. 217.

70. MRC.MSS.36 A93 (i), 'Automation: a report to the UAW-CIO economic and collective bargaining conference held in Detroit, Michigan the 12th and 13th of November 1954', n.d. p.18.

71. MRC.MSS.292/571.81/4, Harle, R., 'American trade unions and automation', n.d. p. 45.

72. Ibid., p. 47.

73. MRC.MSS.292/552.4/2a, letter to V. Tewson from Tonbridge Trades Council, 2 September 1953.

74. MRC.MSS.292/557.35/1, Wright, L. T., 'Sharing the benefits of higher productivity in the United Kingdom', 13 November 1956, p. 1.

75. MRC.MSS.200/F/3/S1/36/36, Evans, L., 'A trade-union view', in 'Unity in industry: a call to labour and management', reprinted from the *Sunday Times*, 16 September 1951, p. 11.

76. MRC.MSS.292/552.4/2a, letter to BPC from Southport Trades Council and Labour Party, 18 September 1953.

77. MRC.MSS.292/552.455/3a, letter to the General Secretary from Morecambe and Heysham Trades Council, 13 August 1956.

78. MRC.MSS.292/557.3/1, 'Labour News Bulletin on European economic cooperation', January 1954.

79. MRC.MSS.200/B/3/2/C1093, pt. B3, 'Letter from Watford LPC', n.d.

80. Ibid., 'British Productivity Council: memorandum from Watford L.P.C. on sharing the proceeds of greater productivity', 7 February 1955.

81. MRC.MSS.292/552.4/3, 'Memorandum, answer to E.P.A. questionnaire', 25 February 1958, p. 6. The BPC effectively functioned as the UK's NPC.

82. MRC.MSS.292/552.4/2a, letter to E. Jones from the Production Secretary, 22 October 1953.

83. MRC.MSS.292/552.434/7, 'Productivity committee off to a good start', 8 June 1954, and letter to A. J. Speakman from Production Department, 29 July 1954.

84. MRC.MSS.292/557.37/1a, Harle, 'American trade unions and automation', n.d. MRC.MSS.292/571.88/1, Colomb, S., 'Automation in the Renault Works', in 'Trade union seminar on automation, final report, London 14–17 May 1956', n.d. MRC.MSS.292/571.81/4, Southwell, E., 'Application of automation in Europe', n.d.

85. MRC.MSS.36 A93 (i) 'UAW ammunition: a report on world automotive labour', July 1956, p. 34.

86. MRC.MSS.200 B/3/3/270 pt. 1, 'Board workers share £34,000: production plan success', *Stroud News and Journal*, 20 February 1959.

87. MRC.MSS.200 B/3/3/275 (58), '20-man firm shows way to raise productivity', BPC, Bulletin, No. 71, 30 November 1959, p. 7.

88. MRC.MSS.292/564.171/1, 'E.R.P. Trade Union Advisory Committee – labour news bulletin on E.R.P. O.E.E.C. news in brief, 30 November 1950', n.d. p. 5. See also, "E.R.P. Trade Union Advisory Committee – labour news bulletin on

E.R.P. O.E.E.C. news in brief, 15 September 1950', No. 23, 15 September 1950', n.d. p. 7.

89. According to the report some 30 delegates attended, representing all the associations which were affiliated to either the International Confederation of Free Trade Unions or the International Confederation of Christian Trade Unions. The seminar was presided over by James Crawford and William Carron, both members of the General Council of the TUC, five papers were given on various aspects of automation in western Europe. This was followed by a question and answer session. Statements were also provided by Crawford, and the TUC on British trade union attitudes towards automation, and Ted Silvey and Nat Weinberg of the AFL-CIO gave a report of American trade union policy on automation.

90. MRC.MSS.292/571.88/1, 'EPA trade union seminar on automation, final report, London 14–17 May 1956', n.d. p. 6.

91. Goodman writing in the 1950s tells us that a transfer machine is essentially a series of machines which are linked by mechanical handling equipment. The part being machined is moved automatically from one machine to the next (Goodman 1957: 45).

92. MRC.MSS.292/571.88/1, Colomb, S., 'Automation in the Renault works', In 'EPA trade union seminar on automation, final report, London 14–17 May 1956', n.d. pp. 32–48.

93. MRC.MSS.292/571.88/1, Liénart, P., 'The development of automation in the administrative techniques of the S.N.C.F', p. 70, in 'EPA trade union seminar on automation, final report, London 14–17 May 1956', n.d. pp. 58–74.

94. Glass manufacture was a 24-hour process, running seven days a week, and production was at the rate of 25 batches of 3000 lb., every hour. That is to say a batch was produced every two minutes and 24 seconds, or 20.83 lb. every second.

95. Automation increased production to batches of 4200 lb. at the rate of one every two minutes and 30 seconds, or 28 lb. every second, a productivity improvement of 34.4 per cent. Production was still 24 hours a day seven days a week.

96. MRC.MSS.292/571.88/1, McLaughlin, J. R., 'Automation in the glass industry', in 'EPA trade union seminar on automation, final report, London 14–17 May 1956', n.d. pp. 49–57.

97. Furthermore that, 'Standard had gone further than most other British firms in sharing authority with labour and in automating the production process. Standard was also one of the first to realise that as capital–labour relations rose, labour could use its control of shop-floor decisions to enhance its bargaining leverage' (Lewchuk 1987: 201).

98. The Standard strike led to the Department of Scientific and Industrial Research compiling its report *Automation*.

99. BPC, *Policy and Progress 1954–55*, October 1955, pp. 17–18. BPC, 'Memorandum submitted by the British Productivity Council', 25 May 1960, p. 279. For more details of the BPC's Work Study Unit see MRC.MSS.200/F/3/S1/36/46, 'British Productivity Council: seventh report upon the activities of the Work Study Unit', 2 March 1956. The BPCs film, 'Introducing Work Study' one amongst 150 BPC films, was to prove one of its most highly demanded films in Norway, and in 1957 was to win first prize in the Industrial Productivity

Section of the Harogate Festival of films in the service of industry, see MRC.MSS.292/552.471/3, BPC, Bulletin No. 59, 27 October 1958, p. 1.

100. Wright, L., 'Work study and the trade unions', in BPC, *Work Study in Theory and – Practice*.

101. TUC, *Trade Unions and Productivity*, p. 51. Carew notes that work study was crucial to the development of scientific management, something the BIM recognised (1987: 169).

102. According to Carew those 'beneath the level of national union leadership' were worried about the BPC's Work Study Unit being heavily reliant upon the personnel and teaching materials of ICI's work study department (1991: 66).

103. MRC.MSS.44/TBN.121/4, 'Application of work study to traffic operation, position as at 22.8.60', 31 August 1960.

104. Jones, R. G., 'Human problems in the application of work study', in BPC, *Work Study in Theory and – Practice*, p. 21.

105. MRC.MSS.44/TBN.55/1 1 of 2, 'Facts and figures about British railways 1958 staff edition', n.d. p. 9.

106. MRC.MSS.44/TBN.69/2, 'British Railways Productivity Council, list of practices examined by the council with their comments, conclusions and recommendations, appendix to report on productive efficiency dated November 1956', November 1956, p. 9.

107. MRC.MSS.44/TBN.60/2 3 of 3, 'British Railways Productivity Council: final report of the sub-committee on productive efficiency on British Railways', November 1956, p. 1.

108. Phillips, 'Decasualisation and disruption', p. 177.

109. BPC, *Productivity Review 24*, pp. 17, 26, 32.

110. Phillips, 'Decasualisation and disruption', p. 170.

111. Batstone and Gourlay (1986) reported in their study that effort levels tended to increase with technical change.

112. On the contentious notion of the issue of effort and the difficulty of measuring it, see Guest (1990).

113. MRC.MSS.292B/552.434/15, letter to Mr Jenner, Oxford and District Trades Council, from Secretary, Production Department, 24 March 1964.

114. Our analysis is superficially similar to that of Lewchuk's who used a game theoretic decision tree approach to outline the strategic possibilities facing labour and capital, but only with reference to automation and the British car industry (1987: 221–5).

115. MRC.MSS.79/AS/3/4, Williamson, T., 'The unions now', *Financial Times: Annual Review of British Industry*, 1955. Tom Williamson himself was in favour of voluntarism. At the 1947 TUC congress he said, 'I am one of those who still believe in the voluntary response of the people of this country if they are told by the government the whole of the facts and what those facts demand' (Wrigley 1996: 77).

116. 'Editors notes', AEUJ, XVI, new ser. No. 12, 1949, p. 353.

117. PRO BT258/1055, untitled minute 662 from M. E. Healy to Miss Ackroyd, 18 November 1959.

118. For example, the BPC stated, 'The Council does not intend to carry out its work by general exhortation.' See MRC.MSS.292/552.4/3, 'The objective', n.d.

119. J. M. Phillips of Coventry Motor Panels was of the opinion as regards the AACP Mechanical Handling Team that '...Trade Union members of the

team have done their part by addressing various union groups'. See MRC.MSS.200/F/3/D3/7/81, letter to T. J. Hutton from J. M. Phillips, 26 April 1950, p. 2.

120. PRO BT258/559, 'Board of Trade Committee on E.P.A. Matters: minutes of meeting held at the Board of Trade at 10.30 A.M. on Wednesday, 16 September 1959', 5 October 1959, p. 2.

121. Interview with Alexander King.

122. MRC.MSS.200/F/4/24/44, 'What FBI members are saying', FBI, *Review*, November 1957, No. 92, p. 61.

4 Britain's relative economic decline and the British state

1. Scultz's model is implicitly monetarist in that it assumes no long-term trade-off between inflation and unemployment.

2. The countries which Boltho measured were Australia, Austria, Denmark, Finland, France, Germany, Italy, Japan, Sweden, United States, and the United Kingdom.

3. It should be emphasised that according to Bacon and Eltis's definition, the non-market sector does not correspond exactly to the public sector, as nationalised industries which make a profit and council houses which are let at a full-cost-covering price are defined as being in the market sector. Only when products of the public sector are not sold at full cost price are they included in the non-market sector (Bacon and Eltis 1978: 31).

4. Rowthorn and Wells (1987: 4) criticise Bacon and Eltis succinctly when they say that Britain's problem has not been one of too few producers, but one of producers working at too low a level of productivity.

5. Interestingly they have turned to game theory and argued that British workers and managers no longer operate in a 'zero-sum' environment and that therefore workers are now co-operative with managers over institutional and organisational changes in the workplace which enhance productivity. The argument however looks tenuously connected to its original form (Bacon and Eltis 1996: Ch. 'Bacon and Eltis after 20 years').

6. Sked (1987: 39) believes there are five predominant factors in the UK's decline, one of these was '... an unavoidable world role after 1945, which imposed a heavy defence burden on her economy'. Kolko and Kolko (1972: 633) wrote with respect to the Korean War that, '... it was rearmament that caused the most serious structural shift in the British economy, dealing the final blow from which it never fully recovered'. Ellwood (1992: 186) wrote 'A wide historical consensus now exists which states that the Korean armament effort set a pattern of gross overspending on defence which caused permanent damage to Britain's economic prospects.' Barnett (1986: 304) wrote that defence expenditure, '... was to impose a heavy dead weight on Britain's sluggish economy and on her fragile balance of payments, suck away from exports scarce manufacturing resources in advanced technology, and continue the wartime concentration of much of Britain's even scarcer R&D resources on defence projects'. Barnett (1983: 10) says 'The country would have been

better off had it not been for futile attempts to remain a Great Power. This is, if you like, a decisive cause of the British disease.' Aaronovitch and Smith (1981: 70, 77) both agree that the Korean War rearmament programme may have led to the relative decline of British capitalism. Lastly Brett (1985: Ch. 6) puts heavy emphasis on Britain's world role and its large military expenditure as contributing to Britain's international decline.

7. Manser is not the only non-economic historian to be candid about the devastating effects the balance of payments has had on the economy. The one-time financial journalist Samuel Brittan said, '... the balance of payments fixation has been a disaster' (Brittan 1988: 7).

8. The 14 countries were Australia, Austria, Belgium, Canada, Denmark, UK, France, West Germany, Italy, Japan, Netherlands, Sweden, Switzerland, and the USA.

9. Others define industrial policy similarly as does Wyn Grant for example, '... industrial policy is a set of measures used by governments to influence the investment decisions of individual enterprises-public and private-so as to promote such objectives as lower unemployment, a healthier balance of payments and a generally more efficient industrial economy' (Grant 1982: 2).

10. For the importance of the manufacturing sector, see also Bazen and Thirlwall (1992).

11. Technically, market failure occurs when the First Fundamental Theorem of welfare economics is violated. Simply this theorem states that a Pareto optimal allocation of resources occurs when all consumers and producers behave competitively, there are 'enough' markets, and when all markets are in equilibrium. If any or all of these conditions do not hold then there is market failure (Ledyard 1989).

12. Ingham like Newton and Porter argues that the campaign for tariff reform, National Efficiency, and Harold Wilson's modernisation programme all floundered on the financial nexus. British capitalism developed in a peculiar way because of Britain's empire and imperialism. The Gold Standard is again seen as the totem by which the financial nexus dominated domestic production. A key component of the dominance of the financial nexus was what came to be called the Treasury View, this taken from the works of Ricardo, was that state interference in a market economy could not logically increase the real wealth of private economic agents (Ingham 1984).

13. This is a point with which Rubinstein in his *Capitalism, Culture, and Decline in Britain 1750–1990*, would most surely agree with, for he wrote, '... Britain was *never* fundamentally an industrial and manufacturing economy; rather it was *always*, even at the height of the industrial revolution, essentially a commercial, financial, and service-based economy whose comparative advantage always lay with commerce and finance' (1993: 24).

14. Marquand similarly traces the origins of the British state's inability to be discretionary and interventionist to the seventieth century, '... thanks in particular, to the victory of the English landed class over the Stuart Kings – one cannot speak of a "British state" in the way that one speaks

of a "French state" or, in modern times, of a "German state" '(Marquand 1988: 152).

15. Edgerton has consistently argued that Britain has been a highly technocratic and modernising state (1991a; 1994a,b).

5 The government and the productivity drive

1. MRC.MSS.292/552.471/3, BPC, Bulletin, No. 63, 26 February 1959, p. 1.
2. PRO BT258/1677, untitled note? to Mr E. Heinemann from Miss E. Llewellyn Smith, 24 June 1963, 'Grant to the British Productivity Council', to Mr O'Connell from G. Parker, 8 August 1963.
3. The Conservatives in 1968 published a policy statement *Fair Deal at Work*, which made the Donovan report look feeble. Tory opposition frontbencher Ian Macleod called the Donovan report a blueprint for inaction (Stewart 1978: 92–5). *Fair Deal At Work* proposed that collective bargaining contracts should normally be legally enforceable and that a conciliation period of 60 days should be enforced before strikes could go ahead and that there should be compulsory ballots of union members before a strike (Pelling 1992: 255–8). The Tory opposition under Edward Health were also promising to bring in a bill, which would end the exceptional immunities of the unions under law (Dell 1999: 385–9).
4. A high court judge and former Labour Member of Parliament, Lord Terence Norbert Donovan, led the Commission. Its members were George Woodcock (General Secretary and President of the TUC in 1965), Sir George Pollock (former director of the British Employers Confederation), Lord Alfred Robens (Chairman of the National Coal Board), John Thomson (Chairman of Barclays Bank), Lord Edwin Savory Tangley (businessman and solicitor), Hugh Clegg (Professor of Industrial Relations at Warwick University and considered to have been the driving intellectual force behind the report), Otto Kahn-Freund (Professor of Comparative Law at Oxford University), Andrew Akiba Shonfield (Director of Studies at the Royal Institute of International Affairs, former journalist, and in 1965 author of the highly influential book *Modern Capitalism*), Eric Wigham (writer and journalist), and Dame Mary Georgina Green (Headmistress of Kidbrooke School) and the only female member.
5. Others from the Oxford Group who undertook research for the Commission were Arthur Marsh, Hugh Clegg, Allan Flanders, John Hughes, and Alan Fox. These were chosen because according to Middlemas they were within the trade unions' reality of existence in contemporary society (Middlemas 1990: 227).
6. Cmnd, 1968 3623, 40, 261.
7. Ibid., 125–7, 203, 290, 300–1.
8. Ibid., 20, 29, 32–3, 37, 77–9, 80, 94, 261–2, 265.
9. Ibid., 14, 18–9, 32, 41–3, 46, 75, 85, 97, 120, 130, 128–30, 135–6, 198.
10. Ibid., 27, 79, 104–6, 179.
11. Ibid., 18, 29, 31, 47, 108, 179–81, 194, 261, 271.
12. Ibid., 26, 28–9, 32, 103–4, 188, 194.
13. Ibid., 79, 282, 284, 257–8.
14. Ibid., 28, 32, 75, 196, 200–2, 211, 216, 272–3.
15. Ibid., 47–8, 211, 263, 275.
16. Ibid., 39, 76, 84, 189, 196, 220, 265.

17. According to Dell the title of the white paper, paid tribute to Aneurin Bevan's book *In Place of Fear* (Dell 1999: 385–9).
18. In 1958 the Council consisted of Lord Cohen, Sir Harold Howitt and the economist Sir Dennis Robertson; in 1959 Professor Henry Phelps Brown succeeded Robbertson; and in 1961 Lord Heyworth and Sir Harold Emmerson succeeded Cohen and Howitt (Knowles 1952: 511).
19. The full-time chair of NIC was Sir Geoffrey Lawrence a barrister. Its members were Prof. H. S. Kirkaldy, Professor of industrial Relations at Cambridge University; Sir Harold Banwell, Secretary of the Association of Municipal Corporations; R. C. Tress Professor of Economics at Bristol University; Mr L. C. Hawkins a member of the London Transport Executive. It had no trade union or industry representatives, which was probably one reason why the TUC would not co-operate with it.
20. During its lifetime, the NBPI had 24 members drawn from trade unions, employers, universities, and 'public life'. They included Professor Hugh Clegg (an industrial relations specialist at Warwick University) who was a member for roughly one year, Joan Mitchell (Reader in Economics at Bristol University), Aubrey Jones (Chair and previously minister of Fuel and Power and Minister of Supply), and Hillary Marquand (former Minister of Pensions and Minister of Health). Jones, Clegg, and Mitchell wrote books either about their involvement with it or the wider issues of incomes and prices (Clegg 1971; Jones 1973; Mitchell 1972).
21. The nine-countries study covered Austria, the Netherlands, Norway, the former Federal Republic of Germany, Sweden, the UK, Denmark, Italy, and France.

6   Employers, managers, and Britain's relative economic decline

1. The concept of the transformation curve although not now widely used in economics is equivalent to the production function concept.
2. Granick's study was based on very large non-governmental enterprises in Britain, France, the Soviet Union, and the USA. The research on which his findings are based was conducted during the middle of the 1960s or earlier for the USA and the Soviet Union, and for France and Britain during 1963–65 and 1967.
3. Such as the Gilchrist-Thomas process in steel, mechanised cutting of coal, the Solvay process for making soda, and the Northrop automatic loom (an English invention) for the weaving of cotton.
4. See the exchanges with McCloskey by Aldcroft, Crafts, Kennedy, and Landes in McCloskey (1981: part 2).
5. In the building industry, failure to recognise the importance of steel frame construction, and in machine tools failure to take up new machinery and its piecemeal introduction leading to jumbled and uneconomic layouts (an industry we shall examine in the next chapter with respect to one specific EPA project), and complacency in the watch-making industry.
6. Gospel has also commented on similar lines, 'In both academic and popular discussion, the management of labour and the practice of industrial relations are often seen as having been major weaknesses of the British economy in the twentieth century' (Gospel 1988: 104).

7. Why Clegg uses the term re-negotiate is unclear for presumably he means abandonment.
8. Chandler defines economies of scale as the reduction in the unit costs of production and distribution as a function of the increased size of an operating unit. Economies of scope are defined as those resulting form joint production or distribution within a single operating unit to produce more than one product (Chandler 1990: 17).
9. Gospel and Palmer define management style as the way an individual or group of managers act on a day-to-day basis and how they manage their employees (1993: 63).
10. The National Training Survey is a nationally representative sample of all adults between the ages of 16 and 64 (59 for women).
11. MRC.MSS.292/557.91/5, 'The *Accountants Journal*: Anglo-American Joint Council on Productivity: some accountancy aspects', September 1948.
12. Caves was neither slow nor illiberal in apportioning blame to one particular group, that is, British workers (1980: 153).

7 British capital and the productivity drive: A comparative perspective

1. The Report also went on to quote approvingly from the TUC's *Trade Unions and Productivity*, which said 'Efficient management set the pace of productivity in American industry – not because of altruistic belief in social progress but from necessity (AACP 1950a: 51).
2. MRC.MSS.200/B/3/3/270 pt. 1, 'Speech by R. W. Mann, Chairman Tyneside LPC and Managing Director, Victor Products (Wallsend) Ltd, at BPC meeting in the TUC Congress Hall, December 1958', n. d. p. 2.
3. PRO BT258/1248, 'Report of the LPC conference held at Ashorne Hill from 5–6 November 1954: second regional conference intended mainly for LPCs in the North & North Midland Regions of England', 1954, n.d. p. 14.
4. MRC.MSS.292/552.471/2, 'British Productivity Council, review of publicity by ad hoc working party', January 1955, p. 4.
5. MRC.MSS.200/F/3/T3/28/3, Young, A. P., 'American management techniques and practices and the bearing on productivity in British industry', n.d. p. 9. Young visited the United States on a scholarship from the Institution of Works Managers. The purpose of Young's visit was to study productivity in the USA and then make known those techniques that might be applied with advantage to UK industry. Young spent 28 days in the USA and 7 in Canada in 1948.
6. Ibid., p. 27.
7. MRC.MSS.200/F/D3/7/30, letter from C. A. Peachey, works manager, Northern Electric Limited, to Sir Norman Kipping, 21 May 1952.
8. MRC.MSS.200/F/3/D3/7/80, letter to C. A. Peachey, Works Manager, Northern Electric Limited, from Sir Norman Kipping, 30 May 1952. The issue of work simplification is important because according to the DSIR Study, in general automation encouraged manufacturers to simplify and standardise their products and components so as to reduce costs as far as possible when introducing new machines (DSIR 1956: 47).

9. MRC.MSS.292/557.3/4, letter to TUC from W. Schevenels European Regional Organisation of the International Confederation of Free Trade Unions, 28 February 1957.

10. The Council of European Industrial Federations was established in 1949, and the FBI and BEC were members, moreover the FBI had been instrumental in its creation. Its prime purpose seems to have been as a conduit by which European views were made known in the USA (Link 1991: 309; Tiratsoo and Tomlinson 1997: 76).

11. PRO BT258/96, letter to Dr King from K. P. Harten, 23 September 1954 and note to Dakin from S. Stewart, 20 September 1954.

12. PRO BT258/559, 'Board of Trade committee on E.P.A. matters: minutes of a meeting held at the Board of Trade, 16 September 1959', 5 October 1959, p. 2. MRC.MSS.200/C/3/EDU/7/4, CBI Memorandum to Mr P. J. Casey from C. M. Woodhouse, 21 August 1969.

13. MRC.MSS.200/F/3/D3/10/11, 'Lord President', by E. M. Nicholson, 25 June 1948, 'Industrial productivity', n. d. Silberman was considered by those at the Treasury to be, '... one of the very small group of first-rate experts on the measurement of productivity in the United States or indeed the world...' The contemporary British productivity expert Rostas, confirmed to the Treasury that Silberman, 'knew his stuff'. Alexander King, recalled of Silberman that he was '... a fanatic, and he regarded productivity with far too much importance, and his kind of model for the kind of society he was wanting to provide, was a strictly American materialistic one...', interview with Alexander King.

14. Phillip Reed Chairman of General Electric and Chairman of the AACP who had lived in Britain for two years during the War and had been back to the UK many times since; also argued that the British economy's tradition of producing 'cut and design' products for foreign markets reduced the scope for volume production, see MRC.MSS.292/552.312/1, 'Anglo-American Council on Productivity at Federation of British Industries, session I, Monday, October 25th, 1948', n.d. pp. 12–44.

15. MRC.MSS.200/F/3/D3/7/83, 'Utilising the hammer', April 1952, p. 7.

16. Ibid., 'Something has been done', April 1952, p. 5.

17. MRC.MSS.200/F/8/D3/7/8, 'Anglo-American Council on Productivity (U.K. Section), interim progress report on the dissemination and implementation of productivity teams' recommendations', 22 November 1951, p. 13. See also MRC.MSS.200/F/3/D3/7/80, 'Progress in productivity: a review of improvements in British steel foundries 1948/1951', 17 August 1951.

18. Tiratsoo and Tomlinson (1998b: 115–16) who argue '... what the Americans wanted to supply was not in fact a self-contained and entire 'model' of production...'.

19. MRC.MSS.292/615.61/1, 'Trades Union Congress: the machine tool industry', 16 April 1958. MRC.ibid., TUC interdepartmental correspondence from V. Beck to Mr. L. Murray, 10 December 1954 (PEP 1966: 28). Machine tools are part of the primary capital goods sector of an economy, and are of the fixed (durable) type, as opposed to the circulating type (goods which get used up in the production process). Machine tools hold a strategic position in the growth process because they are the only ones capable of producing machines for other sectors of the economy (which then produce consumer

goods for example) and of 'self-reproduction'. More importantly shortages of supply can constrain economic growth (Hagemann 1990: 125). The import- ance of machine tools to economic growth is exemplified by the following quote, 'Machine tools have been at the core of manufacturing since the beginning of the industrial revolution. It could be argued that without new and effective machine tools, the industrial revolution which took place in Britain starting in the last quarter of the 18th century would not have taken place when it did' (Carlsson and Jacobsson 1995: 242–3).

20. MRC.MSS.292/615.61/2, 'Labour Party: Home Economic Policy Committee: the machine tool industry, February 1960', n.d. p. 10.

21. MRC.MSS.292/615.61/2, 'OEEC, EPA, promotion of and exchange of information on research in industrial economics: preliminary consideration of the possibility of making economic and technical surveys of the machine tool industry in member countries', 23 October 1959. In his letter of trans- mittal attached to the Report, Melman claimed that he had visited 15 firms and spoke to about a hundred people in the industry. By his own admission the firms he visited were the larger ones.

22. MRC.MSS.292/615/2, OEEC, EPA, 'Promotion of and exchange of informa- tion on research in industrial economics: preliminary consideration of the possibility of making economic and technical surveys of the machine tool industry in member countries', 23 October 1959, p. 26.

23. For example, the Norwegian Productivity Institute did not promote mass production, but instead sought to promote 'batch' production by encouraging Norwegian firms who batch produced to co-operate and network with each other (Amdam and Bjarnar 1998; McGlade 1997: 17–18).

24. MRC.MSS.292/615.61/2, 'OEEC, Machinery Committee: ad hoc meeting held on 2nd February, 1960, with a delegation from the European Committee for co-operation in the machine tool industry', 21 March 1960.

25. PRO BT258/998, 'Board of Trade: Machine Tool Advisory Council: minutes of the seventieth meeting of the Machine Tool Advisory Council held on Wednesday, 2nd December 1959', 17 December 1959.

26. The Machine Tool Advisory Council when considering Melman's Report decided to set up a sub-committee with Sir Stuart Mitchell as chairman to consider the Melman Report and to inform the Machine Tool Advisory Council of what action the UK machine tool industry could undertake following Melman's recommendations in his Report. This sub-committee held over 20 meetings and heard from Professor Melman himself, it included representa- tives from a number of firms, such as Alfred Herbert and General Electric.

27. PRO BT258/809, 'Report by the Sub-Committee of the Machine Tool Advisory Council appointed to consider Professor Melman's Report to the European Productivity Agency on the Machine Tool Industries of western Europe', September 1960.

28. MRC.MSS.292B/147.68/5, 'Automation and British industry: British confer- ence on automation and computing: first report of the research development panel', 1961. The Report was of a Conference which consisted of a number of research institutes and manufactures who noted that there were substan- tial areas of improvement which could be undertaken in British industry. Its members were from: Cambridge University, the British Iron and Steel Research Association, OECD, National Research Development Corporation,

Machine Tool Industry Research Association, Urwick and Orr Partners, Short Brothers and Harland, Unilever Ltd, Lansing Bagnall Ltd, and DSIR. Members of the Conference also thought that industries had let their development of capital equipment lag behind competitors, and that British manufactures usually expected machine builders to tailor their machines to the their special requirements. This left the machine builder with difficulty in selling the machines to other customers and therefore with little room for profit from long production runs and economies of scale, with which to cover their development costs.

29. MRC.MSS.292/564.171/1, 'E.R.P. Trade Union Advisory Committee: Labour News Bulletin on E.R.P. O.E.E.C. – news in brief, 30 November 1950', n.d. p. 5.

30. 'Memorandum submitted by the British Productivity Council: British Productivity Council, 25 May 1960', n.d. supplied by Eric Runacres.

31. PRO BT258/1248, 'Second regional conference intended mainly for LPCs in the North & North Midland regions of England 17 December 1954', n.d. p. 3. According to Alexander King however British industry was in some cases very aloof. Interview with Alexander King. On the other hand some companies could be only too keen to let others see their works. The Stores Controller of Lockheed Hydraulic Brake Co. Ltd Leamington Spa, wrote to Kipping after having read the AACP report *Freight Handling* to ask if the team wanted to come and see their pallet system working. See MRC.MSS. 200/F/3/ D3/7/71, letter to Sir Norman Kipping from L. J. Hoefkens, 5 October 1951.

32. PRO BT258/1248, 'Second Regional Conference intended mainly for LPCs in the North & North Midland regions of England 17 December 1954', n.d. p. 6.

33. Middlemas does not use the term LPC or LPA but instead 'Regional Production Committees'. However it is very difficult to envisage what else Middlemas can be referring to if not LPCs or LPAs (Middlemas 1986: 239).

34. PRO BT258/96, 'Sub-Committee on Technical Assistance: United Kingdom Co-operation with European Productivity Agency', 12 March 1954, pp. 3, 8. PRO BT64/4741, 'Note of a meeting between the President of the Board of Trade and other Ministers to discuss problems connected with productivity', by F. W. Glaves-Smith, April 1954.

35. PRO BT64/4741, 'Note of a meeting between the President of the Board of Trade and other Ministers to discuss problems connected with productivity', by F. W. Glaves-Smith, April 1954, p. 3.

36. MRC.MSS.200/F/3/S1/36/21, McGraw, J. H., 'A businessman looks at Europe', pt. 'Britain: the outlook for its recovery', n.d.

37. MRC.MSS.292/564.1/3, 'The Benton Amendment to the Mutual Security Act: address by Senator William Benton before the Anglo-American Press Association, Paris, November, 7, 1951', 7 November 1951, pp. 3, 8, 12.

38. MRC.MSS.292/564.11/5a, 'Advisory board 4th session: opinion of the Council of European Industrial Federations on the future of the European Productivity Agency, 13 April 1959', n.d. p. 4.

39. Mercer has claimed that every time in the 1940s and 1950s there was a movement to strengthen competition policy there always followed calls for trade union restrictive practices to be tackled (Mercer 1995: 175).

40. MRC.MSS.292/564.1/3, 'The Benton Amendment to the Mutual Security Act: address by Senator William Benton before the Anglo-American Press Association, Paris, November 7, 1951', n.d. p. 5.

41. MRC.MSS.292/552.312/2, 'Anglo-American Council on Productivity, committee B, report of U.K. section: maintenance of productive plant and power', n.d. See also MRC.MSS.292/552.3/1, letter to T. L. Rowan from Secretary, Organisation Department, TUC, 2 November 1948.
42. MRC.MSS.292/552.3/5, letter from H. E. Newbold, Secretary, Manchester and Salford Trades Council to Mr E. P. Harries, Organisation Department, TUC, 19 October 1948.
43. MRC.MSS.200/F/3/E3/2/1, 'Draft: appeal to industry to reduce investment in plant and machinery, 26 November 1947', n.d.
44. MRC.MSS.292/552.471/3, BPC, Bulletin, No. 27, December 1955, p. 1.
45. MRC.MSS.292/552.312/1, 'Anglo-American Council on Productivity at Federation of British Industry, session I, Monday, October 25th, 1948', n.d. p. 26.
46. MRC.MSS.200/F/3/E3/2/2, 'Minutes of the meeting of the Home Economic Policy Committee, 4 October 1948', 12 October 1948.
47. MRC.MSS.36 A93 (i) Goodman, L. L., 'World trends in automation', *Financial Times*, 23 July 1956, p. 56. Leyland writing in the early 1950s also felt the same, 'There is some evidence to suggest that the more generous depreciation allowances for tax purposes in America have played a part in the growth of capital there', see Leyland (1952: 396).
48. PRO, BT190/9, 'West Germany's rising Competition with British exports', extract from the Board of Trade Journal, 28 July 1956.
49. MRC.MSS.200/F/3/D3/10/11, note to Mr Rowan, 'Industrial productivity', n.d.
50. MRC.MSS.200/F/D3/7/30, letter from C. A. Peachey, works manager, Northern Electric Limited, to Sir Norman Kipping, 21 May 1952.
51. MRC.MSS.200 B/3/2/C1162 pt. 2, letter to Mr. Burton BEC, from Tom Normanton, 31 December 1956.
52. MRC.MSS.200 F/3/S1/36/21, McGraw, J. H., 'A businessman looks at Europe', pt. 'Britain: the outlook for its recovery', n.d.
53. MRC.MSS.200 F/3/D3/7/27, letter to Norman Kipping FBI from Guy Locock FBI, 27 September 1950.
54. MRC.MSS.200 F/3/D3/7/27, letter to Sir Guy Locock, FBI, from C. Bailey, L. H. Doulton & Co. Limited, 21 September 1950.
55. According to a paper written by Kipping in 1954, the FBI did '... not deal with questions affecting wages or labour relations; they are the province of the British Employers Confederation...' (Kipping 1954: 2). See also Blank (1973: 16).
56. Victor Products mainly made mining machinery. It is probably the case that Mann was a very progressive employer for he had a wall chart at his works which showed the output of each section of the factory every month. Those sections which did well and beat a production target received a free packet of cigarettes for their workers from management and a bonus from a payment by results system. See MRC.MSS.292/557.97/1, 'The dogs tell the tale', n.d.
57. Harle, R., 'Scientific management-and how!', AEUMJ, Vol. XVIII, new. ser. No. 12 December 1951. Mann, R. W., 'Scientific management – and how!', AEUMJ, Vol. XIX, new ser. No. 2, February 1952.
58. MRC.MSS.200/F/3/E3/2/2, 'Home Economic Policy Committee, 16 December 1948', n.d. and 'Home Economic Policy Committee, 26 January 1949'.

59. MRC.MSS.200/F/3/D3/7/62, 'Recommendations by the National Association of Drop Forgers and Stampers on the findings contained in the Official Report of the Drop Forging Team which visited America in 1949', 2 January 1951.

60. MRC.MSS.200/F/3/E3/2/1, 'Minutes of meeting of Home Economic Policy Committee', 14 July 1949, p. 2. MRC.MSS.200/F/3/E3/2/2, 'Home Economic Policy Committee', 17 July 1948.

61. MRC.MSS.200/F/3/E3/2/1, 'First meeting of the Home Economic Policy Committee of the F.B.I., 26 November 1947', 12 December 1947, p. 5.

62. The team, selected in part by the BIM, comprised company chairmen, educationalists, and managers, and visited 30 universities and colleges, 8 trade unions, and 50 industrial and commercial undertakings.

63. Prominent members in the EPA were also keen on promoting American management methods within Europe. Alexander King was aware that if the technical and economic gap between the USA and Europe was to be reduced then the education of management was crucial (Gemelli 1995). According to the EPA report we discussed earlier American managers, '... were astounded at the general lack of university courses in industrial management' (EPA 1954: 17).

64. BBC Radio 4, 'Club class', 20 November 2003, 20.00–20.30. *The Independent, Review Supplement*, 'fat cat list 2003', 20 May 2003. *The Guardian*, 'Boardroom pay up 23%', pp. 1, 4–5.

65. The claim that specialisation leads to greater efficiency goes at least as far back to the writings of Adam Smith and Andrew Ure.

66. MRC.MSS.292/557.91/5, 'Trades Union Congress: report of a conference of General Council members of the National Production Advisory Service on Industry with the National Association of Unions in the textile trades, 25 February 1949', 3 march 1949.

67. PRO BT258/97, 'Note for Mr. Pollock's talk with the Secretary on 13th March 1956', n.d. 'Consultation with the main industrial organisations about questions concerning the European Productivity Agency', n.d.

68. Preferences are transitive when agent z prefers x to y, y to w, and therefore x to w. Preferences are independent of irrelevant alternatives when agent z prefers any alternative of x and y irrespective of any other alternatives. The criteria of 'universal domain' is fulfilled when the social choice function can be defined for every possible set of individual preferences.

69. Decision cycling at its simplest occurs when individuals or organisations oscillate between judgements. In our case an appropriate example would be a firm that constantly switched back and forth between production institutions such as Fordism and flexible specialisation.

70. MRC.MSS.79/AS/3/4, Seaman, M., 'Automation – some problems for the boardroom, 17 June', in 'The automatic factory what does it mean: conference, Margate, 16–19 June 1955', the Institution of Production Engineers, n.d.

71. MRC.MSS.200/B/3/2/C1162 pt. 3, letter to K. J. Burton, from C. Henniker-Heaton, 7 January 1957, p. 2.

72. MRC.MSS.200/B/3/2/C1162 pt. 2, 'British Employers Confederation Draft of "Automation" Committee: minutes of meeting on 18 October 1956', n.d. pp. 2–4.

73. MRC.MSS.200/B/3/2/C1190 pt. 1, 'Third international conference of manufacturers November/December 1956 New York: the economic and social

implications of continued mechanisation, automation and nuclear energy: problems of management and organisation', 1 August 1956.
74. MRC.MSS.200/B/3/2/C1190 pt. 1, letter to Mr Pollock from W. H. Garrett, 8 August 1956.
75. Ibid., letter to Mr Pollock from A. M. Holbein, 21 August 1956.
76. The EPA, Report, *Steel Workers and Technical Change*, p. 35, also concluded that mechanisation required a greater degree of planned production.
77. PRO BT258/1248, 'Report of the LPC conference held at Ashorne Hill from 5–6 November 1954: second regional conference intended mainly for LPCs in the North & North Midland regions of England: 17 December 1954', n.d. p. 4.
78. MRC.MSS.200/C/4/G2/2, Fraser, C., 'Britain's industrial performance', CBI, *Review*, Winter 1973, No. 11, p. 27.

8 Conclusion

1. Similarly Crafts wrote, 'Britain's early and idiosyncratic industrialisation did influence later growth and structural adjustment ... when a new range of problems and opportunities opened up in the years after 1890 the economy seemed to lack the flexibility easily to respond' (Crafts 1985: 176). Although Crafts later wrote, 'No one has yet produced a fully convincing version of the early "start hypothesis" ...' (Crafts 1994a: 38).

Bibliography

Primary Sources

Interviews

King, A., Chief Scientific Officer DSIR 1950–56, Deputy Director Of The EPA 1957–61, Conducted on 7 April 1997.

Runacres, E. A., BPC 1954–71, Deputy Director 1959–71, Secretary 1960–66, Vice-Chairman of OECD Committee on National Productivity Centres 1960–66, Conducted on 25 March 1997.

Whitehorn, J., Deputy Director CBI 1966–78, Deputy Overseas Director 1960, Overseas Director 1963, 1965–68, Conducted on 19 February 1997.

Files from the Modern Records Centre, University of Warwick

MSS.36 Iron and Steel Trades Confederation and National Union of Blastfurnacemen, Cokemen, and Ore Workers

MSS.44/TBN Confederation of Shipbuilding and Engineering Unions

MSS.79 Association of Scientific, Technical, and Managerial Staffs

MSS.200/B CBI Predecessor Archive: British Employers' Confederation

MSS.200/C Confederation of British Industries

MSS.200/F CBI Predecessor Archive: Federation of British Industries

MSS.202 R. A. Etheridge Papers

MSS.292 and MSS 292B TUC Archive

Files from the Public Record Office, Kew, London

BT64 Industries and Manufacture's No. 1

BT190 National Production Advisory Council on Industry

BT258 Industry and Manufactures

LAB10 Ministry of Labour Industrial Relations Department

T229 Central Economic Planning Staff

Journals

Amalgamated Engineering Union Journal
Amalgamated Engineering Monthly Union Journal
British Productivity Council (Bulletin)
BPC, *Productivity Review*
EPA, *European Productivity*
FBI, *Review*
Target Bulletin of the British Productivity Council
TUC, *Report of Annual Congress* (various issues)

Articles, books, and pamphlets

AACP. 1949. *Simplification in British Industry: Report of an Investigation in the United States of America made by a Group Appointed by the Council.* London: Anglo-America Council on Productivity.

AACP. 1950a. *Management Accounting: Report of a Specialist Team which Visited the United States of America in 1950.* London: Anglo-American Council on Productivity.

AACP. 1950b. *Materials Handling in Industry: Report of an Investigation in the United States of America made by a Group Appointed by the Council.* London: Anglo-American Council on Productivity.

AACP. 1951a. *Education for Management: Report of a Visit to the U.S.A. in 1950 of a Specialist Team Concerned with Education for Management.* London: Anglo-American Council on Productivity.

AACP. 1951b. *Freight Handling: Report of a Specialist team which Visited the United States of America in 1950.* London: Anglo-American Council on Productivity.

AACP. 1953a. *The British Pressed Metal Industry: Report of a Productivity Team From the United States of America Which Visited the United Kingdom in 1951.* London: British Productivity Council.

AACP. 1953b. *Metal Working Machine Tools: Report of a Productivity Team Representing the British Machine Tool Industry which Visited the United States of America in 1951.* London: British Productivity Council.

Bailey, S. B. 1958. *Automation in North America: A Report on Visits to Industrial, Commercial and Research Establishments in the USA and Canada.* London: HMSO.

BPC. 1954. *Progress Report 1953–4.* London: British Productivity Council.

BPC. 1955. *Policy and Progress 1954–55.* London: British Productivity Council.

BPC. April 1955. *Work Study, in Theory and – Practice,* BPC, Bulletin, Supplement.

BPC. July 1955. *What they are Saying About the Circuit Scheme,* BPC, Bulletin, Supplement.

BPC. 1956. *Productivity Review 24: Freight Handling.* London: British Productivity Council.

Castle, B. 1984. *The Castle Diaries 1964–70.* London: Weidenfeld and Nicolson.

Clegg, H. 1971. *How to Run and Incomes Policy and why we made such a mess of the last one.* London: Heinemann Educational Books Ltd.

Cmnd. 1968 3623. *Royal Commission on Trade Unions and Employers' Associations 1965–1968.* London: HMSO.

Cmnd. 1980 7794. *Engineering our Future: Report of the Committee of Inquiry into the Engineering Profession, 1980.* London: HMSO.

Dinning, N. 1955 August. *Automation – Complacency or Realism?.* AEUJ, New Ser. XXII: 246.

EPA. 1954. *Problems of Business Management: American Opinions, European Opinions.* Paris: European Productivity Agency, Organisation for European Economic Co-operation, Technical Assistance Mission No. 129.

EPA. 1958. *Activities and Achievements.* Paris: European Productivity Agency, Organisation for European Economic Co-operation.

EPA. 1959. *Steel Workers and Technical Progress: A Comparative Report on Six National Studies.* Paris: European Productivity Agency, Organisation for European Economic Co-operation.

EPA. 1960. *Activities for the Year 1958–9*. Paris: European Productivity Agency, Organisation for European Economic Co-operation.

EPA. n.d. *Joint Consultation in Practice: A Survey in British Industry*. Paris: European Productivity Agency, Organisation for European Economic Co-operation.

Fourastié, J. 1953. 'Towards Higher Labour Productivity in the Countries of Western Europe'. *International Labour Review*, LXVII: 340–55.

Gomberg, W. 1959. 'Labor's Participation in the European Recovery Program: A Study in Frustration'. *Political Science Quarterly*, 74: 240–55.

Hutton, G. 1953. *We too can Prosper: The Promise of Productivity*. London: George Allen and Unwin Ltd.

Hutton, G. 1980. *What ever Happened to Productivity? Tenth Wincott Memorial Lecture*. London: Institute for Economic Affairs.

Jones, A. 1973. *The New Inflation: The Politics of Prices & Incomes*. London: Andre Deutsch.

Kipping, N. 1954. *The Federation of British Industries: A Paper by Sir Norman Kipping*. London: The Federation of British Industries.

Kipping, N. 1972. *Summing Up*. London: Hutchinson & Co. Ltd.

Mitchell, J. 1972. *The National Board for Prices and Incomes*. London: Secker and Warburg.

Parsons, O. H. 1968. *The Donovan Report: Trade Unions Strikes and Negotiations*. London: Labour Research Department.

Priest, A. 1955. 'Automation Replacing Workers in U.S. Industry'. AEUJ, New Ser. XXII: 217.

Richard, R. 1953. 'Productivity and the Trade Unions in France'. *International Labour Review*, 68: 279–302.

Scarr, A. E. 1947. 'Slog Harder or Work more Effectively?'. AEUJ, New Ser. XIV.

TUC. 1968. *Action on Donovan: Interim Statement by the TUC General Council in Response to the Report of the Royal Commission on Trade Unions and Employers' Associations*. London: Trades Union Congress.

TUC. n.d.a. *Trade Unions and Automation*. London: Trade Union Congress.

TUC. n.d. *Trade Unions and Productivity: The Report and Recommendations of a Team of British Trade Union Officials who Investigated the role of Unions in Increasing Productivity in the United States of America*. London: Trades Union Congress.

Wollard, F. G. 1955. *What Automation Means*, BPC, Bulletin, Supplement, June.

Secondary sources

Aaronovitch, S. and Smith, R., with Gardiner, J. and Moore, R. 1981. *The Political Economy of British Capitalism: A Marxist Analysis*. London: Mcgraw-Hill.

Abramovitz, M. 1986. 'Catching up, Forging Ahead, and Falling Behind'. *Journal of Economic History*, XLVI: 385–406.

Ackrill, M. 1988. 'Britain's Managers and the British Economy, 1870s to the 1980s'. *Oxford Review of Economic Policy*, 4: 59–73.

Addison, J. T. and Addison, A. H. 1982. 'The Impact of Unions on Productivity'. *British Journal of Industrial Relations*, XX: 145–62.

Addison, J. T. and Hirsch, B. T. 1989. 'Union Effects on Productivity, Profits and Growth: Has the Long Run Arrived'. *Journal of Labor Economics*, 7: 72–105.

Addison, J. T. and Chilton, J. B. 1993. 'Can we Identify Union Productivity Effects?'. *Industrial Relations*, 32: 124–32.

Addison, P. 1993. *Churchill on the Home Front 1900–1955*. London: Pimlico.

Albu, A. 1956. 'Automation'. *The Political Quarterly*, 27: 250–9.

Aldcroft, D. H. 1964. 'The Entrepreneur and the British Economy, 1870–1914'. *Economic History Review*, Sec. Ser. XVII: 113–34.

Aldcroft, D. 1982. 'Britain's Economic Decline 1870–1980', In G. Roderick and M. Stephens, eds, *The British Malaise: Industrial Performance, Education and Training in Britain Today*. Sussex: Falmer Press.

Alesina, A. and Rodrik, D. 1994. 'Distributive Politics and Economic Growth'. *Quarterly Journal of Economics*, CIX: 465–90.

Alford, B. W. E. 1988. *British Economic Performance 1945–1975*. London: Macmillan Education Ltd.

Alford, B. W. E. 1992. 'Economic Culture and Economic Growth: The Case of Great Britain', In K. Rohe, G. Schmidt, and H. Pogge Von Strandmann eds, *Deutschland-Grossbritannien-Europa*. Bochum: Arbeitskreis Deutsche England-Forschung.

Alford, B. W. E. 1996. *Britain in the World Economy since 1880*. London: Longman.

Allen, G. C. 1979. *The British Disease: A Short Essay on the Nature and Causes of the Nations Lagging Wealth*. London: Institute of Economic Affairs.

Amdam, R. P. and Bjarnar, O. 1998. 'The Regional Dissemination of American Productivity Models in Norway in the 1950s and 1960s', In M. Kipping and O. Bjarnar, eds, *The Americanisation of European Business: The Marshall Plan and the Transfer of US Management Models*. London: Routledge.

Amdam, R. P. and Yttri, G. 1998. 'The European Productivity Agency, the Norwegian Productivity Institute and Management Education', In T. R. Gourvish and N. Tiratsoo, eds, *Missionaries and Managers: American Influences on European Management Education, 1945–60*. Manchester: Manchester University Press.

Anderson, P. 1987. 'The Figures of Descent'. *New Left Review*, 161: 20–77.

Anderson, P. 1964. 'Origins of the Present Crisis', *New Left Review*, 23: 26–53.

Anthony, P. D. 1986. *The Foundation of Management*. London: Tavistock Publications.

Artis, M. J., ed. 1992. *Prest & Coppock's the UK Economy: A Manual of Applied Economics*. Oxford: Oxford University Press.

Bacon, R. and Eltis, W. 1996. *Britain's Economic Problem Revisited*. Basingstoke: Macmillan.

Bacon, R. and Eltis, W. 1978. *Britain's Economic Problem: Too few Producers*. London: Macmillan.

Bagrit, L. 1966. *The Age of Automation*. Middlesex: Pelican Books.

Balfour, W. C. 1953. 'Productivity and the Worker'. *British Journal of Sociology*, 4: 257–65.

Baily, M. N. 2002. 'Distinguished Lecture on Economics in Government: The New Economy: Post Mortem or Second Wind?', *Journal of Economic Perspectives*, 16: 3–22.

Bain, G. S. and Price, R. 1980. *Profiles of Union Growth: A Comparative Statistical Portrait of Eight Countries*. Oxford: Basil Blackwell.

Barnett, A. 1983. 'The Dangerous Dream'. *New Statesman*, 17 June: 9–11.

Barnett, C. 2002. *The Verdict of Peace: Britain Between her Yesterday and the Future*. London: Pan Books.

Barnett, C. 1986. *The Audit of War: The Reality and Illusion of Britain as a Great Nation*. London: Papermac.

Batstone, E. 1986. 'Labour and Productivity'. *Oxford Review of Economic Policy*, 2: 32–43.

Batstone, E. and Gourlay, S. 1986. *Unions, Unemployment and Innovation*. Oxford: Basil Blackwell.

Bazen, S. and Thirlwall, T. 1992. *Deindustrialisation*. Oxford: Heinemann Educational.

Bean, C. and Crafts, N. F. R. 1996. 'British Economic Growth since 1945: Relative Economic Decline and Renaissance?', In N. F. R. Crafts and G. Toniolo, eds, *Economic Growth in Europe since 1945*. Cambridge: Cambridge University Press.

Berghahn, V. R. 1986. *The Americanisation of West German Industry 1945–1973*. Leamington Spa: Berg.

Bjarnar, O. and Kipping, M. 1998. 'The Marshall Plan and the Transfer of US Management Models to Europe: an Introductory Framework', In M. Kipping And O. Bjarnar, eds, *The Americanisation of European Business: The Marshall Plan and the Transfer of US Management Models*. London: Routledge.

Blank, S. 1977. 'Britain: the Politics of Foreign Economic Policy, the Domestic Economy, and the Problem of Pluralistic Stagnation'. *International Organization*, 31: 673–721.

Blank, S. 1973. *Industry and Government in Britain: The Federation of British Industries*. Hant's: Lexington Books.

Boel, B. 1998. 'The European Productivity Agency: a Faithful Prophet of the American Model?', In M. Kipping and O. Bjarnar, eds, *The Americanisation of European Business: The Marshall Plan and the Transfer of US Management Models*. London: Routledge.

Bok, D. and Dunlop, J. 1985. 'How Trade Union Policy is Made', In W. E. J. Mccarthy ed., *Trade Unions: Selected Readings*. London: Penguin Books.

Boltho, A. 1989. 'Did Policy Activism work?'. *European Economic Review*, 33: 1709–726.

Booth, A. 2003. 'The Manufacturing Failure Hypothesis and the Performance of British Industry during the Long Boom'. *Economic History Review*, LVI: 1–33.

Booth, A. 1996. 'Corporate Politics and the Quest for Productivity: The British TUC and the Politics of Industrial Productivity, 1947–1960', In J. Melling and A. Mckinlay, eds, *Management, Labour and Industrial Politics in Modern Europe: The Quest for Productivity Growth in Britain, Germany and Sweden during the Twentieth Century*. Aldershot: Edward Elgar.

Booth, A., Melling, J. and Dartmann, C. 1997. 'Institutions and Economic Growth: the Politics of Productivity in West Germany, Sweden, and the United Kingdom, 1945–1955'. *Journal of Economic History*, 57: 416–44.

Bowden, S., Foreman-Peck, J. and Richardson, T. 2001. 'The Post-war Productivity Failure: Insights from Oxford (Cowley)'. *Business History*, 43, July, 54–78.

Bowles, S. and Eatwell, J. 1983. 'Between Two Worlds: Interest Groups, Class Structure, and Capitalist Growth', In D. C. Mueller, ed., *The Political Economy of Growth*. London: Yale University Press.

Boyer, R. 1995. 'Capital–Labour Relations in OECD Countries: From the Fordist Golden Age to Contrasted National Trajectories', In J. Schor and Jong-Il You, eds, *Capital, the State and Labour: A Global Perspective*. Aldershot: Edward Elgar.

Brett, E. A. 1985. *The World Economy since the War: The Politics of Uneven Development*. London: Macmillan.

Bright, J. R. 1958. *Automation and Management*. New York: Maxwell Reprint Company.

Brittan, S. 1978. 'How British is the British Sickness?'. *Journal of Law & Economics*, 21: 245–68.

Brittan, S. 1971. *Steering the Economy: The Role of the Treasury*. Middlesex: Penguin Books.

Brittan, S. 1988. *The Economic Consequences of Democracy*. Aldershot: Wildwood House.

Broadberry, S. and Crafts, N. F. R. 1990a. 'The Implications of British Macro-economic Policy in the 1930s for Long run Growth Performance'. *Rivista Di Storia Economica*, 7: 1–17.

Broadberry, S. and Crafts, N. F. R. 1990b. 'The Impact of the Depression of the 1930s on Productive Potential in the United Kingdom'. *European Economic Review*, 34: 599–607.

Broadberry, S. N. and Crafts, N. F. R. 1990c. 'Explaining Anglo-American Productivity Differences in the Mid-twentieth Century'. *Oxford Bulletin of Economics and Statistics*, 52: 375–401.

Broadberry, S. N. and Crafts, N. F. R. 1996. 'British Economic Policy and Industrial Performance in the Early Post-war Period'. *Business History*, 38: 65–91.

Broadberry, S. N. and Wagner, K. 1996. 'Human Capital and Productivity in Manufacturing during the Twentieth Century: Britain, Germany and the United States', In B. Van Ark and Nicholas Crafts, eds, *Quantitative Aspects of Post-war European Economic Growth*. Cambridge: Cambridge University Press.

Broadberry, S. N. 1997a. *The Productivity Race: British Manufacturing in International Perspective, 1850–1990*. Cambridge: Cambridge University Press.

Broadberry, S. N. 1997b. 'The Long Run Growth and Productivity Performance of the United Kingdom'. *Scottish Journal of Political Economy*, 44: 403–24.

Broadberry, S. N. 1998. 'How did the United States and Germany overtake Britain? A Sectoral Analysis of Comparative Productivity Levels, 1870–1990', *Journal of Economic History*, 58: 375–407.

Broadberry, S. and Crafts, N. F. R. 1998. 'The Post-war Settlement: not such a good Bargain after all'. *Business History*, 40: 73–9.

Broadberry, S. and Crafts, N. 2001. 'Competition and Innovation in 1950s Britain'. *Business History*, 43, January, 97–118.

Buchanan, J. M., Burton, J. and Wagner, R. 1978. *The Consequences of Mr Keynes: An Analysis of the Misuse of Economic Theory for Political Profiteering, with Proposals for Constitutional Disciplines*. London: Institute of Economic Affairs.

Buchele, R. and Christiansen, J. 1992. 'Industrial Relations and Productivity Growth: A Comparative Perspective'. *International Contributions to Labour Studies*, 2: 77–97.

Burnham, P. 1990. *The Political Economy of Postwar Reconstruction*. London: The Macmillan Press.

Butler, D. and Sloman, A. 1980. *British Political Facts 1900–79*. London: Macmillan Press Ltd.

Buxton, T., Chapman, P. and Temple, P. eds, 1994. *Britain's Economic Performance*. London: Routledge.

Cain, P. J. and Hopkins, A. G. 1993. *British Imperialism: Crisis and Deconstruction 1914–1990*. London: Longman Group Limited.

Cairncross, Sir A. 1985. *Years of Recovery: British Economic Policy 1945–51*. London: Methuen.

Cairncross, Sir A. 1994. 'Economic Policy and Performance 1945–1964', In R. Floud and D. Mccloskey, eds, *The Economic History of Britain since 1700, 3: 1939–1992*. Cambridge: Cambridge University Press.

Calmfors, L. and Driffill, J. 1988. 'Bargaining Structure, Corporatism and Macroeconomic Performance'. *Economic Policy*, 6: 13–62.

Cameron, G. 2003. 'Why did UK Manufacturing Productivity Growth Slowdown in the 1970s and Speed up in the 1980s?'. *Economica*, 70: 121–41.

Cannon, L. 1955. 'The Productivity Drive'. *Marxist Quarterly*, 2: 88–104.

Capie, F. and Collins, M. 1992. *Have the Banks Failed British Industry? An Historical Study of Bank/Industry Relations in Britain 1870–1990*. London: Institute of Economic Affairs. Hobart Paper 119.

Cardwell, D. 1994. *The Fontana History of Technology*. London: Fontana Press, an imprint of Harper Collins.

Carew, A. 1987. *Labour Under the Marshall Plan: The Politics of Productivity and the Marketing of Management Science*. Manchester: Manchester University Press.

Carew, A. 1991. 'The Anglo-American Council on Productivity (1948–52): The Ideological Roots of the Post-war Debate on Productivity in Britain'. *Journal of Contemporary History*, 26: 49–69.

Carlin, W. and Soskice, D. 1990. *Macroeconomics and the Wage Bargain: A Modern Approach to Employment, Inflation and the Exchange Rate*. New York: Oxford University Press.

Carlsson, B. 1995. 'Introduction', In B. Carlsson, ed. *Technological Systems and Economic Performance: The Case of Factory Automation*. London: Kluwer Academic Press.

Carlsson, B. and Eliasson, G. 1995. 'The Nature and Importance of Economic Competence', In B. Carlsson, ed., *Technological Systems and Economic Performance: The Case of Factory Automation*. London: Kluwer Academic Press.

Carlsson, B. and Jacobsson, S. 1995. 'What makes the Automation Industry Strategic?', In B. Carlsson, ed., *Technological Systems and Economic Performance: The Case of Factory Automation*. London: Kluwer Academic Press.

Carlsson, B. and Stankiewicz, R. 1995. 'On the Nature, Function and Composition of Technological Systems', In B. Carlsson, ed., *Technological Systems and Economic Performance: The Case of Factory Automation*. London: Kluwer Academic Press.

Carlsson, B. and Taymaz, E. 1995. 'The Importance of Economic Competence in Economic Growth: A Micro-to-Macro Analysis', In B. Carlsson, ed., *Technological Systems And Economic Performance: The Case of Factory Automation*. London: Kluwer Academic Press.

Carlsson, B., Taymaz, E. and Tryggestad, K. 1995. 'The Economic Impact of Factory Automation', In B. Carlsson, ed., *Technological Systems and Economic Performance: The Case of Factory Automation*. London: Kluwer Academic Press.

Casson, M. 1991. *The Economics of Business Culture: Game Theory, Transaction Costs, and Economic Performance*. New York: Oxford University Press.

Caves, R. E. 1980. 'Productivity Differences Among Industries', In R. E. Caves and L. B. Krause, eds, *Britain's Economic Performance*. Washington D.C.: The Brookings Institution.

Chalmers, M. 1985. *Paying for Defence: Military Spending and Economic Decline*. London: Pluto Press.

Chalmers, M. 1992. 'British Economic Decline: The Contribution of Military Spending'. *Royal Bank of Scotland Review*, 173: 35–46.

Chandler, A. D. 1990. *Scale and Scope: The Dynamics of Industrial Capitalism*. London: Belknap Press of Harvard University.

Channon, D. F. 1973. *Strategy and Structure of British Enterprise*. London: Macmillan.

Chick, M. 1997. *Industrial Policy in Britain 1945–1951: Economic Planning, Nationalisation, and the Labour Governments*. New York: Cambridge University Press.

Clark, I. 1999. 'Institutional Stability in Management Practice And Industrial Relations: The Anglo-American Council for Productivity, 1948–52'. *Business History*, 41: 64–92.

Clegg, H. 1964. 'Restrictive Practices'. *Socialist Commentary*, No. 12: 9–11.

Clegg, H. 1970. *The System of Industrial Relations in Great Britain*. Oxford: Basil Blackwell.

Coates, D. 1996. 'Introduction', In D. Coates, ed., *Industrial Policy in Britain*. London: Macmillan Press Ltd.

Coleman, D. C. 1973. 'Gentlemen and Players'. *Economic History Review*, Sec. Ser. XXVI: 92–116.

Coleman, D. C. 1987. 'Failings and Achievements: Some British Business, 1910–80'. *Business History*, XXIX: 1–17.

Coleman, D. C. and Macleod, C. 1986. 'Attitudes to New Techniques: British Businessmen, 1800–1950'. *Economic History Review*, Sec. Ser. XXXIX: 588–611.

Collins, B. and K. Robbins, eds. 1990. *British Culture and Economic Decline*. London: Weidenfeld and Nicolson.

Coopey, R. and Woodward, N. 1996. 'The British Economy in the 1970s: An Overview', In R. Coopey and N. Woodward, eds, *Britain in the 1970s: The Troubled Economy*. London: UCL Press.

Cooley, T. F. and Ohanian, L. E. 1997. 'Postwar British Economic Growth and the Legacy of Keynes'. *Journal of Political Economy*, 105: 439–72.

Corden, W. M. 1980. 'Relationships between Macro-economic and Industrial Policies'. *World Economy*, 3: 167–84.

Crafts, N. 2002. *Britain's Relative Economic Performance, 1870–1999*. London: Institute of Economic Affairs.

Crafts, N. F. R. 1985. *British Economic Growth during the Industrial Revolution*. Oxford: Clarendon Press.

Crafts, N. F. R. 1988. 'The Assessment: British Economic Growth over the Long Run'. *Oxford Review of Economic Policy*, 4: I–XXI.

Crafts, N. F. R. 1991a. 'Reversing Relative Economic Decline? The 1980s in Historical Perspective'. *Oxford Review of Economic Policy*, 7: 81–98.

Crafts, N. F. R. 1991b. 'Economic Growth', In N. F. R. Crafts and N. Woodward, eds, *The British Economy since 1945*. Oxford: Clarendon Press.

Crafts, N. F. R. 1991c. 'Economics and history', In D. Greenaway, M. Bleaney and I. Stewart, eds, *Companion to Contemporary Economic Thought*. London: Routledge.

Crafts, N. F. R. 1992a. 'Productivity Growth Reconsidered'. *Economic Policy*, 15: 388–426.

Crafts, N. F. R. 1992b. 'Institutions and Economic Growth: Recent British Experience in an International Context'. *West European Politics*, 15: 16–38.

Crafts, N .F. R. 1992c. 'Productivity Growth in West Germany and the UK, 1950–1990: a British Perspective', In K. Rohe, G. Schmidt and H. Pogge Von Strandmann, eds, *Deutschland-Grossbritannien Europa*. Bochum: Arbeitskreis Deutsche England-Forschung.

Crafts, N. F. R. 1993a. 'Adjusting from war to Peace in 1940s Britain'. *Economic And Social Review*, 25: 1–20.

Crafts, N. F. R. 1993b. *Can De-industrialisation Seriously Damage Your Wealth: A Review of why Growth Rates Differ and how to Improve Economic Performance*. London: Institute Of Economic Affairs.

Crafts, N. F. R. 1993c. 'Was the Thatcher Experiment Worth it? British Economic Growth in a European Context', In A. Szirmai, B. Van Ark and D. Pilat, eds, *Explaining Economic Growth: Essays In Honour Of Angus Maddison*. London: Elsevier Science Publishers B.V.

Crafts, N. F. R. 1994a. 'Managing Decline? 1870–1990'. *History Today*, 44: 37–42.

Crafts, N. F. R. 1994b. 'Labour in Power but not in Control'. *Labour History Review*, 59: 45–7.

Crafts, N. F. R. 1995a. 'The Golden age of Economic Growth in Western Europe, 1950–73'. *Economic History Review*, Sec. Ser. XLVIII: 429–47.

Crafts, N. F. R. 1995b. ' "You've never had it so good?": British Economic Policy and Performance, 1945–60', In B. Eichengreen, ed., *Europe's Post War Recovery*. Cambridge: Cambridge University Press.

Crafts, N. F. R. 1996a. 'Deindustrialisation and Economic Growth'. *Economic Journal*, 106: 172–83.

Crafts, N. F. R. 1996b, 'Economic Growth in the 1970s', In R. Coopey and N. Woodward eds, *Britain in the 1970s: The Troubled Economy*. London: UCL Press.

Crafts, N. F. R. 1997. *Britain's Relative Economic Decline 1870–1995: A Quantitative Perspective*. London: The Social Market Foundation, Paper No. 29.

Crafts, N. 1998a. 'Forging Ahead and Falling Behind: The Rise and Relative Decline of the first Industrial Nation'. *Journal of Economic Perspectives*, 12: 193–210.

Crafts, N. 1998b. *The Conservative Government's Economic Record: An End of Term Report*. London: Institute of Economic Affairs, Occasional Paper No. 104.

Crafts, N. F. R. 1999a. 'Economic Growth in the Twentieth Century', *Oxford Review of Economic Policy*, 15: 18–34.

Crafts, N. F. R. 1999b. 'The Great Boom: 1950–73', In M-S. Schulze, ed. *Western Europe: Economic and Social Change since 1945*. London: Longman.

Crafts, N. F. R. and Woodward, N. 1991. 'The British Economy since 1945: Introduction and Overview', In N. F. R. Crafts and N. Woodward, eds, *The British Economy since 1945*. Oxford: Clarendon Press.

Creedy, J. 1984. *Economics: An Integrated Approach*. London: Prentice/Hall International.

Crockett, G. and Elias, P. 1984. 'British Managers: A Study of their Education, Training, Mobility and Earnings'. *British Journal of Industrial Relations*, 22: 34–46.

Crouch, C. 1985. 'Conditions for Trade Union Wage Restraint', In L. N. Lindberg and C. S. Maier, eds, *The Politics of Inflation and Economic Stagnation: Theoretical Approaches and International Case Studies*. Washington D.C.: The Brookings Institution.

Crouch, C. 1993. *Industrial Relations and European State Traditions*. New York: Oxford University Press.

Dahlin, K. 1995. 'Diffusion and Industrial Dynamics in the Robot Industry', In B. Carlsson, ed., *Technological Systems and Economic Performance: The Case of Factory Automation*. London: Kluwer Academic Press.

Dahrendorf, R. 1982. *On Britain*. London: BBC Publications.

Daly, A., Hitchens, D. M. W. N. and Wagner, K. 1985. 'Productivity, Machinery and Skills in a Sample of British and German Manufacturing Plants'. *National Institute Economic Review*, 111: 48–61.

Dartmann, C. 1996a. *Re-distribution of Power, Joint Consultation or Productivity Coalitions? Labour and Postwar Reconstruction in Germany and Britain, 1945–1953*. Bochum: Arbeitskreis Deutsche England – Forschung.

Dartmann, C. 1996b. 'Labour–management Relations, the Marshall Plan and the Politics of Productivity Growth in Germany', In J. Melling and A. Mckinlay, eds, *Management, Labour and Industrial Politics in Modern Europe: The Quest for Productivity Growth in Britain, Germany and Sweden during the Twentieth Century*. Aldershot: Edward Elgar.

Dasgupta, P. 1989. 'Applying Game Theory: Some Theoretical Considerations'. *European Economic Review*, 33: 619–24.

Daunton, M. J. 1989. ' "Gentlemanly Capitalism" and British Industry 1820–1914'. *Past & Present*, 122: 119–58.

David, P. 1985. 'Clio and the Economics of QWERTY'. *American Economic Review*, 75: 332–37.

Davis Smith, J. 1990. *The Attlee and Churchill Administrations and Industrial Unrest, 1945–55: A Study in Consensus*. London: Pinter.

Dell, E. 1996. *The Chancellors: A History of the Chancellors of the Exchequer 1945–90*. London: Harper Collins Publishers.

Dell, E. 1999. *A Strange Eventful History: Democratic Socialism in Britain*. London: Harper Collins Publishers.

Denny, K. and Nickell, S. 1991. 'Unions and Investment in British Manufacturing industry'. *British Journal of Industrial Relations*, 29: 113–21.

Denny, K. and Nickell, S. J. 1992. 'Unions and Investment in British Industry'. *Economic Journal*, 102: 874–87.

Dimmock, W. J. 1951. 'Mechanical Handling in Industry and its Effect on Costs'. *The Time Study Engineer*, June: 167–78.

Dintenfass, M. 1992. *The Decline of Industrial Britain 1870–1980*. London: Routledge.

Donnelly, T. and Thoms, D. 1989. 'Trade Unions, Management and the Search for Production in the Coventry Motor car Industry, 1939–75'. *Business History*, 31: 98–113.

Donovan, R. J. 1987. *The Second Victory: The Marshall Plan and the Postwar Revival of Europe*. New York: Madison Books.

Dore, R. 1990. 'Two kinds of Rigidity: Corporate Communities and Collectivism', In R. Brunetta and C. Dell'Aringa, eds, *Labour Relations and Economic Performance: Proceedings of a Conference held by the International Economic Association in Venice, Italy*. London: Macmillan, in Association with the International Economic Association.

Dorwick, S. and Spencer, B. J. 1994. 'Union Attitudes to Labour-saving Innovation: When are Unions Luddites?'. *Journal Of Labor Economics*, 12: 316–44.

Dow, J. C. R. 1970. *The Management of the British Economy 1945–60*. Cambridge: Cambridge University Press.

Drucker, P. F. 1951. *The New Society: The Anatomy of the Industrial Order*. London: Heinemann.

DSIR (Department Of Scientific and Industrial Research). 1956. *Automation: A Report on the Technical Trends and their Impact on Management and Labour.* London: HMSO.

Dumke, R. 1990. 'Reassessing the Wirtschaftswunder: Reconstruction and Postwar Growth in West Germany in an International Context'. *Oxford Bulletin of Economics & Statistics,* 52: 451–91.

Duncan Macrae, C. 1977. 'A Political Model of the Business Cycle'. *Journal of Political Economy,* 85: 239–63.

Dunkerley, J. and Hare, P. G. 1991. 'Nationalised Industries', In N. F. R. Crafts and N. Woodward, eds, *The British Economy since 1945.* Oxford: Clarendon Press.

Dunning, J. H. 1998. 'US-owned Manufacturing Affiliates and the Transfer of Managerial Techniques: The British Case', In M. Kipping and O. Bjarnar, eds, *The Americanisation of European Business: The Marshall Plan and the Transfer of US Management Models.* London: Routledge.

Edgerton, D. 1991a. 'The Prophet Militant and Industrial: The Peculiarities of Correlli Barnett'. *Twentieth Century British History,* 2: 360–79.

Edgerton, D. 1991b. *England and the Aeroplane: An Essay on a Militant and Technological Nation.* London: Macmillan Academic and Professional Ltd.

Edgerton, D. 1992. 'Whatever Happened to the British Warfare State? The Ministry of Supply, 1945–1951', In H. Mercer, N. Rollings and J. D. Tomlinson, eds, *Labour Governments and Private Industry: The Experience of 1945–1951.* Edinburgh: Edinburgh University Press.

Edgerton, D. 1994a. 'British Industrial R&D, 1900–1970'. *Journal of European Economic History,* 23: 49–67.

Edgerton, D. 1994b. 'The Rise and Fall of British Technology'. *History Today,* 44: 43–8.

Edgerton, D. 1996. 'The "White Heat" Revisited': the British Government and Technology in the 1960s'. *Twentieth Century British History,* 7: 53–82.

Eggertsson, T. 1990. *Economic Behaviour and Institutions.* Cambridge: Cambridge University.

Ehrnberg, E. and Jacobsson, J. 1995. 'Technological Discontinuities and Company Strategies-machine Tools and Flexible Manufacturing Systems', In B. Carlsson, ed., *Technological Systems and Economic Performance: The Case of Factory Automation.* London: Kluwer Academic Press.

Eichengreen, B. 1994. 'Institutional Prerequisites for Economic Growth: Europe after World War II'. *European Economic Review,* 38: 883–90.

Eichengreen, B. 1996a. 'Explaining Britain's Economic Performance: A Critical Note'. *Economic Journal,* 106: 213–18.

Eichengreen, B. 1996b. 'Institutions and Economic Growth: Europe after World War II', In N. F. R. Crafts and G. Toniolo, eds, *Economic Growth in Europe since 1945.* Cambridge: Cambridge University Press.

Elbaum, B. and Lazonick, W. 1986. 'An Institutional Perspective on British Decline', In B. Elbaum and W. Lazonick, eds, *The Decline of the British Economy.* Oxford: Clarendon Press.

Ellwood, D. W. 1992. *Rebuilding Europe: Western Europe, America and Postwar Reconstruction.* New York: Longman.

Elster, J. 1984. *Ulysses and the Sirens: Studies in Rationality and Irrationality.* Cambridge: Cambridge University Press.

Elster, J. 1989. *The Cement of Society*. Cambridge: Cambridge University Press.

Eltis, W. 1996. 'How low Profitability and weak Innovativeness Undermined UK Industrial Growth'. *Economic Journal*, 106: 184–95.

Feinstein, C. 1990. 'Benefits of Backwardness and Costs of Continuity', In A. Graham and A. Seldon, eds, *Government and Economies in the Post-war World: Economic Policies and Comparative Performance 1945–85*. London: Routledge.

Feinstein, C. 1994. 'Success and Failure: British Economic Growth since 1948' In R. Floud and D. Mccloskey, eds, *The Economic History of Britain since 1700: Volume 3: 1939–1992*. Cambridge: Cambridge University Press.

Fels, A. 1972. *The British Prices and Incomes Board*. London: Cambridge University Press. Occasional Paper 29.

Flanagan, R. J., Soskice, D. W. and Ulman, L. 1983. *Unionism, Economic Stabilization, and Incomes Policies: European Experience*. Washington D.C.: The Brookings Institution.

Flanders, A. 1964. *The Fawley Productivity Agreements: A Case Study of Management and Collective Bargaining*. London: Faber and Faber Ltd.

Forester, T. 1977. 'Do the British Sincerely want to be Rich?'. *New Society*, 40: 158–61.

Freeman, R. 1988. 'Labour Market Institutions and Economic Performance', *Economic Policy*, 6: 64–80.

Gamble, A. 1981. 'Symposium: the Decline of Britain'. *Contemporary Record*, 2: 18–23.

Gamble, A. 1994. *Britain in Decline: Economic Policy, Political Strategy and the British State*. London: St Martin's Press.

Gilbert, D. 1996. 'Strikes in Postwar Britain', In C. Wrigley, ed. *A History of British Industrial Relations, 1939–1979: Industrial Relations in a Declining Economy*. Cheltenham: Edward Elgar.

Golden, M. A., Wallerstein, M. and Lange, P. 1999. 'Postwar Trade-Union Organization and Industrial Relations in Twelve Countires', In H. Kitschelt, P. Lange, G. Marks, and Stephens, J. D., eds, *Continuity and Change in Contemporary Capitalism*. Cambridge: Cambridge University Press.

Goldthorpe, J. H., Lockwood, D., Bechhofer, F., and Platt, J. 1968. *The Affluent Worker: Industrial Attitudes and Behaviour*. Cambridge: Cambridge University Press.

Goodman, L. L. 1957. *Man and Automation*. Middlesex: Penguin Books Ltd.

Gospel, H. F. 1979. 'Employer's Labour Policy: A Study of the Mond-Turner Talks 1927–23'. *Business History*, XXI: 180–97.

Gospel, H. F. 1988. 'The Management of Labour: Great Britain, the US, and Japan'. *Business History*, XXX: 104–15.

Gospel, H. F. 1992. *Markets, Firms and the Management of Labour in Modern Britain*. Cambridge: Cambridge University Press.

Gospel, H. F. and Palmer, G. 1993. *British Industrial Relations*. London: Routledge.

Gourevitch, P., Martin, A., Ross, G., Allen, C., Bornstein, S., and Markovits, A. 1984. *Unions and Economic Crisis: Britain, West Germany and Sweden*. London: George Allen and Unwin.

Gourvish, T. R. 1987. 'British Business and the Transition to a Corporate Economy: Entrepreneurship and Management Structures'. *Business History*, XXIX: 18–45.

Gourvish, T. R. and Tiratsoo, N. eds, 1998. *Missionaries and Managers: American Influences On European Management Education, 1945–60*. Manchester: Manchester University Press.

Granick, D. 1972. *Managerial Comparisons of Four Developed Countries: France, Britain, United States, and Russia.* Massachusetts: The MIT Press.

Grant, W. 1982. *The Political Economy of Industrial Policy.* London: Butterworths.

Grant, W. and Marsh, D. 1977. *The Confederation of British Industry.* London: Hodder and Stoughton.

Grout, P. A. 1984. 'Investment and Wages in the Absence of Binding Contracts: A Nash Bargaining Approach'. *Econometrica*, 52: 449–60.

Grove, J. W. 1962. *Government and Industry in Britain.* London: Longmans.

Guest, D. E. 1990. 'Have British Workers been Working Harder in Thatcher's Britain? A Re-consideration of the Concept of Effort'. *British Journal of Industrial Relations*, 28: 293–312.

Gustafsson, B. 1998. 'Some Theoretical Problems of Institutional Economic History', *Scandinavian Economic History Review*, XLVI: 4–31.

Hagemann, H. 1990. 'Capital Goods', In J. Eatwell, M. Milgate and P. Newman, eds, *The New Palgrave: Capital Theory.* London: W. W. Norton & Company.

Hall, P. 1986. 'The State and Economic Decline', In B. Elbaum and W. Lazonick, eds, *The Decline of the British Economy.* Oxford: Clarendon Press.

Hampden-Turner, C. and Trompenaars, F. 1993. *The Seven Cultures of Capitalism: Value Systems for Creating Wealth in the United States, Britain, Japan, Germany, France, Sweden, and the Netherlands.* London: Piatkus.

Hampsher-Monk, I. 1992. 'Prices as Descriptions: Reasons as Explanations', In J. Melling and J. Barry, eds, *Culture in History: Production, Consumption and Values in Historical Perspective.* Exeter: University Of Exeter Press.

Hannah, L. 1983. *The Rise of the Corporate Economy.* London: Methuen.

Hannah, L. 1992. 'Human Capital Flows and Business Efficiency', In K. Bradley, ed., *Human Resource Management: People and Performance.* Aldershot: Dartmouth.

Hannah, L. 1994. 'The Economic Consequences of the State Ownership of Industry, 1945–1990', In R. Floud and D. Mccloskey, eds, *The Economic History of Britain since 1700: Volume 3: 1939–1992.* Cambridge: Cambridge University Press.

Harris, J. 1990. 'Enterprise and Welfare States: A Comparative Perspective'. *Transactions of the Royal Historical Society*, Fifth Ser. 40: 175–95.

Harvie, C. 1985. 'Liturgies of National Decadence: Wiener, Dahrendorf and the British Crisis', *Cencrastus*, 21: 17–23.

Haskel, J. 1991. 'Imperfect Competition, Work Practises and Productivity Growth'. *Oxford Bulletin of Economics and Statistics*, 53: 265–79.

Hatton T. J. and Chrystal, K. A. 1991. 'The Budget and Fiscal Policy', In N. F. R. Crafts and N. Woodward, eds, *The British Economy since 1945.* Oxford: Clarendon Press.

Hayek, F. A. 1984. *1980s Unemployment and the Unions: Essays on the Impotent Price Structure of Britain and Monopoly in the Labour Market.* London: Institute of Economic Affairs.

Henderson, D. 1990. 'Comparative Economic Performance of the OECD Countries 1950–87: A Summary of the Evidence', In A. Graham and A. Seldon, eds, *Government and Economies in the Post-war World: Economic Policies and Comparative Performance 1945–85.* London: Routledge.

Hennessy, P. 1989. *Whitehall.* New York: The Free Press.

Hennessy, P. 1993. *Never Again: Britain 1945–1951.* London: Vintage.

Hinton, J. 1994. *Shop Floor Citizens: Engineering Democracy in 1940s Britain.* Aldershot: Edward Elgar.

Hoel, M. 1978. 'Distribution and Growth as a Differential Game Between Workers and Capitalists'. *International Economic Review*, 19: 335–50.

Hogan, M. J. 1987. *The Marshall Plan: America, Britain, and the Reconstruction of Western Europe, 1947–1952*. Cambridge: Cambridge University Press.

Honkapohja, S. 1988. 'Discussion'. *Economic Policy*, 6: 48–51.

Hutber, P. ed. Forward by Lord Home. 1978. *What's Wrong with Britain: Fifteen Answers to an Urgent Contemporary Question*. London: Sphere Books Ltd., Published in Association with the Sunday Telegraph.

Hyman, R. and Elger, T. 1981. 'Job Controls, the Employers Offensive and Alternative Strategies'. *Capital and Class*, 15: 115–49.

Ingham, G. 1984. *Capitalism Divided? The City and Industry in British Social Development*. London: Macmillan.

Jessop, B. 1977. 'Recent Theories of the Capitalist State'. *Cambridge Journal of Economics*, 1: 353–73.

Jones, G. and Barnes, M. 1967. *Britain on Borrowed Time*. (Harmondsworth: Penguin Books, 1967).

Jones, R. 1987. *Wages and Employment Policy 1936–1985*. London: Allen & Unwin.

Kaplinsky, R. 1984. *Automation: The Technology and Society*. Essex: Longman.

Katzenstein, P. J. 1985. *Small States in World Markets: Industrial Policy in Europe*. London: Cornell University Press.

Keeble, S. P. 1992. *The Ability to Manage: A Study of British Management 1890–1990*. Manchester: Manchester University Press.

Keefe, J. H. 1991. 'Do Unions Influence the Diffusion of Technology?'. *Industrial and Labour Relations Review*, 44: 261–74.

Kidron, M. 1970. *Western Capitalism since the War*. Harmonsworth: Penguin Books.

Kilpatrick, A. and Lawson, T. 1980. 'On the Nature of Industrial Decline in the UK'. *Cambridge Journal of Economics*, 4: 85–102.

Kipping, M. 1998. 'Operation Impact: Converting European Employers to the American Creed', In M. Kipping and O. Bjarnar, eds, *The Americanisation of European Business: The Marshall Plan and the Transfer of US Management Models*. London: Routledge.

Kipping, M. and J-P, Nioche. 1998. 'Much ado About Nothing? The US Productivity Drive and Management Training in France, 1945–60', In T. R. Gourvish and N. Tiratsoo, eds, *Missionaries and Managers: American Influences on European Management Education, 1945–60*. Manchester: Manchester University Press.

Kirby, M. W. 1989. 'Institutional Rigidities and Britain's Industrial Decline', *Business History Review*, 63: 930–37.

Kirby, M. W. 1991. 'Supply-Side Management', In N. F. R. Crafts and N. Woodward, eds, *The British Economy since 1945*. Oxford: Clarendon Press.

Kirby, M. W. 1992. 'Institutional Rigidities and Economic Decline: Reflections on the British Experience'. *Economic History*, Sec. Ser. XLV: 637–60.

Kitson, M. and Michie, J. 1996. 'Britain's Industrial Performance since 1960: Underinvestment and Relative Decline'. *Economic Journal*, 106: 196–212.

Knight, J. 1992. *Institutions and Social Conflict*. Cambridge: Cambridge University Press.

Knight, K. G. 1989. 'Labour Productivity and Strike Activity in British Manufacturing Industries: Some Quantitative Evidence'. *British Journal of Industrial Relations*, 27: 365–74.

Knowles, K. G. J. C. 1952. 'Wages and Productivity', In G. D. N. Worswick and P. H. Ady, eds, *The British Economy 1945–1950*. Oxford: Oxford University Press.

Koestler, A., ed. 1963. *Sucide of a Nation*. London: Hutchinson.

Kolko, J. and Kolko, G. 1972. *The Limits of Power: The World and United States Foreign Policy, 1945–1954*. New York: Harper & Row.

Kramer, A. 1990. *The West German Economy 1945–1955*. Oxford: Berg.

Kuisel, R. F. 1993. *Seducing the French: The Dilemma of Americanisation*. London: University Of California Press.

Lancaster, K. 1973. 'The Dynamic Inefficiency of Capitalism'. *Journal of Political Economy*, 81: 1093–109.

Lange, P. 1984. 'Unions, Workers and Wage Regulation: The Rational Basis of Consent', In J. H. Goldthorpe, ed., *Order and Conflict in Contemporary Capitalism*. New York: Oxford University Press.

Lansbury, M. and Mayes, D. 1996. 'Productivity Growth in the 1980s', In D. G. Mayes, ed., *Sources of Productivity Growth*. Cambridge: The National Institute of Economic and Social Research and Cambridge University Press.

Lazonick, W. 1986. 'The Cotton Industry', In B. Elbaum and W. Lazonick eds, *The Decline of the British Economy*. Oxford: Clarendon Press.

Lazonick, W. 1990. 'Labour Process', In J. Eatwell, M. Milgate and P. Newman, eds, *The New Pelgrave: Marxian Economics*. London: The Macmillan Press Ltd.

Lazonick, W. 1994. 'Employment Relations in Manufacturing and International Competition', In R. Floud and D. Mccloskey, eds, *The Economic History of Britain Since 1700: Volume 2: 1860–1939*. Cambridge: Cambridge University Press.

Ledyard, J. O. 1989. 'Market Failure', In J. Eatwell, M. Milgate and P. Newman, eds, *The New Pelgrave: Allocation, Information and Markets*. London: The Macmillan Press Ltd.

Lee, S. 1996. 'Manufacturing', In D. Coates, ed., *Industrial Policy in Britain*. London: Macmillan Press Ltd.

Lewchuk, W. 1986. 'The Motor Vehicle Industry', In B. Elbaum and W. Lazonick, eds, *The Decline of the British Economy*. Oxford: Clarendon Press.

Lewchuk, W. 1987. *American Technology and the British Vehicle Industry*. Cambridge: Cambridge University Press.

Leyland, N. H. 1952. 'Productivity', In G. D. N. Worswick and P. H. Ady, eds, *The British Economy 1945–1950*. Oxford: Oxford University Press.

Link, W. 1991. 'Building Coalitions: Non-Governmental German–American Linkages', In C. S. Maier, ed., *The Marshall Plan and Germany: West German Development Within the Framework of the European Recovery Program*. Oxford: Berg.

Locke, R. R. 1985. 'Business Education in Germany: Past Systems and Current Practice'. *Business History Review*, 59: 232–53.

Locke, R. R. 1989. *Management and Higher Education since 1940: The Influence of America and Japan on West Germany, Great Britain, and France*. Cambridge: Cambridge University Press.

Lorenz, E. and Wilkinson, F. 1986. 'The Shipbuilding Industry 1880–1965', In B. Elbaum and W. Lazonick, eds, *The Decline of the British Economy*. Oxford: Clarendon Press.

Lupton, T. 1971. *Management and the Social Sciences*. Middlesex: Penguin Books.

Machin, S. and Wadhwani, S. 1991. 'The Effects of Unions on Investment and Innovation: Evidence from WIRS'. *Economic Journal*, 101: 324–30.

MacInnes, J. 1987. *Thatcherism at Work: Industrial Relations and Economic Change*. Milton Keynes: Open University Press.

Macmillan, R. H. 1956. *Automation: Friend or Foe*. Cambridge: The Syndicates of the Cambridge University Press.

Maddison, A. 1987. 'Growth and Slowdown in Advanced Capitalist Economies: Techniques of Quantitative Assessment'. *Journal of Economic Literature*, XXV: 649–98.

Maddison, A. 1988. 'Ultimate and Proximate Growth Causality: A Critique of Mancur Olson on the Rise and Decline of Nations'. *Scandinavia Economic History Review*, XXXVI: 25–9.

Maddison, A. 1991. *Dynamic Forces in Capitalist Development: A Long-Run Comparative View*. Oxford: Oxford University Press.

Maguire, P. 1991. 'Designs on Reconstruction: British Business, Market Structures and The Role of Design in Post-war Recovery'. *Journal of Design History*, 4: 15–30.

Maguire, P. 1996. 'Labour and the Law', In C. Wrigley, ed., *A History of British Industrial Relations 1945–79: Industrial Relations in a Declining Economy*. Cheltenham: Edward Elgar.

Maier, C. S. 1977. 'The Politics of Productivity: Foundations of American Economic Policy after World War II'. *International Organization*, 31: 607–33.

Maier, C. S. 1991. 'Introduction to Part II', In C. S. Maier, ed., *The Marshall Plan and Germany: West German Development Within the Framework of the European Recovery Program*. Oxford: Berg.

Mankelow, R. and Wilkinson, F. 1998. 'Industrial Relations in Iron and Steel, Shipbuilding and the Docks, 1930–1960', In N. Whitside and R. Salais, eds, *Governance, Industry and Labour Markets in Britain and France: The Modernising State in the Mid-Twentieth Century*. London: Routledge.

Manning, A. 1994. 'How Robust is the Microeconomic Theory of the Trade Union', *Journal of Labor Economics*, 12: 430–59.

Manser, W. A. P. 1971. *Britain in Balance*. London: Longman and the Institute for Economic Affairs.

Mant, A. 1977. *The Rise and Fall of the British Manager*. London: The Macmillan Press Ltd.

March, J. G. and Olsen J. P. 1989. *Rediscovering Institutions: The Organisational Basis of Politics*. London: The Free Press – Macmillan.

Marglin, S. A. 1974. 'What do Bosses do? The Origins and Functions of Hierarchy in Capitalist Production'. *Review of Radical Political Economics*, 6: 60–112.

Marquand, D. 1988. *The Unprincipled Society: New Demands and Old Politics*. London: Fontana Press.

Marquand, D. 1990. 'Political Institutions and Economic Performance', In A. Graham and A. Seldon, eds, *Government and Economies in the Post-war World: Economic Policies and Comparative Performance 1945–85*. London: Routledge.

Matthews, D. 1999. 'Accountants vs. Engineers: The Professions in Top Management in Britain since the Second World War'. *Contemporary British History*, 13: 82–104.

Matthews, D., Anderson, M., and Edwards, J. R. 1997. 'The Rise of the Professional Accountant in British Management'. *Economic History Review*, Sec. Ser. L: 407–29.

Matthews, R. C. O. 1968. 'Why has Britain had full Employment since the War'. *Economic Journal*, LXXVII: 555–609.

Matthews, R. C. O. 1986. 'The Economics of Institutions, and the Sources of Growth'. *Economic Journal*, 96: 903–18.

Mayes, D. G. 1996. 'Introduction', In D. G. Mayes, ed., *Sources of Productivity Growth*. Cambridge: The National Institute of Economic and Social Research and Cambridge University Press.

Mayr, O. 1986. *Authority, Liberty & Automatic Machinery in Early Modern Europe*. London: The Johns Hopkins University Press.

McCloskey, D. N. 1973. *Economic Maturity and Entrepreneurial Decline: British Iron and Steel*. Massachusetts: Harvard University Press.

McCloskey, D. N. 1981. *Enterprise and Trade in Victorian Britain: Essays in Historical Economics*. London: George Allen and Unwin.

McCombie, J. S. L. and Thirlwall, A. P. 1994. *Economic Growth and the Balance-of-Payments Constraint*. London: Macmillan.

McDonald, G. W. and Gospel, H. F. 1973. 'The Mond-Turner Talks, 1927–33: A Study in Industrial Co-operation'. *Historical Journal*, XVI: 807–29.

McGlade, J. 1998. 'From Business Reform Programme to Production Drive: The Transformation of US Technical Assistance to Western Europe', In M. Kipping and O. Bjarnar, eds, *The Americanisation of European Business: The Marshall Plan and the Transfer of US Management Models*. London: Routledge.

Mckinsey Global Institute. 1998. *Driving Productivity and Growth in the UK Economy*. Washington D.C.: Mckinsey Global Institute.

McLoughlin, I. and Clark, J. 1994. *Technological Change at Work*. Buckingham: Open University Press.

Mee, C. L. 1984. *The Marshall Plan Revisited: The Launching of the Pax Americana*. New York: Simon and Schuster.

Mercer, H. 1992. 'Anti-monopoly Policy', In H. Mercer, N. Rollings and J. D. Tomlinson, eds, *Labour Governments and Private Industry: The Experience of 1945–1951*. Edinburgh: Edinburgh University Press.

Mercer, H. 1995. *Constructing a Competitive Order: The Hidden History of British Antitrust Policies*. Cambridge: Cambridge University Press.

Metcalf, D. 1989. 'Water Notes Dry Up: The Impact of the Donovan Reform Proposals and Thatcherism at Work on Labour Productivity in British Manufacturing Industry'. *British Journal of Industrial Relations*, XXVII: 1–31.

Metcalf, D. 1990a. 'Trade Unions and Economic Performance: The British Evidence', In R. Brunetta and C. Dell'Aringa, eds, *Labour Relations and Economic Performance: Proceedings of a Conference held by the International Economic Association in Venice, Italy*. London: Macmillan, in Association with the International Economic Association.

Metcalf, D. 1990b. 'Union Presence and Labour Productivity in British Manufacturing: A Reply to Nolan and Marginson'. *British Journal of Industrial Relations*, 28: 248–55.

Meyer, F. V., Corner, D. C. and Parker, J. E. S. 1970. *Problems of a Mature Economy: A Text for Students of the British Economy*. London: Macmillan and Co. Ltd.

Middlemas, K. 1979. *Politics in Industrial Society: The Experience of the British System since 1914*. London: André Deutsch Limited.

Middlemas, K. 1983. *Industry, Unions and Government: Twenty one Years of NEDC*. London: Macmillan.

Middlemas, K. 1986. *Power, Competition and the State: Volume 1: Britain in Search of Balance, 1940–61*. London: The Macmillan Press Ltd.

Middlemas, K. 1990. *Power, Competition and the State: Volume 2: Threats to the Postwar Settlement Britain, 1961–74.* London: The Macmillan Press Ltd.

Middleton, R. 1996. *Government Versus the Market: The Growth of the Public Sector, Economic Management and British Economic Performance, c. 1890–1979.* Cheltenham: Edward Elgar.

Millar, J. 1979. *British Management Versus German Management: A Comparison of Organisational Effectiveness in West German and UK Factories.* Hampshire: Saxon House.

Miller, G. 1992. *Managerial Dilemmas: The Political Economy of Hierarchy.* Cambridge: Cambridge University Press.

Milward, A. S. 1984. *The Reconstruction of Western Europe 1945–51.* London: Routledge.

Milward, R. 1994. 'British Industry since the Second World War'. *History Today,* 44: 49–54.

Mirowski, P. 1986. 'Institutions as a Solution Concept in a Game Theory Context', In L. Samuelson, ed., *Microeconomic Theory.* Lancaster: Kluwer-Nijhoff Publishing.

Moene, K. O., Wallerstein, M. and Hoel, M. 1993. 'Bargaining Structure and Economic Performance', In R. J. Flanagan, K. O. Moene and M. Wallerstein, eds, *Trade Union Behaviour, Pay-Bargaining, and Economic Performanc.:* New York: Oxford University Press.

Mokyr, J. 1992. 'Technological Inertia in Economic History'. *Journal of Economic History,* 52: 325–38.

Mokyr, J. 2000. 'Innovation and its Enemies: The Economic and Political Roots of Technological Inertia', In M. Olson and S. Kähkönen, eds, *A Not-so-Dismal Science: A Broader View of Economies and Societies.* New York: Oxford University Press.

Muellbauer, J. 1996. 'Productivity and Competitiveness', In T. Jenkinson, ed., *Readings in Macroeconomics.* Oxford: Oxford University Press.

Musgrave, R. and Musgrave, P. 1968. 'Fiscal Policy', In R. Caves, ed., *Britain's Economic Prospects.* London: George Allen & Unwin Ltd.

NEDC (National Economic Development Office) 1976. *Cyclical Fluctuations in the United Kingdom Economy.* London: National Economic Development Office. Discussion Paper No. 3.

Nevin, M. 1983. *The Age of Illusions: The Political Economy of Britain 1968–1982.* London: Victor Gollancz Ltd.

Newell, A. and Symons, J. 1990. 'The Passing of the Golden Age', In R. Brunetta and C. Dell'Aringa, eds, *Labour Relations and Economic Performance: Proceedings of a Conference held by the International Economic Association in Venice, Italy.* London: Macmillan, in Association with the International Economic Association.

Newton, C. 1983. 'How Successful was the Marshall Plan?'. *History Today,* 33: 11–15.

Newton, S. and Porter, D. 1988. *Modernisation Frustrated: The Politics of Industrial Decline in Britain since 1900.* London: Unwin Hyman.

Nichols, T. 1986. *The British Worker Question: A New Look at Workers and Productivity in Manufacturing.* London: Routledge and Kegan Paul.

Noble, D. F. 1978. 'Social Choice in Machine Design: The Case of Automatically Controlled Machine Tools, and a Challenge for Labor'. *Politics and Society,* 8: 313–47.

Nolan, P. and Marginson, P. 1990. 'Skating on Thin Ice? David Metcalf on Trade Unions and Productivity'. *British Journal of Industrial Relations*, 28: 227–47.

North, D. C. 1981. *Structure and Change in Economic History*. New York: W.W. Norton.

North, D. C. 1990. *Institutions, Institutional Change and Economic Performance*. Cambridge: Cambridge University Press.

North, D. C. 1991. 'Institutions'. *Journal of Economic Perspectives*, 5: 97–112.

North, D. C. 1993. 'Institutions and Credible Commitment'. *Journal of Institutional and Theoretical Economics*, 149: 11–23.

North, D. C. 1994. 'Economic Performance Through Time'. *American Economic Review*, 84: 359–68.

North, D. C. 1999. *Understanding the Process of Economic Change*. London: Institute of Economic Affairs. Occasional Paper 106.

Olson, M. 1982. *The Rise and Decline of Nations: Economic Growth, Stagflation and Social Rigidities*. London: Yale University Press.

O'Mahony, M. 1999. *Britain's Productivity Performance 1950–1996: An International Perspective*. London: National Institute of Economic and Social Research.

Oswald, A. 1985. 'The Economic Theory of Trade Unions: An Introductory Survey'. *Scandinavian Journal of Economics*, 87: 160–93.

Oulton, N. 1995. 'Supply side Reform and UK Economic Growth: What ever Happened to the Miracle?'. *National Institute Economic Review*, No. 154: 53–70.

Oulton, N. and O'Mahony, M. 1994. *Productivity and Growth: A Study of British Industry, 1954–1986*. Cambridge: Cambridge University Press.

Oulton, N. and Young, G. 1996. 'How high is the Social rate of Return to Investment?'. *Oxford Review of Economic Policy*, 12: 48–69.

Overbeek, H. 1990. *Global Capitalism and National Decline: The Thatcher Decade in Perspective*. London: Unwin Hyman.

Panitch, L. 1976. *Social Democracy and Industrial Militancy: The Labour Party, the Trade Unions and Incomes Policy, 1945–1974*. Cambridge: Cambridge University Press.

Paqué, K.-H. 1996. 'Why the 1950s and not the 1920s?' In N. F. R. Crafts and G. Toniolo, eds, *Economic Growth in Europe since 1945*. Cambridge: Cambridge University Press.

Park, J. 1987. *Profit-sharing and Industrial Co-partnership in British Industry, 1880–1920: Class Conflict or Class Collaboration?* New York and London: Garland Publishing Inc.

Pass, C., Lowes B. and Davies, L. 1988. *Dictionary of Economics*. London: Collins.

Pelling, H. 1992. *A History of British Trade Unionism*. London: Penguin Books.

Pelling, H. 1996. *The Third Revolution: Professional Elites in the Modern World*. London: Routledge.

PEP (Political and Economic Planing) Report, 1966. *Attitudes in British Management*. Org. Published as *Thrusters and Sleepers*, Middlesex: Pelican Books.

Phelps Brown, H. 1977. 'What is the British Predicament?'. *Three Banks Review*, 113: 3–29.

Pisani, S. 1991. *The CIA and the Marshall Plan*. Kansas: University of Kansas Press.

Ploeg, F. and Van Der. 1987. 'Trade Unions, Investment and Employment: A Non-coopertaive Approach'. *European Economic Review*, 31: 1465–92.

Pollard, S. 1968. *The Genesis of Modern Management: A Study of the Industrial Revolution in Great Britain*. Middlesex: Penguin Books.

Pollard, S. 1982. *The Wasting of the British Economy: British Economic Policy 1945 to the Present*. London: Croom Helm.

Pollard, S. 1994. 'Entrepreneurship, 1870–1914', In R. Floud and D. Mccloskey, eds, *The Economic History of Britain since 1700: Volume 2: 1860–1939*. Cambridge: Cambridge University Press.

Porter, M. E. and Ketels, C. H. M. 2003. *UK Competitiveness: Moving to the Next Stage*. London: Economic and Social Research Council. DTI Economics Paper No. 3.

Prais, S. J. 1981. *Productivity and Industrial Structure: A Statistical Study of Manufacturing Industry in Britain, Germany and the US*. Cambridge: Cambridge University Press.

Prais, S. J. 1995. *Productivity, Education and Training: An International Perspective*. Cambridge: Cambridge University Press. Occasional Paper XLVIII.

Pratten, C. 1976. *Labour Productivity Differentials Within International Companies*. Cambridge: Cambridge University Press.

Pratten, C. F. and Atkinson, A. G. 1976. 'The Use of Manpower in British Manufacturing Industry'. *Department of Employment Gazette*, June: 571–6.

Prest, A. R. 1968. 'Sense and Nonsense in Budgetary Policy'. *Economic Journal*, LXXVIII: 1–18.

Pursell, C. 1995. *The Machine in America: A Social History of Technology*. Baltimore: The Johns Hopkins University Press.

Radice, H. 1984. 'The National Economy: A Keynesian Myth'. *Capital & Class*, 22: 111–40.

Raven, J. 1989. 'British History and the Enterprise Culture'. *Past & Present*, 123: 178–204.

Rees, A. 1985. 'Economic Functions and Objectives', In W. E. J. Mccarthy, ed., *Trade Unions: Selected Readings*. Middlesex: Penguin Books.

Reid, A. 1991. 'Employers' Strategies and Craft Production: The British Shipbuilding Industry 1870–1950', In S. Tolliday and J. Zeitlin, eds, *The Power to Manage? Employers and Industrial Relations in Comparative-historical Perspective*. London: Routledge.

Reynolds, P. and Coates, D. 1996. 'Conclusion', In D. Coates, ed., *Industrial Policy in Britain*. London: Macmillan Press Ltd.

Richardson, R. 1991. 'Trade Unions and Industrial Relations', In N. F. R. Crafts and N. Woodward, eds, *The British Economy since 1945*. Oxford: Clarendon Press.

Roderick, G. and Stephens, M. 1982. 'Introduction', In G. Roderick and M. Stephens, eds, *The British Malaise: Industrial Performance, Education, and Training in Britain Today*. Sussex: The Falmer Press.

Romero, F. 1992. *The United States and the European Trade Union Movement 1944–1951*. Chapel Hill: University of North Carolina Press.

Rowlinson, M. 1997. *Organisations and Institutions: Perspectives in Economics and Sociology*. London: The Macmillan Press Ltd.

Rowthorn, R. E. and Wells, J. R. 1987. *De-industrialisation and Foreign Trade*. Cambridge: Cambridge University Press.

Rubinstein, W. D. 1993. *Capitalism, Culture, and Decline in Britain 1750–1990*. London: Routledge.

Rutherford, D. 1992. *Dictionary of Economics*. London: Routledge.

Rutherford, M. 1996. *Institutions in Economics: The Old and the New Institutionalism*. Cambridge: Cambridge University Press.

Rutherford, M. 2001. 'Institutional Economics: Then and Now'. *Journal of Economic Perspectives*, 15: 173–94.

Salmon, J. 1988. 'Wage Strategy, Redundancy and Shop Stewards in the Coventry Motor Industry', In M. Terry and P. K. Edwards, eds, *Shopfloor Politics and Job Controls: The Post-war Engineering Industry*. Oxford: Basil Blackwell.

Sanderson, M. 1988. 'Education and Decline, 1890–1980s'. *Oxford Review of Economic Policy*, 4: 38–50.

Sawyer, M. 1992. 'Industry', In M. J. Artis, ed., *Prest & Coppock's the UK Economy: A Manual of Applied Economics*. Oxford: Oxford University Press.

Schott, K. 1984. 'Investment, Order and Conflict in a Simple Dynamic Model of Capitalism', In J. H. Goldthorpe, ed., *Order and Conflict in Contemporary Capitalism*. New York: Oxford University Press.

Schultz, K. A. 1995. 'The Politics of the Business Cycle'. *British Journal of Political Science*, 25: 79–99.

Scranton, P. 1997. *Endless Novelty: Specialty Production and American Industrialisation, 1865–1925*. Princeton: Princeton University Press.

Segreto, L. 1998. 'Sceptics and Ungrateful Friends vs. Dreaming Social Engineers: The Italian Business Community, the Italian Government, the United States and the Comitato Nazionale per la Produttività', In T. R. Gourvish and N. Tiratsoo, eds, *Missionaries and Managers: American Influences on European Management Education, 1945–60*. Manchester: Manchester University Press.

Shanks, M. 1972. *The Stagnant Society*. Harmondsworth: Penguin Books. Rev. Ed.

Shonfield, A. 1969. *Modern Capitalism: The Changing Balance of Public and Private Power*. London: Oxford University Press.

Sked, A. 1987. *Britain's Decline: Problems and Prospects*. Oxford: Basil Blackwell.

Smith, O. E. 1980a. 'Collective Bargaining', In W. P. J. Maunder, ed., *The British Economy in the 1970s*. London: Heinemann.

Smith, R. P. 1980. 'Military Expenditure and Investment in OECD Countries 1954–1973'. *Journal of Comparative Economics*, 4: 19–32.

Soskice, D. 1990. 'Reinterpreting Corporatism and Explaining Unemployment: Co-Ordinated and Non-co-ordinated Market Economies', In R. Brunetta and C. Dell'Aringa, eds, *Labour Relations and Economic Performance: Proceedings of a Conference held by the International Economic Association in Venice, Italy*. London: Macmillan, in Association with the International Economic Association.

Stewart, M. 1978. *Politics and Economic Policy in the UK since 1964: The Jekyll and Hyde Years*. London: Pergamon Press.

Streeck, W. 1992. *Social Institutions and Economic Performance: Studies of Industrial Relations in Advanced Capitalist Economies*. London: Sage Publications.

Supple, B. 1994a. 'Fear of Failing: Economic History and the Decline of Britain'. *Economic History Review*, Sec. Ser. XLVII: 441–58.

Supple, B. 1994b. 'British Economic Decline since 1945' In R. Floud and D. Mccloskey, eds, *The Economic History Of Britain since 1700: Volume 3: 1939–1992*. Cambridge: Cambridge University Press.

Swords-Isherwood, N. 1980. 'British Management Compared', In K. Pavitt ed. *Technical Innovation and British Economic Performance*. London: The Macmillan Press Ltd.

Tauman, Y. and Weiss, T. 1987. 'Labor Unions and the Adoption of New Technology'. *Journal of Labor Economics*, 5: 471–501.

Taylor, R. 1980. *The Fifth Estate: British Unions in the Modern World*. London: Pan Books. Rev. Ed.

Taylor, R. 1982. 'Trades Union Influence on Industrial Performance', In G. Roderick and M. Stephens, eds, *The British Malaise: Industrial Performance, Education, and Training in Britain Today*. Sussex: The Falmer Press.

Taylor, R. 1993. *The Trade Union Question in British Politics*. Oxford: Blackwell.

Taylor, R. 1996. 'The Heath Government, Industrial Policy and the "New Capitalism" ', In S. Ball and A. Seldon, eds, *The Heath Government 1970–74: A Reappraisal*. London: Longman.

Taymaz, E. 1991. 'The Impact of Trade Unions on the Diffusion of New Technology: The Case of NC Machine Tools'. *British Journal of Industrial Relations*, 29: 305–11.

Terry, M. 1988. 'Introduction: Historical Analyses and Contemporary Issues', In M. Terry and P. K. Edwards, eds, *Shopfloor Politics and Job Controls: The Post-war Engineering Industry*. Oxford: Basil Blackwell.

Thain, C. 1984. 'The Treasury and Britain's Decline'. *Political Studies*, XXXII: 581–95.

Theakston, K. 1996. 'Whitehall, Westminster and Industrial Policy', In D. Coates, ed., *Industrial Policy in Britain*. London: Macmillan Press Ltd.

Thirlwall, A. P. and Gibson, H. D. 1992. *Balance-of-Payments Theory and the United Kingdom Experience*. London: Macmillan Press.

Thompson, E. P. 1981. *The Making of the English Working Class*. Middlesex: Penguin.

Thoms, D. and Donnelly, T. 1985. *The Motor car Industry in Coventry since the 1890s*. London: Croom Helm.

Tiratsoo, N. 1995. 'Standard Motors 1945–55 and the Post-war Malaise of British Management', In Y. Cassis, F. Crouzet and T. Gourvish, eds, *Management and Business in Britain and France: The age of the Corporate Economy*. Oxford: Clarendon Press.

Tiratsoo, N. 2000. 'The United States Technical Assistance Programme in Japan, 1955–62'. *Business History*, 42: 117–36.

Tiratsoo, N. and Gourvish, T. R. 1996. ' "Making It Like In Detroit": British Managers and American Productivity Methods, 1945-c.1965 " '. *Business and Economic History*, 25: 206–16.

Tiratsoo, N. and Tomlinson, J. 1993. *Industrial Efficiency and State Intervention: Labour 1939–51*. London: Routledge/LSE.

Tiratsoo, N. and Tomlinson, J. 1994. 'Restrictive Practices on the Shopfloor in Britain, 1945–60: Myth and Reality'. *Business History*, 36: 65–84.

Tiratsoo, N. and Tomlinson, J. 1997. 'Exporting the "Gospel of Productivity": United States Technical Assistance and British Industry 1945–1960'. *Business History Review*, 71: 41–81.

Tiratsoo, N. and Tomlinson, J. 1998a. *The Conservatives and Industrial Efficiency, 1951–64*. London: LSE/Routledge.

Tiratsoo, N. and Tomlinson, J. 1998b. 'Americanisation beyond the mass Production Paradigm: The case of the British', In M. Kipping and O. Bjarnar, eds, *The Americanisation of European Business: The Marshall Plan and the Transfer of US Management Models*. London: Routledge.

Tolliday, S. 1986. 'High Tide and After: Coventry Engineering Workers and Shopfloor Bargaining, 1945–80', In B. Lancaster and T. Mason, eds, *Life and Labour in a Twentieth Century city: The Experience of Coventry*. Coventry: Cryfield Press.

Tolliday, S. and Zeitlin, J. 1991. 'Introduction: Employers and Industrial Relations Between Theory and History', In S. Tolliday and J. Zeitlin, eds, *The Power to*

Manage? Employers and Industrial Relations in Comparative-historical Perspective. London: Routledge.

Tomlinson, J. 1991a. 'The Failure of the Anglo-American Council on Productivity'. *Business History*, 33: 82–92.

Tomlinson, J. 1991b. 'A Missed Opportunity? Labour and the Productivity Problem 1945–51', In G. Jones and M. Kirby, eds, *Competitiveness and the State: Government and Business in Twentieth Century Britain.* Manchester: Manchester University Press.

Tomlinson, J. 1991c. 'The Labour Government and the Trade Unions, 1945–51', In N. Tiratsoo, ed., *The Atlee Years.* London: Pinter Publishers.

Tomlinson, J. 1992. 'Productivity Policy', In H. Mercer, N. Rollings and J. D. Tomlinson, eds, *Labour Governments and Private Industry: The Experience of 1945–1951.* Edinburgh: Edinburgh University Press.

Tomlinson, J. 1993. 'Mr Atlee's Supply-side Socialism'. *Economic History Review,* Sec. Ser. XLVI: 1–22.

Tomlinson, J. 1994a. 'British Economic Policy since 1945', In R. Floud and D. Mccloskey, eds, *The Economic History of Britain since 1700: Volume 3: 1939–1992.* Cambridge: Cambridge University Press.

Tomlinson, J. 1994b. *Government and the Enterprise since 1900: The Changing Problem of Efficiency.* New York: Oxford University Press.

Tomlinson, J. 1994c. 'The Politics of Economic Measurement: The Rise of the "Productivity Problem" in the 1940s', In A. G. Hopwood and P. Miller, eds, *Accounting as a Social and Institutional Practice.* Cambridge: Cambridge University Press.

Tomlinson, J. 1995. 'The Iron Quadrilateral: Political Obstacles to Economic Reform under the Attlee Government'. *Journal of British Studies*, 34: 90–111.

Tomlinson, J. 1996a. 'Inventing 'Decline': The Falling Behind of the British Economy in The Postwar Years'. *Economic History Review*, Sec. Ser. XLIX: 731–57.

Tomlinson, J. 1996b. 'Productivity, Joint Consultation and Human Relations in Post-war Britain: The Atlee Government and the Workplace', In J. Melling and A. Mckinlay, eds, *Management, Labour and Industrial Politics in Modern Europe: The Quest for Productivity Growth in Britain, Germany and Sweden during the Twentieth Century.* Aldershot: Edward Elgar.

Tomlinson, J. 1996c. 'British Industrial Policy', In R. Coopey and N. Woodward, eds, *Britain in the 1970s: The Troubled Economy.* London: UCL Press.

Tomlinson, J. 1997. *Democratic Socialism and Economic Policy: The Attlee Years, 1945–51.* Cambridge: Cambridge University Press.

Tomlinson, J. 2001. *The Politics of Decline: Understanding Post-war Britain.* London: Pearson Education Limited.

Tomlinson, J. 2002. 'The British "Productivity Problem" in the 1960s'. *Past and Present*, 175: 188–210.

Tomlinson, J. and Tiratsoo, N. 1998. 'An Old Story Freshly Told'? A Comment on Broadberry and Crafts' Approach to Britain's Early Post-War Economic Performance'. *Business History*, 40: 62–72.

Tsuru, S. 1993. *Institutional Economics Revisited.* Cambridge: Cambridge University Press.

Veblen, T. 1990. Org. 1919. 'The Limitations of Marginal Utility', In T. Veblen, *The Place of Science in Modern Civilization and other Essays.* London: Transaction Publishers.

Wadhwani, S. 1990. 'The Effect of Unions on Productivity Growth, Investment and Employment: A Report on Some Recent Work'. *British Journal of Industrial Relations*, 28: 371–85.

Walker, C. D. and Guest, R. H. 1952. *The Man on the Assembly Line*. Massachusetts: Harvard University Press.

Warwick, P. 1985. 'Did Britain Change? An Inquiry into the Causes of National Decline'. *Journal of Contemporary History*, 20: 99–133.

Wendell, G. 1980. *Institutional Economics: The Changing System*. London: University of Texas Press.

Wexler, I. 1983. *The Marshall Plan Revisited: The European Recovery Program in Economic Perspective*. London: Greenwood Press.

Whiting, A. 1976. 'An International Comparison of the Instability of Economic Growth: Is Britain's Poor Growth Performance due to Government Stop-Go Induced Fluctuations'. *Three Banks Review*, 109: 26–46.

Wiener, M. 1981a. *English Culture and the Decline of the Industrial Spirit*. Cambridge: Cambridge University Press.

Wiener, M. 1981b. 'Conservatism, Economic Growth and the English Culture'. *Parliamentary Affairs*, 34: 409–21.

Wigham, E. 1961. *What's Wrong with the Unions?* Harmondsworth: Penguin Books.

Wigham, E. 1973. *The Power to Manage: A History of the Engineering Employers Federation*. London: Macmillan.

Wilkinson, B. 1983. *The Shopfloor Politics of New Technology*. London: Heinmann Educational Books.

Wilks, S. 1984. *Industrial Policy and the Motor Industry*. Manchester: Manchester University Press.

Williams, J., Haslam, C. and Williams, K. 1990. 'Bad Work Practices and Good Management Practices: The Consequences of the Extension of Managerial Control in British and Japanese Manufacturing since 1950'. *Business History Review*, 64: 657–88.

Williams, K., Williams, J. and Thomas, D. 1983. *Why are the British bad at Manufacturing?* London: Routledge and Kegan Paul.

Willman, P. 1986. *Technological Change, Collective Bargaining and Industrial Efficiency*. Oxford: Clarendon Press.

Wilson, T. 1966. 'Instability and the Rate of Growth'. *Lloyds Bank Review*, 81: 16–32.

Witt De, D. 1994. *The Shaping of Automation: A Historical Analysis of the Interaction Between Technology and Organisation, 1950–1985*. Hilversum: Verloren.

Worswick, G. D. N. 1962. 'The British Economy 1950–59', In G. D. N. Worswick and P. H. Ady, eds, *The British Economy in the Nineteen-Fifties*. London: Oxford University Press.

Wrigley, C. 1996a. 'Trade Unions, Strikes and the Government', In R. Coopey and N. Woodward, eds, *Britain in the 1970s: The Troubled Economy*. London: UCL Press.

Wrigley, C. 1996b. 'Introduction', In C. Wrigley, ed., *A History of British Industrial Relations, 1939–1979: Industrial Relations in a Declining Economy*. Cheltenham: Edward Elgar.

Wrigley, C. 1996c. 'Trade Union Development', In C. Wrigley, ed., *A History of British Industrial Relations 1939–1979: Industrial Relations in a Declining Economy*. Cheltenham: Edward Elgar.

Wrigley, C., ed., 1997. *British Trade Unions 1945–1995*. Manchester: Manchester University Press.

Yankelovich, D. and Immerwahr, J. 1985. 'Putting the American Work Ethic to Work', In D. Yankelovich, H. Zetterberg, B. Strümpel, M. Shanks, J. Immerwahr, E. Noelle-Neumann, T. Sengoku, and E. Yuchtman-Yaar, eds, *The World at Work: An International Report on Jobs, Productivity, and Human Values*. New York: Octagon Books.

Yankelovich, D., Zetterberg, H., Strümpel, B., Shanks, M., Immerwahr, J., Noelle-Neumann, E., Sengoku, T., and Yuchtman-Yaar, E. 1985a. 'The Changing World Of Work', In D. Yankelovich, H. Zetterberg, B. Strümpel, M. Shanks, J. Immerwahr, E. Noelle-Neumann, T. Sengoku, and E. Yuchtman-Yaar, eds, *The World At Work: An International Report on Jobs, Productivity, and Human Values*. New York: Octagon Books.

Yankelovich, D., Zetterburg, H., Strümpel, B., Shanks, M., Immerwahr, J., Noelle-Neumann, E., Sengoku, T., and Yuchtman-Yaar, E. 1985b. 'The Core Problem', In D. Yankelovich, H. Zetterberg, B. Strümpel, M. Shanks, J. Immerwahr, E. Noelle-Neumann, T. Sengoku, and E. Yuchtman-Yaar, eds, *The World at Work: An International Report on Jobs, Productivity, and Human Values*. New York: Octagon Books.

Zeitlin, J. 1991. 'The Internal Politics of Employer Organization: The Engineering Employers Federation 1896–1939', In S. Tolliday and J. Zeitlin, eds, *The Power To Manage? Employers and Industrial Relations in Comparative-historical Perspective*. London: Routledge.

Zeitlin, J. 1998. 'Americanisation and its Limits: The Reconstruction of Britain's Engineering Industries', In N. Whitside and R. Salais, eds, *Governance, Industry and Labour Markets in Britain and France: The Modernising State in the Mid-Twentieth Century*. London: Routledge.

Zeitlin, J. and Herrigel, G., eds, 2000. *Americanization and its Limits: Reworking US Technology in Post-war Europe and Japan*. New York: Oxford Univeristy Press.

Secondary sources – not published

Boel, B. 1994. 'The European Productivity Agency and the Development of Management Education in Western Europe in the 1950s', Unpublished Typescript.

Bufton Mark, W. 1998. *The Productivity Drive in Britain c. 1948–63: An Institutional Analyses with Particular Reference to the Discussion of Technical and Organisational Change*. Unpublished PhD., University of Exeter.

D'Attorre, P.P. 1985. *ERP Aid and the Politics of Productivity in Italy during the 1950s*. Florence: European University Institute. EUI Working Paper No. 85/159.

Gemelli, G. 1995. *American Influence on European Management Education: The Role of the Ford Foundation*. Florence: European University Institute. EUI Working Paper RSC No. 95/3.

Hargreaves Heap, S. P. 1991. *Institutions and (Short-run) Macroeconomic Performance*. Norwich: Economics Research Centre, School of Economic and Social Studies, University of East Anglia. Discussion Paper No. 9124.

McGlade, J. 1995. *The Illusion of Consensus: American Business, Cold War Aid and the Industrial Recovery of Western Europe, 1948–1958*. Unpublished PhD., George Washington University.

McGlade, J. 1997. *Whose Plan Anyway? An Examination of Marshall Plan Leadership in the United States and Western Europe*. Paper Presented to the Marshall Plan and its Consequences: A 50th Anniversary Conference May 23–24, University of Leeds.

Romero, F. 1997. *Where the Marshall Plan Fell Short: Industrial Relations in Italy*. Paper Presented to the Marshall Plan and its Consequences: A 50th Anniversary Conference May 23–24, University of Leeds.

Smith, S. C. 1990. *On the Economic Rational for Codetermination Law*. Florence: European University Institute. EUI Working Paper ECO No. 90/12.

Index

236